CONQUEST

OF THE PAST

Conquest

OF THE PAST

AN AUTOBIOGRAPHY

PRINCE HUBERTUS ZU LOEWENSTEIN

ILLUSTRATED

Boston

HOUGHTON MIFFLIN COMPANY

The Riverside Press Cambridge

1938

The Riverside Press
CAMBRIDGE · MASSACHUSETTS
PRINTED IN THE U.S.A.

PRINCE HUBERTUS ZU LOEWENSTEIN TODAY

Who is my mother? And who are my brethren?

St. Matthew XII, 48.

Contents

Illustrations

I. *A Park is the World*

I WAS born on Sunday, October 14, 1906, in the castle of Schoenwoerth, near Kufstein, in the Tyrol. It seems that I was in no hurry to enter a world that had already awaited my arrival for five weeks. The doctors were compelled to induce artificial labour.

My birthday coincided with the centenary of the battle of Jena and Auerstaedt, in which Napoleon defeated the Prussians, and with the millennial anniversary of the death of my ancestor Luitpold, Margrave of Austria, who was killed fighting against the Hungarians.

Astrologists may be interested to learn the exact hour of my birth — 4 h. 59 m. A.M. My zodiacal sign is Libra, which at the time of my birth had just ascended above the horizon (1 47), and the sun, also in Libra, was not far behind. My ruling planet, therefore, is Venus, in the Jovian sign of Sagittarius. Jupiter, the planet of reign, in conjunction with Neptune, the planet of intuition, were near the zenith in Cancer, the sign of the people, benevolently aspected to Mercury in Scorpio and Saturn in Pisces. Opposing them, in the Nadir, there was Uranus in Capricorn, the planet of revolution and revival in the sign of the State.

I was the youngest of five children — two sisters and two brothers were born before me — but I was the first to have a birthplace suited to my rank according to the ideas prevailing in a certain class of society, even if it was far removed from all the bigger towns. The castle of Schoenwoerth is a very old building of which the foundations date back to the ninth century. Every owner, however, had added something, and also my father built a new wing for which he himself made the plans and measurements.

My birth was very thoroughly celebrated. We had some ancient cannon, which were fired off a hundred and one times, to the despair of my mother. One of them exploded and wounded several bystanders, among them my father. The whole valley still remembers the noise that announced my arrival in the world. Certainly there was no lack of warlike omina, and belief in peace was not instilled into me in my cradle. In addition my father gave me as my first name that of Saint Hubertus, the Patron Saint of huntsmen and archers.

My christening on October 24 took place, not in the chapel of the castle, but in my father's armoury amidst mediaeval swords, lances, helmets, shields, and bucklers. There was nearly an accident when my brother Leopold — then three years old — held his head too near the lighted candles.

When shortly afterwards my sisters returned from their convent school for the Christmas holidays, they were excitedly assailed by my brothers with the complaint that it was intolerable that I should enjoy special privileges. Like all other sensible children they had been baptized with water, I, however, had been baptized with methylated spirit ('Spiritus'). For they had, with their own ears, heard the priest say, 'Spiritus Sanctus,' as he besprinkled my head.

So strongly are my earliest memories bound up with the Tyrol and its mountains, and so much did I take its meadows, woods, and brooks for granted that for many years I could not imagine how anyone could tolerate another landscape.

My first memories of people, soil, and events date very far back and soon also came the moment when for the first time I said 'I.' I cannot have been more than two years old at that time. We had travelled from Schoenwoerth to the South Tyrol, somewhere near Bozen. My elder brothers' French governess, Mademoiselle Jex, my sisters' German governess Fräulein Skomal, and my nurse Anna were all present. I was wheeled in my pram to a meadow, a clearing

2

in the forest. I remember this journey like the time between sleeping and waking. On reaching the meadow my
nurse lifted me out of my pram and set me upon a stool.

'He sits there like a pasha,' said the German governess.
This was the final impetus. 'He?' I thought to myself,
'*I* am sitting!' ('Like a pasha?' That was merely incidental.
In any case I did not know what a pasha was.)

I, I, I — sit, move, eat. Those were the thoughts which
occupied my mind during the succeeding days. 'Children
who are always saying "I" end in hell,' old Anna warned me.
Undoubtedly she was in earnest and did not say it merely in
order to prevent my waking her during the night. 'Anna, I
cannot sleep any more. I want to whistle. I want to go out.
I want you to read to me ——' However, whether she
meant it or not, the effect was the same.

From that time onward she told me more about supernatural things than was good for me. Everything she told
me took on terrifying aspects. From morning till night —
and especially at night — I was fed with devils and poor
souls. There was, for instance, the following tale: 'And one
night I hear a voice calling "Clara, Clara." Three days
later my sister Clara went mad. A poor soul had called
her.' I became terribly afraid on hearing this lest a poor
soul should suddenly call out "Anna, Anna" — would she
not go mad too?

I imagined how mad people looked: they look at you over
their shoulder grinning and scratching. One is very helpless
as a child of two, and to be scratched without being defended
by anybody would be very unpleasant. How souls could
call was difficult to understand, though. I imagined them
to be thin white disks that sit in the back of the head. In
order to fly to heaven (Anna had impressed this upon me as
the most important task set to souls), they twirled round very
rapidly after the manner in which a top flies when it is spun.

The second dogma which I learned from Anna was that
everyone had a guardian angel (who stood by one's right
side) and a devil (who stood by the left side). It seemed to
me as if she intended to convey that the devil was as a rule

3

the more powerful. This I wanted to remedy, therefore for years afterward before going to sleep I used to kiss the right side of my pillow and hit the left with my clenched fist.

A whole tribe of lesser and greater spirits — scaly, horny, and double-tailed demons — played an important part in Anna's stories. But of God I did not hear before my third year. I may even have been three and a half. In my room at Schoenwoerth — a mysterious and comfortable room panelled with stone pine, with small leaded glass windows — there hung pictures of the Infant Jesus, with whom, however, I did not yet connect any clear idea. Our Blessed Lady, His Mother, meant far more to me, especially as I seldom saw my own mother.

This stone-pine panelled room was my first and my most personal realm. All kinds of wooden and plush animals stood on a shelf. I owned bricks with which I built houses that invariably collapsed very quickly. Of great importance was a toy motor car which wound up with a crank. I loved to let it crash into the houses, whereby in the end it was irreparably wrecked.

In these days my elder brothers took no part in my games. They were not even very clearly in my mind, they were too big and too remote. After all, Hans was five and Leopold three years older than myself. My sisters Sophie and Fanny, who were educated at the Sacré Coeur and came home only for the holidays, were tenderly loved by me, though they were even ten and eight years my seniors. It may have been because during the short holidays they mothered me and showed their personal pride in their youngest brother quite openly. Subsequently I learned that this pride in me had been properly displayed to their school friends — they could even tell them that something like a portent of my birth had happened during the summer holidays two months before I was born: a flash of lightning had struck through the window at which my mother was standing. It touched her without doing her any harm.

Now, there is hardly another place in Europe where thunderstorms are as terrific as at Schoenwoerth. Sometimes they continue for forty-eight hours above the castle. On such nights we children were hauled out of bed — the whole castle had wooden staircases, panelled rooms, and wooden shingles — and sat for hours downstairs round an oak table in the stone hall. The walls of the castle, many yards thick, shook continuously as if war or earthquake threatened the house, and I can still hear the anxious voice of our superintendent as he knelt before a crucifix with two red wax candles burning, to invoke the protection of Heaven.

The castle was supposed to be the home of innumerable ghosts, which for me as a child possessed absolute reality. There was, for instance, the 'White Lady of Schoenwoerth.' Her husband was killed while hunting bears, whereupon she committed suicide. Every three months, the peasants declared, she came back to the place where she had killed herself, and of course the souls of earlier owners of the castle who had maltreated the peasants were unable to rest easily in their graves. The descendants of those who had been fleeced revenged themselves upon the descendants of the wrongdoers by placing their forefathers in hell!

My father, though, was on friendly terms with the peasants. There was no celebration of any kind in the village at which he was not present. He drank and threw dice with them, and listened to all their stories of personal pleasures and grievances. One of the fundamental principles of my education was: 'Only one class is related to, though not equal to the nobility — the peasants; of course only as long as they acknowledge the nobles as their masters and do not rebel!'

Of the working classes it was said that they were 'red' and always in revolt against the landowners, the monarchy, and the Church. Therefore they were profoundly evil, and it was an absolute necessity that they should be kept in subjection. Still — as my father used to say in later years — they are better than the commercial classes. Those were the worst of all. They were without exception criminals — and were bound to be so from the nature of their calling. 'Why?' I asked him once when I was ten years old. 'That's

5

very simple,' he replied. 'The rascals make their living by selling dearer than they buy. Is that honest?'

There were also certain historical reasons for my father's preference for the working above the trading classes. He always had a sort of *haine d'amour* for the peasants who in the sixteenth century rebelled against their feudal lords and often strung them up to the towers of their own castles. In those days it would have been possible, with the help of the peasantry, to establish anew the supreme power of the Emperor over the German Princes — what an opportunity missed in our history! And so my father thought, at least in certain moments, that one might even try to understand socialism so as to shape it into an imperial monarchy based upon justice and the will of the people.

It never occurred to me in those days to wonder what was my father's profession. When I was still quite young, I was taught that decent people did not need any. Only a plebeian follows a profession; a gentleman passes his time — my father used to say — by being either a diplomatist, an officer, or simply himself. As a young man he had served in the German Army, and had resigned at an early age. This was a great mistake as he had extraordinary strategic talents. At the manoeuvres in which he took part soon after his marriage he was singled out from all the other young officers of the Bavarian Army for praise. It was said of him that he might one day play an important part on the Great General Staff.

I can remember as a child watching him in his leisure hours drawing military sketches and strategical plans of classical, mediaeval, and modern warfare. As soon as they were finished, he threw them into the wastepaper basket and started again — this time on fortresses and buildings with all architectural requirements. I never remember having seen my father idle. I am sure that he never knew what boredom was during his whole life, for he was interested in so many things, knowing something about them all without being a real expert.

He was in truth a brilliant amateur in everything he took

6

up. His collection of mediaeval coins and arms had a certain fame in Europe in their day, but it was always incomplete. He wrote books both in prose and verse on historical subjects, some of which were really beautiful, but on the whole he lacked seriousness in his work. He was interested in rural social problems, and agricultural experiments. At the same time he lost four estates successively within a few years. He was pious without being devout. He had a vast knowledge of French literature, but of France all he wanted to see was the Montmartre and the Riviera.

After his father's death a cousin named Ernest contested his inheritance. In consequence a superb property on the Chiemsee in Bavaria had to be sold in order that an adequate income could be provided for his mother and that he might supplement his lieutenant's pay.

My grandfather, at the time of his marriage, had signed an agreement renouncing his claims upon the family property both for himself and his heirs. Against this agreement nothing availed. Indeed, my grandfather himself had unsuccessfully attempted to restore their rights to his children — rights that he had too hastily signed away in order to obviate possible disputes over his marriage.

When his marriage took place, it was still generally known that my grandmother was a natural child of King Maximilian II of Bavaria by his cousin the Empress Dowager of Brazil, a daughter of Eugène Beauharnais, Duke of Leuchtenberg. When my grandmother was ten years old, her mother had her adopted by commoners in Hamburg, from whom she acquired the surname of Wollrabe. Subsequently the King of Bavaria ennobled her with the title of baroness.

My grandfather's marriage was not regarded as morganatic and therefore my grandmother bore the title of princess, just as my father and the other children of the marriage were born and brought up as princes and princesses.

It is perhaps interesting to note that the Court *Almanach de Gotha*, in order to draw a discreet veil over the affair, gives the date of my grandmother's birth as eleven years

7

after the actual one, given by the *Graefliche Gotha*. If the date given by the Court *Gotha* were correct, my grandmother, of course, could not have been the child of Max of Bavaria and the Duchess of Leuchtenberg; but on the other hand, she could only have been twelve and a half years of age at the time of her marriage to my grandfather!

A few years after my father's birth, King Ludwig II of Bavaria conferred on my grandmother — his stepsister — the additional hereditary name and title of Countess of Loewenstein-Scharffeneck. She was also given the original coat of arms of the family with the addition of purpure and ermine. The right to bear the princely name and title was not thereby affected.

After the death of my grandfather, however, which occurred at about the time when the money which he had received in exchange for the renunciation of his appanage was exhausted, my father only used the title of Count von Loewenstein-Scharffeneck. He held that in society the title of prince or count made no difference, as everybody knew his rank in any case, but that in the eyes of the world a prince was expected to live on a greater style, which he could not afford. Hence my brothers and sisters, and I myself, grew up and went to school bearing the titles of count and countess.

The name Count von Loewenstein-Scharffeneck was the original name of my family. The first to bear it was Ludwig of Bavaria, the son of the Elector Palatine Friedrich the Victorious of the House of Wittelsbach, at the beginning of the sixteenth century. Loewenstein and Scharffeneck were sovereign counties of the Holy Roman Empire, conferred by the Emperor on my ancestor Ludwig of Bavaria.

Our family, therefore, is the senior branch of the House of Wittelsbach, the progenitors of which — the Counts of the Nordgau, near Regensburg, are first mentioned in the pages of history in the year 770. We are related by marriage to every dynasty that rules or has ruled in Europe. We are direct descendants of the Carolingian, Hohenstaufen, and Franconian emperors, Rudolf von Habsburg, the Planta-

8

FIRST TO BEAR THE TITLE WAS LUDWIG OF BAVARIA, SON OF THE
ELECTOR PALATINE FRIEDRICH OF THE HOUSE OF WITTELSBACH

genets, the House of Savoy, the House of Aragon in Sicily and Spain, and the Przemyslid rulers of Bohemia and Poland. Our coat of arms is practically identical with that of the Bavarian Royal House; our colours are the same, white and blue. Our flag shows them either fusilly bendy like the inescutcheon, or in two stripes, horizontal and equally broad.

Our family has never ceased to lay claim to the Bavarian throne, which it should have inherited according to ancient family agreements. When the branch of the House of Wittelsbach, then occupying the throne of Bavaria, died out in 1777, and my own family should have succeeded to the throne, we were passed over in favour of a younger branch which was wealthier and controlled a large military force.

As after the overthrow of the German monarchies a special style of living was no longer expected of a prince, my father in 1920 decided to resume the title for himself and his children. Thereupon the governments of Prussia and Bavaria furnished the necessary documents through the German Legation in Vienna, and the *Graefliche Gotha* for the same year contained an announcement of these facts. My father's decision was in conformity with an agreement concluded in 1912 between him and his cousin Prince Ernest. At that time my father brought an action against Prince Ernest as head of the family to compel him to pay appanage, but he was defeated on the ground of the same agreement which his father had first signed and then tried to contest.

In the course of the action, as well as in the judgment that concluded it, it was definitely stated that the question of the princely title was not to be raised. Since Prince Ernest considered it to be exceedingly doubtful whether he could prevent my father from resuming the princely name and title, he undertook at the time of this action not to question his right to the title if he continued to reside in Austria.

It was a matter of course during my childhood that my father should wield the highest — and the unquestioned —

authority in the house. His authority was all the greater because we saw comparatively little of him. Only after meals were we children allowed to appear in order to kiss our parents' hands. But sometimes after dusk, too, I would see my father, when we were all gathered in the Great Hall, where petroleum lamps shadowed rather than lighted up the family portraits and panelled walls, and he told us stories of knights and ghosts. He often said that the sound of knocking was to be heard behind one of the portraits whenever the name of the sitter was mentioned. I cannot confirm this, as it never happened in my presence. The mysterious power of another picture, however, was described to me in the same way by so many different people, that really I am still in doubt as to whether or not it was only a family tale.

This is what is supposed to have happened: Once there was a large shooting party staying at the castle, when my father told an astonishing story about a remarkably brave stag. Nobody believed him and everyone declared that he was drawing the long bow. Then my father called out laughingly: 'If I have exaggerated, that picture over there will fall.' And the picture fell. The bottom of the frame was cracked by the fall. My father never had it mended.

The Great Hall was the main room of the castle. In later years it appeared to me rather significant that we received daylight there only filtered through the stained glass of the armorial windows.

One evening among others in the Great Hall I remember clearly. There is summer lightning behind the mountains, the air is heavy and oppressive, and an uncanny feeling over everything. Suddenly my father comes in and seems very excited.

'Come quickly to the armoury. Something extraordinary is going on.'

We run downstairs. There stands a being in full armour surmounted by a steel helmet from which a lighted skull grins at us.

'Don't dare run away,' says my father. 'Boys of noble blood are never afraid.'

10

Nevertheless I was afraid. Indeed, it was this experience that first taught me what fear was.

But there were better ways than this of teaching us the knightly virtues. When I was a little older I was allowed to wear a suit of armour myself. True, it was made of tin, but what did that matter? I also received a long sword and on my fourth birthday a medal with the effigy of Saint George the dragon-killer. He was to be my exemplar.

There is an early likeness of me that shows all this very clearly. I am standing on the steps before the entrance to Schoenwoerth, guarding it with my sword. What did I look like then?

I was always tall for my age and slim. As a child I was golden-haired, and until I was eight I wore my hair coming down to my shoulders. Between the age of eight and ten my hair was cut like that of a page — cut to my ears at the side of the head and with a fringe over my forehead. Usually I was dressed in Russian blouses of various colours. It was not until I was ten that I went into sailor suits.

I was supposed to have a will of my own, and to be a thoughtful child full of weird notions. Grown-ups used to amuse themselves at times by making me angry in order to see me bang the table with my fist and defend my rights vigorously.

I possessed a strongly marked sense of order and discipline. One day when I was still very small I felt sick at table. I left the room, thought better of it, reopened the dining-room door, stood at attention and said: 'I have to report that I am being sick!' This episode also shows the military atmosphere that surrounded us.

It was an atmosphere upon which my mother exercised no influence — if indeed she ever exercised any influence at all over our education. I retain hardly a memory of her from these years, and since I remember much else very clearly, I can only conclude that her will never prevailed in Schoenwoerth. I cannot tell whether this was due to her own character or rather to the surroundings, very different from ours, in which she was born and brought up.

Her father was Baron Henry de Worms. His father had settled in England. But the family had lived in Germany since 1520. A distant relative of my grandfather once showed me some old books and papers from which I learnt that my grandfather's family, and also that of his mother, was descended from the Spanish statesman, scholar, philosopher, and poet Abarbanel, who lived in the days of Ferdinand the Catholic. Abarbanel, who must have been one of the most universal minds of his time, traced his ancestry back in a direct line to King David.

My grandfather was a Conservative Member of Parliament when he was still quite a young man, and soon made a name for himself as one of the most important leaders of the Conservative Party. A whole series of books from his pen on such subjects as English policy in the Far East, English trade and commercial policy, and the development and history of Austria-Hungary have not yet become archaic. He was a brilliant lawyer. At a relatively early age he became Parliamentary Secretary to the Board of Trade, and was subsequently Under-Secretary of the State for the Colonies for many years. When Lord Salisbury became Prime Minister for the third time, he raised him to the peerage as Baron Pirbright of Pirbright. He is said to have contributed largely to the political and economical development of the British Empire.

My grandmother was a Baroness Todesco and came from a Viennese family. Her house was a meeting-place for writers and artists. She herself was one of the most beautiful — and also the most frivolous — women of her time. Hence the marriage of my grandfather was not a happy one. They were divorced soon after the birth of my mother, who spent her infancy in London and was subsequently brought up in Baden-Baden and Vienna.

It was a curious world in which my mother grew up. I have read the diaries which she kept from the time she was sixteen until she was nineteen. Her life was passed in Vienna, Munich, and Wiesbaden amidst luxurious surroundings. Her family never thought of a country estate as other than a place in which to pass six weeks in the summer. There seems to have been no notion of money. An artificial took the place of the real world. Everyone was dissatisfied and filled with an immense and terrible boredom.

Her diaries end a few months before she and my father met for the first time. It was at a Court Ball in Munich. They were married after they had been engaged for a very short time. My father was then twenty-four, my mother twenty years of age.

For the first few years their marriage — at least outwardly — appears to have been a happy one. But my father was tempted by the prosperity brought to him through his marriage to resign prematurely from the army. He bought one estate after another and had to give them up. My mother on her part could not accustom herself to a country life; she had never been used to it. They began to live in a luxury that far exceeded their means. An army of servants, expensive journeys — they frequently hired special trains — horses, clothes, jewellery, all these things ruined them financially, thereby causing quarrel and dissent.

Schoenwoerth was bought with the remainder of the money which my grandfather Pirbright had left to them. It was intended to become the scene of a new life and to afford the family a permanent home. It was already too late. At the time of my birth my parents were already so estranged from one another that not even my arrival could prevent the coming of the end. Moreover, shortly before my birth my mother handed over the household duties at Schoenwoerth to a lady companion and thus became, as it were, a guest at her own table, a guest indeed whose presence was only barely tolerated as time went on, until finally she was a total stranger.

I was four years old when my mother left Schoenwoerth forever. On the day of her departure the stone shield bearing her coat of arms, which stood beside that bearing my father's above the entrance gate, split in two of itself.

I barely grasped what her departure meant. I was told that she was ill and was travelling for her health's sake.

13

I could not understand it. Why could she not get better in Schoenwoerth, in the park, beneath the great chestnut trees, in the meadows, beside the brook? Something was wrong — I felt it — and it made me miserable.

I stood in the inner courtyard of the castle and watched the horses being harnessed — four snow-white Lippizaner with red nostrils. My mother was dressed entirely in black. She kissed us children and spoke some words of farewell. The scene only lasted a short time. For the 'lady companion' led me back into the castle before the gates were opened and the carriage drove away. I went with my brothers into our playroom, and suddenly I began to cry.

In harsh and angry tones Mademoiselle Jex reproached me for crying. Thereupon I sprang upon her lap with a shriek of rage and bit her nose. I must have bitten it pretty hard, because the red marks were visible for a long time afterward. She revenged herself very thoroughly on me for this bite, and had many opportunities of doing so, for she remained with us for another three years. In this way she was responsible for filling me with a dislike of three things for years to come. The first was arithmetic. I still remember how she explained to me that the serious side of life begins when one comes to numbers and figures. 'Un deux, un deux,' she said. 'That's what you have to learn! It will be be a bad lookout for you if you don't.' Her way of saying 'un deux' was so malevolent that for years afterward I never opened an arithmetic book without shuddering.

Secondly, she is to blame that I learned to read French only comparatively late. Her method of teaching consisted in laying herself at full length on her stomach on the floor beside me and opening the book. If I could not pronounce the word, she seized me by the hair and bumped my head and nose against the book. I disliked this and thought that all learning consisted of such unpleasant procedure.

Finally, she aroused in me a dislike that lasted for years of everything French. I looked on her as the embodiment of France, and thought that all French people, or at least all French women, resembled her.

14

My dislike for Mademoiselle Jex was also due partly to the fact that I could not understand why she had any rights at all over me. Neither my brothers nor I looked upon her as anything more than a superior servant, and my father had taught us that such people were far beneath us. How, then, did she dare to order us about and actually to punish us?

After all, the other servants were given precise instructions that even in talking to us children they were always to use the third person. Also, the sons of our superintendent — one called George was about my age — were absolutely forbidden to be 'familiar' with us, and if I did not insist upon the observance of this rule, I was reprimanded by my father. It is nearly indecent, he would say, to mix in that way with the lower classes: it spoils their character, and makes them impertinent.

For a long time I dissented from his opinion. But one day I noticed George secretly riding my tricycle and telling people that it was his. 'Papa is right, after all,' I said to my sister. 'From now onward we will only talk French so that George won't be able to understand what we are saying. That shall be his punishment.' Well, that worked for some time, until something happened which made me change my mind.

A large brook — a fierce stream in my childish eyes — flowed through the park. Beyond the park this brook passed over a weir and beneath a mill. We were strictly forbidden to go near the place. Undoubtedly it was dangerous for children. Naturally this induced me to go frequently to that very place. I saw with fear and trembling how the waters fell down into what seemed to me an enormous depth. A small bridge joined the mill to the bank of the brook. I knew that I was easily dizzy and that was just what lured me.

I left the firm earth feeling that I was about to achieve something tremendous. I looked down at the waters below with a feeling of wonderful horror, and then I fell. If Paul — elder brother of George — had not been there, and immediately fished me out, I should certainly have been drowned.

15

There was great excitement at home. I was carried back
to the castle, dripping and shivering, and had to go to bed
for the rest of the day. I could not be quieted for days, and
I was worse because Anna told me that I should certainly
get the plague and die. I did not quite believe her, but said,
'Then you will die too.' For I was convinced, I cannot tell
why or how, that everybody in the world died at the same
moment. But still I was somehow frightened, although I
comforted myself a little with the thought that Mademoiselle
Jex would then die too.

The most important result of the episode was that from
that time onward I was allowed to play with the superintendent's children, though my father still insisted that a
certain restraint should be used.

Neither was this changed by another incident that happened soon after I fell into the mill race.

There are two kinds of animal at Schoenwoerth that are
better avoided by man: a particularly poisonous snake called
'sand viper' and hornets. The hornets live in ball-like nests
that they fix to walls. The sand vipers, on the other hand,
prefer warm and sandy places where they lie maliciously —
from the human point of view — pretending to be a piece
of greyish-brown wood.

One day I was in the park with Anna and Mademoiselle
Jex. My elder brothers were also there, armed with bows
and arrows for the purpose of bringing down some huntable
animal, as my father would have said. Instead of which they
suddenly saw a hornets' nest and shot at it.

The effect was unpleasant. Hundreds of hornets flew out
from their so unkindly damaged home and whizzed round
us. My brothers stood rooted to the ground in horror, one
even with his mouth open. To cut the story short — they
were ill for weeks and nearly died of blood poisoning.

Immediately after this fateful shot, when the hornets
were massing to the attack, Anna noticed one of those greyish-brown sticks lying at our feet. She was not a Tyrolese
and therefore trusted it, probably she wanted to use it for
my defence. Just as she was stretching out her hand to

16

ON MY TRICYCLE — THE ONE GEORGE TOOK

BEFORE THE ENTRANCE TO SCHOENWOERTH, GUARDING IT
WITH MY SWORD

pick it up, the superintendent's eldest son ran out of the house, seized hold of us and hurried us inside. Outside the infuriated hornets buzzed round the windows, while the greyish-brown 'stick' disappeared rapidly in the nearest bush.

That episode with bow and arrows is not wholly without significance. We grew up surrounded by weapons of all kinds. With a sabre which I received later I knocked out one of my brother's front teeth. The arrows we used were not supposed to be sharpened; actually they were, and as the bows that we used when we grew older were fairly strong they could be used for better purposes than shooting at hornets' nests.

My brothers at one time fought a duel with bow and arrow that resulted in many wounds. But when it was discovered that an arrow had pierced the hat of my elder brother, and that therefore we evidently did not pay much heed to where our arrows went, we were obliged to play this game secretly for a long time.

We had no punishment to fear as the result of such peccadilloes. We knew very well that my father would encourage our military leanings as far as he could. In old times — he would say — one could rid money-bags this way of their goods and chattels, thereby realizing social justice much better than by all this modern humanitarian balderdash.

To Schoenwoerth and its childhood liberties I owe much. I had my places in the park which nobody else knew, and trees to be climbed, if I did not want to be found.

'Now I can view my entire kingdom,' I said to myself. 'And now I must rule it.' But who are my subjects? Not only the superintendent's children, George and Paul, or their somewhat younger sister who often brought me flowers and did 'homage' — they were only the representatives of innumerable invisible beings.

All lands belonged to me, all woods, even a part of the mountains. All round I could claim loyalty, even if they did not know it.

17

At night in my bed I prayed that God would protect them and make them happy. I took this very seriously, as one of the duties of my office that I could not leave undone.

Children's kingdoms, children's empires — hundreds of tiny springs filled the park of Schoenwoerth: to me they were both streams and voices. Trees and bushes had names and souls: the mightiest among them, the great ash, centuries old, deep-rooted in the wall, touched the roof with its topmost leaves. 'Wotan's sacred tree,' I was taught. 'Germany's God protected your cradle,' my father said once.

Christianity and paganism often meet in our part of the world. Why not Wotan's ash, if bonfires are lit in honour of Saint John on all the mountain peaks — Midsummer's Eve in a Christian mantle? Not a mantle — the fulfilment of the pagan sagas, the Germanic revelation no less than the fulfilment of the Old Testament prophecies.

I can still hear the wind in the branches of the ash as when I lay in bed in the dark stone-pine panelled room. I can hear the river at its feet, and what they spoke to me I shall never forget. Their primeval words, from the mouth of creation, come so clearly to me from this enchanted land behind all mountains and forests that I can feel them always, in my country and in a thousand exiles.

II. *Surprising Experiences*

*A*S A RULE we went to the South Tyrol in the late autumn. But for the winter of 1909 our parents decided to take us down to Bordighera on the Italian Riviera. The people there spoke a language, so I was told, of which I should not understand a word. In fact the only one of us who would understand it would be Mademoiselle Jex. This was surprising. But what surprised me still more was the enormous stretch of water that I saw from Genoa onward. Hardly had I grown accustomed to this when I was thrilled by the line beyond which the sea seemed to come to an end, although the ships could go farther. The only explanation I could think of for this was that they probably had concealed wheels which they let down once they got beyond the line which was called the horizon. This seemed all the more probable since Mademoiselle Jex had told me that Africa began beyond where I could see and that it was full of sand.

Also the new plants I saw — orange trees, lemons, and pumpkins — deeply impressed me, especially the pumpkins, for lanterns could be made out of them. It annoyed me, however, to hear that there was no snow at Christmas time and that the Child Christ — as we say in Germany — could not bring real fir trees, and I told Mademoiselle Jex that I thought Italy was a very silly country.

She was not at all pleased, but replied brusquely that we ought to be thankful to be allowed such a wonderful tour, and that anyhow we had much too good a time.

I could not understand why she said this, and wondered

what was the matter with her. But just as my brothers and I regarded her as only a servant, though a superior one, she on her side may have harboured an individual piece of class-hatred — 'the revenge of the fourth estate,' as Strindberg calls it, working itself out on the children of the upper classes, whose education is handed over to them.

It was a bad day for us when her feelings got the better of her. One morning the German governess had been obliged to stay at home, and we had gone to the beach with Mademoiselle Jex, neatly dressed and behaving nicely. Little Italian urchins were playing round us. We hardly noticed them; it probably did not even dawn on us that one might notice them. Nor did they make any attempt to talk to us, though they may have been making remarks about us and other children from afar.

Suddenly Mademoiselle Jex's face changed, she spat out a few abusive words and rushed across to the street boys. She said something to them in Italian, mouthing and shrieking like a fishwife, whereupon the boys made a united set at us, whistling and cat-calling, and razed our sand castles to the ground. We ran crying to Mademoiselle Jex, who received us sneeringly. The poor little Italians were quite right, she said, it was irritating enough to see us playing here every day, haughty and well-fed.

The whole affair was so strange that we said nothing about it at home. Only among ourselves we talked of it and decided that Mademoiselle Jex was a very common person and liked to make friends with the lower classes.

When on the following day the same boys disturbed the games of some English youngsters, and at last it threatened to be quite impossible for 'nice' children to play on the beach, something of what had happened came out. Mademoiselle Jex would have been dismissed except that my parents feared the inconvenience. However, my father severely forbade her any repetition of her behaviour and called her a 'Red.' From this time onward she was obliged, furious though she was, to keep the Italians away from us.

The word a 'Red' made a deep impression on me. At first

I thought it referred to Mademoiselle Jex's nose, a theory which was soon upset by a fresh occurrence.

One day as my brothers and I were playing on the beach, we climbed over the wall that separated the promenade from the railway. On the rails we found a thick bamboo cane. We cracked it and found a little iron bottle inside—it was a bomb. Fräulein Skomal, who had been watching, exclaimed: 'This the Reds must have done to blow up the train!' If she had said 'anarchists' she would probably have been right, but the word would have meant even less to me. An association of ideas was immediately established between the bomb and Mademoiselle Jex, and I was convinced that it was she who had placed it on the line. My brothers thought the same. We stood round the bomb and watched it with curiosity.

At last one of us said: 'What fools the Reds are. It wouldn't be good fun to blow up a train. It must be much jollier to see a shipwreck.' Unhindered by Fräulein Skomal, who was in a half-fainting condition, we picked up the bomb and threw it into the sea. Then we performed war-dances on the beach and waited to see what happened. Of course nothing did.

Shortly before we left Bordighera, my first political idea came to me — less an idea perhaps than a sort of vision. We had a footman called Michael, of whom my father thought a good deal at that time. We children were particularly fond of him, as he was very good at making wooden swords, spears, and shields.

One evening he and I were standing looking out of a window, in front of which there grew a tall eucalyptus tree.

'I want a new sword,' I said to Michael. But he replied that he had not got time to make it, because he had to go back to Germany to join his regiment for the manoeuvres.

'Must you or do you want to?' I enquired.

'I don't want to, but I have got to. The German Emperor has commanded it.'

'Well,' I said, 'if the German Emperor commands people to do things they don't want to, he must go! Under me it would be different ——'

21

Perhaps Michael thought someone might have overheard the conversation — anyway, he went and repeated it to my father, who was furious with me.

'Never say a thing like that again,' he said. 'I suppose some Red must have put that idea into your head.'

I was astonished at how many different things these Reds will do. First they force small children to lie on their stomachs and look at French books, and if they don't understand them their noses are bumped on the books. Secondly, they lay bombs on railway lines (instead of blowing up ships), and thirdly, they are against the German Emperor. And all the time I knew that it was I who was furious with the Emperor, and not the Reds! After all, who was it that was not getting a sword because Michael had to go and join the army — the Reds or myself? And Michael would much rather have carved a sword for me than have gone to the manoeuvres.

At about the same time, my life nearly came to a violent end. It must have been on December 28 when I went down to the beach with Mademoiselle Jex at an unusual hour. It was already dark and I was a little bit afraid. The sea looked quite different; there was a treacherous greenish light on it, long threads of waves strained themselves along the shore, while far off on the horizon a thunderstorm seemed to be brewing. Sky and sea met in an arch; each appeared to have been bent over towards the other, with no more than a thin yellow line to show the division.

On shore everything was frighteningly still. Not a leaf quivered, not an animal was to be heard. I picked up a stone and threw it into the sea. It fell with a dull thud, as though the sound had been swallowed up in the water. I was going to draw Mademoiselle Jex's attention to this when I found that I was alone on the beach. She had remained up above on the promenade talking to some Italian friends while I had come down beside the water. She was so deep in conversation that she did not notice what was going on below.

I picked up another stone, a flatter one this time. Once again it gave back a muffled sound, but it was more long-drawn-out and seemed to be radiating in every direction from the place where the stone had sunk. My head felt numb. Could it be that the sound remained caught below the waters? A sensation like that before fainting came over me, when men and trees cease to be corporal, but planes take solid form, the sky, the roads, and all the fields. And yet I knew I was wide awake and that what I saw and heard was real. While the air remained still, the sea began to hum like a forest of glass; it quivered as though countless stones had fallen into it, or rather as though they were coming up from the bottom and as if the great circles were down below and those on top were only their last faint reflections.

This grew ever stronger; now there was a sound like the booming of the deep notes of an organ — whence could it come? Surely from that very blue wave there — no, from that reddish one! But was not that the one that had just been hissing? Then I knew: it was not from close by at all, it was from far, far away that the organ tone came; from where the yellow zigzag line was. Now it is no longer a narrow zigzag — it has become quite wide, as wide as my hand and phosphorescent.

And then — at first the sea had been simply curved upward, now it was toppled over like the uncurving of an enormous steel spring; it tightened and became one gigantic wave reaching all across the horizon, and came nearer. Faster and faster it approached, rolling towards me with furious speed; I had to raise my head to see the top — the sea, the whole sea.

I turned round — it was as though a hand pushed me — away, for Heaven's sake away, it will roll over you, in another moment you will be underneath, and it will be cold and stifling.

'Mademoiselle!' I cried, 'Mademoiselle!' while the sand under my feet began to slip. I scrambled through holes from which leapt fountains, I fell over clefts that grew broader as I fell.

Now I had reached the top. At last Mademoiselle Jex had noticed what was happening. But what did 'top'

23

mean when there was no more bottom? Together with me the first wave reached the promenade. I was so exhausted that Mademoiselle Jex had to carry me. She ran like mad, pursued by the suddenly forthbursting storm. She must have run knee-deep through water, because even in our garden the waves were already slapping against the sides of the house.

I can still remember the anxious night that followed. We sat in the second story, and did not dare to sleep. Over and over again the storm beat at the house, and now and then waves splashed up to the windows. Amid all the noise we heard the screams of the people who were fleeing up from the lower parts of the town.

Later I was told that this was the night in which Messina was swallowed up in an earthquake.

After spending the winter in Bordighera, we returned to Schoenwoerth by way of the South Tyrol. There was a glorious spring in Bozen and Meran. Thousands of blossoming trees, the mountain brooks, the early spring flowers — as in a trance I ran through the gardens and did not come home for hours. My love of the South Tyrol dates from that time. It is the only country that ever fills me with a kind of ecstasy. This most southern land of the German tongue, this land of Walther von der Vogelweide, where Italy and Germany mingle — no, not mingle, but where the unity of the western world, of the truly Holy Roman Empire, of the German Nation is made manifest.

At that time I did not realize it, not clearly at least. But later I was taken to castles and strongholds, where my father told me of the battles of German knights against the Lombards, who were merchants and enemies of the Empire — of course, for what else could one expect of them! It was here in the South Tyrol, he said, that our House rose to its first glory when Otto von Wittelsbach, risking his own life, saved that of his cousin the Emperor Frederick Barbarossa.

I knew fairy tales in which there were kings and emperors. They were not like the German Emperor who forced Michael

24

to do things he did not want to. The emperors in my books of fairy tales went into battle themselves and did not stay comfortably at home while their men fought. But in times of peace they sat on golden thrones and were merciful and just.

Thus fairy tales were the door through which I first entered German history. But nowhere was it more vivid to me than in the mountains of the South Tyrol.

My father once found an old arrowhead as we were clambering through a ruin together. When he gave it to me, I said: 'I'm going to be a knight too and kill dragons and journey to the Holy Land.' But the reply was: 'There aren't any dragons nowadays, nor any knights. The days of chivalry are over.' I did not understand what he meant, but it gave me a momentary pang. Then I said: 'I shall be a knight all the same; I shall be the only one there is.'

A little while later I and my brothers were given a volume of *Germanic Sagas*, with a dedication in it from my father to his three sons. I liked this so much that I always wanted it read to me. I still remember its last words — 'the heart of German gold, of German steel the sword.'

This book gave me Dietrich of Berne, Siegfried and Hagen, Beowulf, and Ruediger of Pechlarn, as the constant companions of my childhood. They came with me wherever I went. They kept the longing alive to be like them, even when I was no longer surrounded by castles and strongholds, by mountains and a southern land. And this was good. For all at once, not long after my mother had left, when we were in the South Tyrol again, we were told that we were not going back to Schoenwoerth, not this winter, nor yet in the following spring or summer. Why? I asked. That was not my affair, I was told, possibly we might return some day; there was no need for me to know more than that.

Soon afterward we set out on a long railway journey. When I woke up I was told that we were now in Vienna and that life would begin in earnest. My nurse, Anna, had not come with us, and Mademoiselle Jex would take complete charge of me. Before I was able to make any comment —

or possibly begin to cry — I found myself sitting in a carriage, and in the excitement of looking at the great city, I completely forgot what I had just been told.

As my brothers were now eight and ten years of age, they had a tutor whom my father addressed as 'Herr Doctor.' At first I thought he was a doctor of medicine and that somebody in the family was ill. When I discovered my mistake, it seemed to me ridiculous to call him Doctor, until my brothers explained that to call him 'Herr Lehrer' would be an insult.

In the intervals between my brothers' lessons, the Doctor-Tutor gave me my first lessons in writing, which I found very entertaining. I was proud for a week once when I had made a specially successful M.

As a result of the comparatively narrow quarters of the town house, which was situated in a pleasant district, quite near a large park, my brothers and I saw more of each other than we had done at Schoenwoerth. And I remember that at the very beginning of this new epoch in our lives, an ill-omened word came to haunt us — 'War.' It became a word of such mighty import that everything we did seemed to revolve round it. I can remember no peaceful games, nothing that, carried to its logical conclusion, did not imply war. This is true alike of the external impressions that we received and of everything that we did together in work or play.

The first impetus was given by the news of the Turco-Italian war and a little later of the Balkan wars. We children took sides in them passionately, and fought out the battles daily in miniature with our toys. I don't know how it happened, but I was on the side of the Italians and my brothers on the side of the Turks. 'I'm going to help the Italians,' we expressed it, and 'We're going to help the Turks.' It was considered disgraceful to be helping the Italians — probably on account of our experiences at Bordighera. So I was fighting a really desperate battle, first on account of 'public opinion,' and secondly, because the toys belonging to one child are fewer than the toys belonging to two children, more especially when these two are older.

26

During the war between the Bulgarians and the Turks, the latter suddenly ceased to enjoy the sympathies of our family. It was looked upon as the decent thing to 'help' the Bulgarians. Whereupon, of course, I had to be on the Turkish side.

My championship of Italy had done me considerable damage. But my anti-Bulgarian attitude finally stamped me as a small Power of the lowest grade for at least two years.

Now everybody has been a child once. But most people forget what their views and feelings were at the time. Therefore it is not easy to recall the rules of childish thought.

In our earliest days together, we lived in a purely ideal, visionary world. During my fifth and sixth years we did not even need our animals to help us fight our wars and battles. The conflict was carried on in words. My eldest brother would say, for example: 'I am invading your country and I am going to conquer a seaport.' Whereupon I replied: 'But my men take it back from you and go a long way into your country' — after which my second brother, who was very strong, intervened, and inflicted a decisive defeat on me.

What we said was reality to us. We always knew exactly where our 'troops' were, and we knew the laws that determined victory or defeat. Not until a little later did these battles take on more concrete form by games with our animals and toy soldiers. The last stage of development before the final collapse of the children's order was reached when we learnt to play chess. We made maps and drew fresh frontiers after winning or losing games.

Our animals included every kind existing: tigers, hippopotami, camels, frogs, and so on. Every Christmas, every birthday, added some new ones.

My most important animal was a white elephant. It always had to be a white one. I called him 'The Commander-in-Chief' and put him over all the animals. How I happened to light on that name I cannot recollect. I only remember that once I asked my father which was higher, a general or a commander-in-chief. His answer, that a

27

commander-in-chief was always a general, but that a general need not necessarily be a commander-in-chief, left me no wiser than I was before.

The lords set over my brothers' animals were of a much more traditional type — lions in fact. In our nursery speech they were referred to as 'levi,' until my father said we were not to call them that any longer because it sounded Jewish.

My eldest brother's lion exercised immense power, not only over my brother's animals but also over the subjects of the Commander-in-Chief. He had the right to turn out our animals from a large motor omnibus in which during times of peace the most respected ones went home at nights. Moreover, he could give and take away patents of nobility and riches. Very soon, however, a permanent alliance was concluded between my two elder brothers' animals, and alas, it was an alliance of offence against myself.

A terrible reign of arbitrary government set in. It went so far that the Commander-in-Chief was deprived of his royal rank, and was only accorded a new title after long negotiations. The moral justification for this lay in a great sea-battle which had taken place in Vienna in my sixth year between my brothers' animals and the Commander-in-Chief's subjects. We had built little boats of paper and wood and had received permission for the battle to take place in the evening by candlelight. The Commander-in-Chief was hopelessly beaten, and forced to adopt the cognomen of 'War-Ruin,' since he had been ruined in war.

This seems a convenient place to say a few words about Pipopil, although his importance lasted over a number of years. Pipopil was a very real figure — to call him a fairy king would not be sufficient. He was, in fact, the power that animated my animals and fought his battles in their persons. Even the Commander-in-Chief was to some extent dependent upon him.

What was the origin of Pipopil and how he came into existence, I cannot remember. It is only certain that he was the successor to Whirl Red. Why Whirl Red was overthrown and eventually had to be shot is, however, veiled in the darkness of prehistory.

The one sure thing is that Pipopil suddenly existed and that his name was Pipopil. Members of his family known by name are only his wife, Pipopa, and her brother, Tibetal, who was king of a neighbouring country.

The characteristics and functions of Pipopil were many and various. He was allowed to do the oddest things with impunity and had evolved more or less original solutions to many of the problems of life. (Psychoanalysts would call him a 'super-ego,' a desire-impulse, to whom everything was permitted that I would have liked to do. But that need not trouble us here.)

Since my brothers had similar beings at their command — who were called Queech and Zimzamzo — and these were allied against Pipopil just as the lions were allied against the Commander-in-Chief, Pipopil's situation was somewhat difficult. It is therefore not surprising that he soon began to believe that only the greatest severity within his own country would give him the necessary power of resistance to external attack. Hence he first of all caused all the remaining members of Whirl Red's family to be executed, that is Whirl Blue, Whirl Green, Whirl Yellow, and Whirl Black. Even his marriage to Pipopa was a political move, whereby a considerable portion of Tibetalia was brought under Pipopilian rule, thus greatly increasing Pipopil's power.

The actual geographical situation of Pipopilia could never be established with certainty. According to the most ancient records, it had been built inside the earth because none of the existing countries had sufficiently pleased Pipopil.

The castle in which he lived was very much like Schoenwoerth, but was built beside a great river called Quam. Part of this river flowed through Pipopil's bathroom and was very warm even in winter.

The family of Pipopil must undoubtedly have ruled over a part of the country even in the days of Whirl Red. Otherwise it could not have been said that Pipopil's grandfather had been a very popular ruler.

29

Pipopil was very jealous of his grandfather. What he disliked most was that he himself was Pipopil III, for he regarded the III after his name as a grave personal insult. But when my brothers brought home from school the use of negative numbers, Pipopil evolved an idea that was worthy of Solomon — from that time onward he called himself Pipopil I and never referred to his grandfather except as Pipopil the Minus Second.

Not satisfied with that, he tried to think of some way in which he might still further weaken the respect in which Pipopil the Minus Second was held without rousing the people against himself.

Now one must know that all the Pipopils had very large round heads, and Pipopil the Minus Second was said to have had the largest of any. Hence Pipopil had a solemn proclamation issued saying that he intended to do special honour to his grandfather's memory and that he purposed raising a memorial to him.

Work was carried on for a long time on this memorial, which cost enormous sums — something between ten and twenty Austrian crowns was mentioned. The astonishment of the people may be imagined when it was at length unveiled in the marketplace of the capital — it was nothing but an enormous ball, typifying with obvious cynicism the head of the beloved ruler Pipopil the Minus Second. Pipopil countered the indignation of the masses with the innocent explanation that the body was of course not visible, because his beloved grandfather had been more deeply rooted than any in his people.

This did not altogether silence the voice of the people. But once about this time when my father was speaking of the reasons for and against freedom of the press, I suddenly piped up: 'Pipopil does these things quite differently. He allows all the papers to print what they like, even if it is about himself. Only the language in which they have to be written is announced every day anew. Anyone who uses the language of the day before is executed.'

My father said: 'But how can one print a newspaper in a

30

language which is only announced in the morning? No one would understand it.' 'That doesn't worry Pipopil,' I said. 'He says that if people are so stupid it's their own lookout.'

Pipopil dealt somewhat differently with pacifist literature. This was found out one day when my father was telling us about Berta von Suttner's book *Down with Arms!* He said it would do a lot of harm among the people to take away their pride in militarism. Suddenly he turned to me and enquired: 'Now I should like to know what Pipopil thinks about it?' 'That's quite simple,' I replied. 'Pipopil allows the publication of all books against war. Only he has commanded that every sentence must end with the word Hurrah!'

Many another laudable and original act of Pipopil's is known; for example, his new fiscal policy. The currency unit was the Pipax which was composed of a hundred Pilis. Both coins were the same size. Anyone who was owed money by a Pipopilian and who was not himself a Pipopilian was handed the full sum in Pipax, upon which, however, had been written 'now a Pili,' and then he was obliged to leave as quickly as possible. On the other hand, if a foreigner owed money to a Pipopilian the process was reversed. The money thus gained was used by Pipopil to carry on the war against Queech and Zimzamzo.

When at last he had come to terms with these two, it was not difficult for him to conquer all the other neighbouring states. He simply issued a stern prohibition to them to shoot at his soldiers. If they did it in spite of this, he would be obliged to take a very serious view of the matter and to designate it as mean. It appears that they did in fact conform to it. As regards Tibetal, at all events, this is fully proved. Pipopil invaded his country once while they were supposed to be at peace, and Tibetal handed over to him all he possessed — land, treasure, and arms. 'For,' said he, 'there's no point in it. If I'm not allowed to shoot in time of war, it'll be all the worse if I shoot in time of peace.'

With which anecdote I will end the history of Pipopil, although he was at least thirty years before his time, and has since then found active imitators in various countries, who are now called 'Leaders,' and who are addressed in diplomatic parlance as 'Your Excellency.'

Among all the turmoil of real and imaginary wars during my time in Vienna, the most terrible news was that of the wreck of the *Titanic*. It made such an impression on me that soon afterward I enquired: 'Has anyone ever come back alive from a war or a sea voyage?'

I was suffering from scarlet fever at that time, and when my brother Leopold developed it too, we spoke of nothing else all day long. These conversations mixed themselves up in my feverish dreams and resulted in all kinds of horrible visions that made a deep impression on me. I saw shapes and men that terrified me; nor could everyone's assurances that they were not real soothe me.

I remember one dream that haunted me for a long time. I dreamt that I went into the room next door which was dark and suddenly felt under me a creature of an indeterminate kind. Before I could get down from it, it whizzed away with me, and when I tried to hold on to it, I found that the creature's forehead was soft. My fingers went right inside its head.

Long after I was well again I had another strange dream, which I also remember very well. I should say by way of introduction that at that time I had no idea what Byzantine mosaics looked like. Not until I was in Sicily as a grown man did it occur to me that I had seen this type of art before.

My dream was this: As a boy of some twelve years of age — thus several years older in my dreams than in reality — I was kneeling in front of the altar in a vast church built in the Byzantine style. I was wearing stiff garments woven of purple and gold, such as the Paleologues might have worn. Before me stood a bishop with a glittering mitre on his head. In his hand he held a crown and was about to set it on my head. The whole church was filled with incense and a strange and solemn music. In my dreams I already felt the touch of the gold upon my brow, when the bishop snatched a dagger from the folds of his robe and plunged it into my heart. I fell, in the midst of a sudden deadly hush, and was carried into a vestry. When death approached me, I woke up.

After we had recovered from the scarlet fever, my father moved with us to Gmunden in Upper Austria. This is a little town of about six thousand inhabitants, on the banks of a wonderful lake.

Gmunden was looked upon as the refuge of impoverished Austrian and German aristocrats. It used to be said that if you accidentally trod on the toe of an unknown man in the street, it was perfectly safe to say, 'I beg your pardon, my dear Count,' for you would be sure to be right. This was typical of the whole atmosphere of the place, or rather of the people with whom one had social intercourse. 'Abysmal ignorance' is a mild term to apply to it. The entire conversation turned on the *Almanach de Gotha*, and upon who had married whom. This could not remain without influence on our family.

My father took very little interest in us at this time. We were left to be brought up by the lady companion, who declared anything to do with literature, poetry, or art to be 'ungentlemanlike' and unworthy of the attention of 'nice people.' Nice in this sense included only the aristocracy and a certain section of the patrician families. Among these were reckoned government officials, and one or two doctors and lawyers, but only those who went shooting.

There was a school at Gmunden — 'Gymnasium' as we say — which my elder brothers attended and where I also was entered when the time came. But for the present I had not reached that stage, being only six. For the first two years I was taught by the lady companion only, whose sole idea of pedagogy was to make me copy bits out of my reading book. Later I was fortunate in getting very pleasant tutors. They aroused my interest in the natural sciences and in German literature. And it was high time.

For years I suffered from the dulling effects of the first method of teaching me. It is a disgraceful fact that I was

33

seven years old before I was able to read a whole story through by myself — and was even very proud of it! Until I was eleven I read very haltingly, which in no way, however, prevented my writing my first poems at the age of seven. The first one I ever wrote was called 'Happiness,' and was very elegiac.

The first house we lived in at Gmunden was called 'Playfield Villa.' Its windows overlooked the city tennis courts that were used as a skating rink in the winter. In the evenings lamps were lighted above it — it was a very pretty sight. At about Christmas time I often stood a long time at the windows looking out. I never told anyone what my secret hope was — it was to see the Christ Child, who would surely pass here at this time of year. After all, He came to us, the children, why then did only the grown-ups have the right to see Him and talk to Him? All we had to do was to write down a list of what we wanted, which was laid on the window-sill and collected by the Christ Child. And then all at once, about a fortnight before Christmas as a rule, a silver or a golden hair would be found somewhere about the house. 'Christ Child's hair,' we called it; it was a sign of the fulfilment of Advent.

It was at such a time, when I was seven years old, that my two brothers went to their First Holy Communion. I was filled with an immense awe of them. They had been allowed to receive the Body of the Lord. For days I hardly dared speak to them. Something new had happened, something that separated my elder brothers from me.

This feeling of being left behind on a road so far travelled in common, grew even stronger, it became almost the fear of eternal damnation after a terrible thing had happened — the list of the things I wanted for Christmas, which had already been taken from the window-sill, was suddenly returned to me. I had been guilty of some childish misdemeanour, and my father had said: 'I shall not punish you because it is Christmas time. But go downstairs and open the window, you'll find your list there again!' And, merciful heavens, he was right. The Christ Child Himself was pun-

ishing me, He rejected me and had brought back my list.
I felt lost and an outcast, trembling with fear lest I should
die suddenly and be eternally damned.

My brothers noticed my altered looks, but thought I was
only putting them on so as not to be left out when it came
to present-giving. For a long time after that I had the reputation of being a liar, and was quite unable to defend myself
against the charge.

Naturally I told lies when I was a child, as every child
does. But not because I had any pleasure, conscious or unconscious, in lying for its own sake. I lied in self-defence.
And being the youngest and surrounded by many older
'enemies,' perhaps I told more lies than my brothers.
Though I always asserted, of course in childish words, that
they told incomparably more lies than I did; only they were
better able to make their lies credible; mine were more
easily found out.

Something else is connected with this — it forms a very
black chapter in my life. It happened not infrequently that
I blushed when my brothers had done something naughty.
Thereupon I was punished until I 'owned up,' and because
I generally refused to do so, my reputation as a liar was
intensified. Very soon nobody believed a word I said, while
anything anyone said about me was taken as truth.

Thus, long before I knew what it meant, I was suspected
of having certain youthful 'bad habits.' All the terrors of
hell, in the truest sense of the word, were loosed on me. It
was enough for my brothers to say at breakfast that I had
pushed my blankets against the sides of my cot to hide
behind them. And once I had after long denial 'owned up,'
I was regarded as capable of every crime.

My first admission was extorted from me in this way. My
father came into the room disguised in a black devil's head
mask with horns and clanking chains — I did not recognize
him. I must own up, he said, or else I should be fetched
away to hell. When I howled and swore by all that was holy
that I had nothing to confess, he vanished for a few moments, only to reappear in a red mask. Then of course I gave

35

in and admitted everything that they wanted me to, without knowing what I was saying.

Yes, that was a grim chapter. In order to eradicate my 'viciousness,' a doctor was brought in in addition to the devils. He arrived with a large pair of scissors and told me in unmistakable terms what he proposed to use them for if there were any repetition of the episode. My father was not in the least prudish or hypocritical in other ways. But no doubt he thought it necessary for hygienic reasons to act as he did — in those days it was seriously believed that children went off their heads as a result of such habits. It probably never dawned on him that his remedy was, from a psychological standpoint, by far the worst thing he could have done.

All this increased my childish fear of death. I was afraid of the terrors of the Beyond; that the flames of hell gave out no light, that there should be eternal darkness was the most horrifying to my mind. Night after night for years on end I was afraid that I might die in my sleep or that I might be the victim of an accident that prevented my receiving the last sacraments. I had no one, no adviser, to tell me that God is the God of Love and not of Torture — and that Christ had promised the Kingdom of Heaven to the children and damnation to their tormentors.

Religious problems did not exist for us. Christianity was regarded as the natural ordinance. I don't think we ever knew anyone who was not a Christian. Even Protestants, who from time to time came within our line of vision, surprised us very much. We regarded them as only half Christians, who must be looked upon with pity, since for them it was still harder than for Catholics to get heaven. (If even we found it enormously difficult to escape hell, what must it be for the adherents of false religions!) The argument upon which all this was based was striking and primitive — who lived first, Christ or Luther? Who was the greater? Who was God and who was man? The answer was obvious. So also were the conclusions to be drawn from the following — Christ founded the Catholic Church,

Luther the Protestant. Only the fact that we were almost forbidden to have anything to do with Protestants or, worse still, to go into a Protestant church, gave Protestantism a certain charm. The atmosphere in which we lived, therefore, was one of unquestioned Catholicism — though not one to be absolutely approved of, as it lacked mercy and understanding.

The stories of the martyrs which my eldest sister brought back with her from the convent and read to us impressed me deeply. The fact that there were boys among the martyrs not much older than myself gave me the greatest shock. There was, for instance, the story of the youthful Saint Pancras. He had been tortured to death because he refused to deliver into the hands of the heathen the sacred Host which he was carrying to Christian prisoners. I was filled with the longing also to die for Christ, to die a martyr's death, the only death that would quite certainly preserve me from hell. For years I included the petition to be allowed such a death in my evening prayers.

O desire, O reality! I longed to equal the martyrs, not to be shamed by holy boys like Saint Pancras — and yet I was terrified of any sort of pain. I even cried if I ran a splinter into my finger, said my father; a nice kind of martyr! That was quite a different matter, I replied; a splinter for no reason hurt so much more than being tortured for Christ's sake. I did not know how right I was; I did not really believe in my own excuse, and prayed to be made braver and less of a cry-baby.

What has remained of all this? I should not like to die for something of no importance, or by an evil chance. I should like to give this life, this most comprehensive gift that comes but once, in exchange for a millennium, a prefiguration of what is to come, and as a sacrifice for truth, freedom, and justice.

In those years, too, I dreamt of many lands and duties. There was a fairy tale in one of my books that I wanted to hear again and again:

37

A king is overthrown by upheaval and mutiny. His child, the heiress to the realm, has to flee with the queen into distant forests. There she lives unrecognized, in a hut with trees and animals as her companions. She herself knows nothing of the secret of her birth. But a longing is in her that tells the truth louder than any memory could. It is the longing for purple and gold, the longing for the crown which had lain in her cradle.

She goes to the waters of a lake deep in the woods. There she sees the water nymphs dancing, they bear glittering jewels, laughing and teasing, enticing and threatening. An old servant who loves the princess wishes to save her from a fate which he fears for her. It is better to live, poor and unrecognized, in the forest than to die clothed in purple. But he cannot stave off the day which by all the stars was bound to come.

The king of the country, the man who had once been a rebel and had overthrown her father, loses his way while he is out hunting and comes to the hut. He takes her to the capital and crowns her as his queen. She walks among the people, who fall on their knees before her, though they do not realize that she is actually by birth and inheritance the ruler of the country.

Nor is the king aware of it. But one day, when he is believed to be far away, she goes down into the dungeon where her old father still lies in chains. Jealous courtiers report this to the new king. He surprises the queen as she is opening the door of the dungeon. Utterly beside himself with the violence of his rage, he knocks her down the iron stairs.

Then the last picture. Clothed in purple, as she had dreamt as a child, she lies in the interior of the palace, while outside bells ring storm and the people rise to avenge the wounds of their dying queen. The king's young brother, who has loved the queen from afar, sees what has happened. With his sword he stabs the king, who sinks beside the queen. She is ruler over all the tumult, over the ruins into which the king's throne has fallen. The turmoil outside loses sense and meaning.

Thus fairy tales also first introduced me to rebellion, guilt and expiation. Through a second book these things were translated into reality. It was not a good book, not a book upon which reliance could be placed. It was an extremely biased history of the French Revolution. Nevertheless it impressed me greatly.

Like the book of martyrs my sister brought it home from the convent. It had been written and designed for convent-bred girls. Louis XVI was presented in the most favourable light. On principle the book referred to him only as the 'noble king.' The queen, of course, was equally kindly treated, while the revolutionaries were depicted as the lowest scum of humanity. Of the social and intellectual problems of the day, of the rights of men, of the corruption of the aristocracy, the extravagance of the court, not a word was said. Thus I knew nothing of it either.

At first the whole thing seemed to me inconceivable. To overthrow a king and set up another in his place — there would have been nothing in that. I was familiar with that idea. But to overthrow the monarchy in order to found a republic? Anyhow, what was a republic? How was such a thing allowed to exist?

After the departure of Mademoiselle Jex another French governess had been engaged who was really a Swiss. 'Why hasn't Switzerland got a king?' I often asked her. And now I discovered that a much larger country was also without a king and *how* that had come to pass.

If I had been alive then, this would never have happened! I would have had the people shot down, ruthlessly. I would have killed thousands of the godless rabble. And if the king hadn't liked it, I would have had them shot just the same and made him abdicate. If I'd been king I wouldn't have stood that sort of thing. Simply to address him as 'Citizen Capet,' to put the head of the Princess de Lamballe (also an ideal person in the book) on the end of a pike — had the Reds anything to do with it? It was a pity that Mademoiselle Jex was no longer with us. I might have asked her. She would certainly have been embarrassed.

39

And then the speech on the scaffold: 'Frenchmen, I die innocent! I wanted the best ——' Was he actually making excuses? 'A little while afterward the Queen followed him on the dark path,' was the next thing I heard. What a good thing that the rascals began cutting each other's heads off after that. If only the little dauphin had escaped! I wondered what I should do if I had to go and be apprenticed to a cobbler, didn't have enough to eat, and had to wear ragged clothes and be addressed as 'Citizen Löwenstein'? Anyhow 'citizen' was an unpleasant appellation. In our family it was synonym with 'commoner,' and we used it as a term of abuse.

'Don't behave like a commoner' we would say, but only in extreme cases. And this was supposed to be an honourable mode of address?

Hardly one of the girls for whom the book was intended was likely to have had revolutionary tendencies. Hence it was not quite clear to me why they were so seriously warned against them. I began to get suspicious. Might there after all be something attractive about revolution? Nonsense, such a cesspool, such meanness could never be attractive.

Then we suddenly came to a passage where I was swept away with the excitement of the story. What happened was simply monstrous. Nevertheless it did happen, possibly against my own will. I felt the stir of feelings that slumbered deep down below the surface, of an unrealized joy in freedom and revolution.

This was the passage: 'The Vendée was in revolt. A four-teen-year-old boy led a division of Republican troops against the rebels. (Yes, the word really was 'rebels,' the author must have been writing carelessly!) Another boy carried a tricolour flag. The whole unit was made up of very young soldiers. Then they fell into an ambush and were overpowered. Every one was slain save the youthful leader and the standard-bearer. They were placed against a wall. 'If you will cry Vive le Roi! you shall have your lives,' said the officer commanding the royalists. The boys looked down the barrels of the guns that were pointing at them —

only for a moment. Then they looked at one another: 'Vive la République!' they cried, and fell.

I leapt up. 'How glorious! Vive la République! La République! La République! I'd have said that too, and Vive la Liberté! as well, if I'd had time.'

The scene that followed was indescribable. My sister dropped the book, my brothers stared at me, horror-stricken, the Swiss lady grew pale ('I'll be blamed,' was evidently the thought that passed through her mind). My father was fetched. 'I'll show you what happens to young noblemen who shout Vive la République!' he said, and then I had one of the most thorough thrashings I can remember. Moreover, I was locked up in my room for several hours, while my brothers sat in the garden eating chocolate, and making faces at me when I looked out of the window.

Thus the book about the French Revolution made certain of the fundamental principles of my life problematic if it did not exactly shake them to their foundations. If kings can be overthrown and have their heads cut off, there must be something wrong about the divine right of kingship. Napoleon affected me quite differently from the way in which Louis XVI did, although the book had little good to say of him. I began to have a kind of personal interest in him when I was told that my maternal grandmother had known him very well. It is true that that was Napoleon III, but the distinction was not very clear in my mind.

Thus the 'revolutionary poison' seeped into our feudally guarded nursery through the most various and unexpected channels. Who could have imagined that the volumes published by the *Bibliothèque Rose* could have contained revolutionary ideas? These were children's stories of the nineteenth century, written for young French Catholic aristocrats, some of them very charming and picturesque and stimulating. The author of most of them was a Comtesse de Ségur, who probably wrote them originally for her own immediate friends and relations. The scene of the stories is always a French château, the characters are the children of noble families, some of whom are good and some naughty.

41

The stories always end happily for the good ones and badly for the naughty ones.

Sometimes they show traces of social feelings — like the story of the wicked little son of a count and the good son of the steward. The little count is converted to better ways by the steward's son, who is given a gold watch as reward, as well as a new suit for his confirmation, and eventually a post as overseer.

Or the wonderful story of the boy Gribouille, who is slightly off his head: he wants to make things look nice, so he puts moss all round the inside of the bowl of fruit salad for the master's dinner. And take the two volumes about the rich, irascible, but kind-hearted Russian, General d'Ouraquine. It was through this work that I first heard of the Polish struggle for independence — again a revolt against the existing order. Yes, but in this case a justifiable one, for the Poles are Catholic and the Russians infidels, despite the fact that they call themselves Orthodox.

So far so good. But then came a book about the Italian *risorgimento*. Where was the confessional justification in this case? With the good Comtesse de Ségur, the anti-Austrian feelings of her heart caused her to ignore what her Catholicism must have wished to say — that Cavour and Garibaldi and Victor Emmanuel inflicted much unpleasant-ness upon the Pope, while Austria, and France, too, defended him.

Thus I heard of more revolutions, of green, white, and red flags, of liberty and equality. A king by the will of the people — I began to feel that there was something in the idea. The fact that from a national standpoint I was pro-Austrian became a matter of indifference. Every nation is served by anyone who is fighting for liberty, even if it hap-pens to be for the moment a hostile nation that is fighting. Did I think so then? Certainly not clearly or in any detail. For what did I know of the struggle for freedom of my own people? Little enough.

It so happened, however, that at about this time I went with my father to a little place near Gmunden called Pinsdorf. There, in the year 1626 an army of rebellious peasants had been annihilated by a Count von Pappenheim. Rebellious? Yes, against the princes, against the black coats, against the oppressors. They had fought for the Emperor, for the Empire, and for Evangelical Freedom.

A thousand peasants had fallen at Pinsdorf, and they were buried in a vast common grave. My father showed me the mound that still remained, with the memorial cross and its inscription. A curious legend I heard about it, too, an old peasant saying that when the mound had become flat enough for a horse and cart to drive over it, then there would be a great war, and more peasants would die in it than ever before in history. The slaughter would not cease until the Emperor Awaited would come to set up the reign of justice, crushing the oppressors of the people and the power of black coats, to the joy and salvation of the united German Nation. Now the mound was flat enough and it was the year 1913.

As I said before, my father sympathized with both sides, that of the peasants and that of the princes who misused the Emperor's name when they beat down the peasants. In the figure of Götz von Berlichingen he saw a solution, to put oneself at the head of the peasants and to lead them. Also one of our ancestors, Count George of Wertheim, had done so. But — shame on him! — he afterward betrayed the peasants and became one of their bloodiest tyrants.

The seventh year of my life seems to have been chosen to teach me a first lesson in many things. All at once something that had happened while we were in Vienna became clear to me; I had not understood it at the time. We were visiting our grandmother at a hotel in the Ringstrasse, when we suddenly heard a violent commotion. The streets were black with people, demonstrating against the Government, and possibly against the Emperor of Austria too. It was hours before we were able to get out. They are bandits and criminals, I was told then, and I accepted the statement as the obvious truth. Seeing the grave of the peasants at Pinsdorf a doubt crept into my mind. Perhaps the people

43

who had cried 'Down!' were quite decent and the police who dispersed them were in the wrong?

I could still see how they attacked, brutally riding into the crowd, into men and women, and children who were no bigger than I myself. True, they were children who went barefoot and had their hair cropped short, who wore grey or blue jackets instead of sailor or velvet Lord Fauntleroy suits and who did not have long curls that were brushed and combed morning, noon, and night.

I realized more and more clearly that the world was not as we had seen it from our nursery. There was conflict in it, but not a fair one between equals. It was a struggle between a great poor unarmed majority and a small well-armed minority. Count Pappenheim had had the better horses and the better guns; the Viennese police had been more brutal and armed with swords which they used relentlessly. No doubt I took my family's precepts more seriously than they were intended, or I may have taken them in a different sense — a young nobleman should fight for the right; he hates injustice and loves truth.

But where was truth? No one could tell me. And above all, could truth suffer compromise? Was it permissible to restrict recognition of a truth, to suppress it, to withstand it if it demands sacrifice? My father answered this in the affirmative.

'One should always uphold one's own class,' he said. 'The aristocracy and the monarchy are bound to one another for better and worse. The aims of the peasantry may have been excellent. Nevertheless their victory would have meant the loss of our privileges.'

'But,' said I, 'if the Emperor had led the peasants against the princes, if he had given them land and liberty —— You said yourself once ——'

'Yes, I did. But it is nonsense all the same. The Emperor could not have remained in power without the princes. We should be a republic today.' (And that was the worst abomination he could think of.)

I said nothing for a long time while I thought this over, till I was quite certain. Then I ventured hesitantly:

'Supposing we had a republic with an Emperor at the head of it — that would be nice.'

'Don't be silly,' he protested. 'How can a republic have an Emperor at the head of it?'

'If there are no princes between him and the people and the Emperor is a republican, like Napoleon.'

I got no further answer.

A few days later I ran away from home to have another look at the mound at Pinsdorf. I thought about the peasants and their faith, how they had been oppressed and how the Emperor had disappointed them. I stood still and said the Lord's Prayer. When I passed the memorial to Count Pappenheim, I shook my fist at it.

III. *Playing at War*

ROUND the house in which we lived there was a lovely garden full of trees and with a little mound in it. This mound we called the 'Fortress' and built walls and trenches round it. Our servant Joseph — the most faithful of servants — who had taken Michael's place, was equally clever at making wooden swords and shields. He painted our entire coat of arms on my shield. It was supposed to render me invulnerable, but it did not do so.

I was often wounded during the daily battles in which we fought each other to exhaustion. We looked upon these contests as preliminary training for our future career. For there was no question that we were all going to be soldiers. I rejoiced — though for different reasons from those my father assumed — at the prospect. That one has to be cautious with grown-ups I had already learnt, and therefore I kept silence about my most secret thoughts. Once I am a soldier, I thought to myself, and subsequently a field marshal, and when all the soldiers have to obey me, then I can do what I like — then I can depose the German Emperor!

It was at this time — the winter of 1913–14 — that I first heard of Caesar and the Romans. I got hold of my brother's history books and also his Latin grammar. Unknown to anyone, I learnt the various declensions and conjugations by heart until one day I triumphantly disclosed my knowledge, which was far greater than my brother's. After that there existed open warfare between us that lasted for many a long day, our sword duels deteriorated into free fights, and I was always the defeated party.

46

Playing at soldiers loses its attraction when one is invariably beaten, no matter what one tries. I was the smaller
and weaker and therefore the most bruised and battered.
I felt this to be unfair and longed for revenge. But how to
achieve it if my sword and my spear failed me? At first I
consoled myself with the thought that presently — 'when
I am big' — I would repay everything. But in my daily
defeats the hopes of future revenge did not go far in com-
forting me.

Therefore it was — though ashamed, I must confess it —
that one day I was led to do a dark deed. I shall not seek to
excuse myself because there is no excuse. It was deliber-
ately planned crime carried out with all the resources of
criminal technique. In short, an exceedingly clever crime.

I knew that metal, especially copper, acted as a conductor
for electricity. I therefore stole a piece of copper wire from
Joseph's tool-box, attached one end to the lightning conductor which passed down beside our bedroom window, drew
the wire through a hole in the window-frame and placed
the other end of it in my brother's bed directly under his
pillow. As soon as I had done this I was immensely happy,
well-behaved, and good-humoured. I never lost my temper
all day, laughed softly and spoke kindly. But when we went
to bed I prayed fervently that God would send a really heavy
thunderstorm that night — a truly tremendous storm —
and also that He would not forget to cause a flash of lightning to pass along my piece of copper wire.

I suffered no pangs of conscience at the time. It would
therefore be hypocritical for me to invent them now. I was
merely disappointed that there was no thunderstorm and
that my prayer had therefore proved unavailing. It suddenly occurred to me, however, that I too might be struck
if the lightning were to strike my brother's bed. The following morning, therefore, I quietly removed the copper wire.

Whenever I hear stories of youthful crimes I always
remember this attempt at murder, which was only distinguished from similar exploits by its originality and a somewhat unusual conception of the nature of God. Every child

47

is at bottom capable of any crime, its instinctive sense of good and evil is destroyed by the grown-ups. Our playing at soldiers, for example, our battles — what were they except playing at killing?

A child makes no distinction between the real world and that of make-believe. The real world for him is the one he plays in. Everything else is incidental, strange and without meaning. If I was allowed to 'kill' my brother in playing, and he me, why should I not actually kill him? Merely because my attempt with the copper wire was cowardly? But children are taught to value deceptions as the weapons of the weak against the strong. Just as a child is told of all sorts of military deceptions or ruses such as the Trojan Horse, Odysseus' trick upon the Cyclops, the killing of the giant Goliath by the boy David.

Every day at home we children heard talk of war. The war of 1870–71 played a great part in all my father's conversations. 'Ten thousand, fifty thousand, a hundred thousand Frenchmen were killed — a glorious victory,' and 'thousands more were wounded.' Terrible? No, heroic! an example to the young.

Tin soldiers in the French and German uniforms of 1870–71 (they were soon to be fitted with new uniforms) helped to intensify these impressions. We shot them to pieces. 'Hurrah! Your officer has lost both his legs!' 'Twenty more men killed!' — and so on and so forth, and in every home that could spare a few pence to buy toys. The same games wherever there were children; their prayers asked to protect the lives of their fathers while their games were invocations of the dark Angels of Death! When will these games played by German children again be played in all seriousness? The game is in truth always played in earnest — only earnestness has its gradations.

In those days I played it as a matter of course. I knew no better. It never occurred to me that there could be anything wrong about it. I had never heard of the heroism of peace. How should I? War seemed to me to be the most natural thing in the world and the fundamental condition of

48

existence, and peace only a short interval between two wars.

In this connection I remember a dreadful thing. One day during the winter of 1913–14 I exclaimed loudly: 'I'll be glad when the World War comes!' This exclamation epitomized all that I had hitherto heard — 'The next time we march against France'; 'In the next war'; 'Once the World War begins,' etc. Gay and lively that will be, marching with bands playing and colours flying; we'll shoot down the French like wild beasts, one will be covered with glory, and a great hero; there will be new battle pictures to take the place of those we already know; lively marches will be played on barrel organs and songs of victory will be sung on Sundays in the inns. To talk of misery and suffering, of festering wounds, of men with their intestines torn to bits — that was cowards' talk.

My exclamation, 'I'll be glad when the World War comes!' drew aside the veil for an instant. The others suddenly became aware of what the future might be. Hence their disgust and horror, their justifiable horror. My exclamation burst upon them like a flash of lightning, like Mephistopheles' song of triumph sung by a child.

There was dead silence in the room. I grew white through fear and shame. I felt as if I had done something monstrous. Shocked and confused by my words, my father said after a few minutes' silence that it was a mortal sin to wish such a thing and that I must never do it again. His warning was unnecessary.

Christmas, 1913, brought us good news. Among all our pleasures it was the greatest. We were returning to Schoenwoerth in the middle of May! I did not then know that we were only returning in order that the castle might realize a higher price when sold. All I knew was that I should once more be among the scenes of my childhood. I had not seen them for so long, it seemed a lifetime: three and a half years.

It was a marvellous Christmas. To make it even more wonderful my sister Sophie returned home from her convent school earlier than usual. I was very fond of her in

those days. It was very late before we turned on the lights.
A room in semi-darkness is the place in which to talk about
Christmas and the coming summer. We discussed what we
should do, and how big the superintendent's children must
now be — as big and grown-up as myself? — and whether
there would still be hornets and sand vipers, whether the
tricycle would still be fit to ride or whether George had
smashed it. My armour, too, would certainly need cleaning,
it must surely have grown rusty.

We also talked about the rooms we were going to live in,
and wondered whether we should be allowed to enter the
room that had been our mother's. It looked out upon the
farm buildings over which there hung a stork. 'The stork
that brought you,' my father once said. 'I shot it so that
it shouldn't bring any more children.' We should soon find
out for ourselves. Spring would soon be here!

The year 1914 thus began joyfully for us. On January 6
we witnessed for the last time for many a year a curious
custom that is apparently only kept up in Upper Austria.
Groups of men and boys go round the houses and gardens
and dance. On their heads they carry paper houses lighted
up from within — peasant houses, churches, palaces. Entire towns dance mysteriously to the ringing of tiny bells
hung about the dancers. Nobody knows the origin of this
custom. But it is almost certainly a Christianized survival
from pagan times — like so many other things in our country.

As I said before, pagan and Christian mingled even in
our own home. We should never have left three doors open
in succession in the sacred Twelve Nights after Christmas,
as this brings bad luck upon the house. These are the nights
in which Wotan and his wild followers ride the skies. The
Church turned them into the devils and evil spirits, the Wild
Huntsman who rides through the night and knows no rest
until the end of the world. The legend tells how he hunted
on Christmas Day and murdered someone. My father
never mentioned this legend except casually. He preferred
to tell about Wotan.

When one goes into the woods in autumn one should cut

three crosses in the tree stumps in order that the good spirits of the forest — gnomes, elves, and woodland fairies — may find sanctuary there from Wotan and his following. The three crosses that are to be seen on most of the tree stumps in Upper Austria testify to the extent to which such customs still live among the people. I never tried to find out if they are compatible with Christian beliefs. After hundreds of years everything is so intermingled that it is impossible to distinguish between the component parts.

I do not know whether this applies as well to all the magic and superstition in which I suddenly became passionately and lastingly interested. At any rate I am not going to proffer it as an excuse.

I compiled for myself an entire code of good and evil omina for which I was constantly on the watch. There was, for instance, the 'Rain Oracle.' If the drops fell with a dull sound into the runnels on the roof, it portended evil; each drop ought to fall with a clear, distinct sound. Or I made two little arches of wood and put a worm — or a snail — in front of them. If the worm or snail passed through the right-hand arch, it was a good sign, but if it went through the left-hand arch, the future was black indeed. At other times I wrote certain words on a piece of paper that I subsequently burnt. The last word to remain legible was the sign.

While all these superstitions can be explained by peasant customs taught to me by our servants, there is no rational explanation for another action of mine that seems to me to be of importance in my life-story.

When I was seven years old I piled up two heaps of stones in the garden and set a round stone the size of a fist on top of each pile. I painted them in barbaric fashion, giving them each a nose, mouth, and eyes, and then I knelt down before them and said, 'Now you are idols.' Whenever I was unobserved, I visited them and brought them gifts of flowers, crumbs of bread, and gay pebbles. This continued for about a fortnight until I suddenly got a fearful headache and moreover was very frightened.

51

'That's what comes of setting up idols. You will certainly die,' I said to myself. Thereupon I rushed off to the garden and destroyed the idols. As my headache ceased soon afterward, I never again 'worshipped idols.'

The day of our departure for Schoenwoerth came at last. It was more than usually exciting for me because my brothers and my eldest sister were not to follow us until the beginning of the summer holidays in July. ('Us' meant my father, Joseph, our cook Toni, a parlour maid, the Swiss governess — still called by us children the 'Frenchwoman' — and myself.) I was full of self-importance and bade my brothers and sister a very haughty farewell.

We travelled as far as Kufstein by train. Dear old Kufstein, the frontier between Bavaria and Austria, with its fortress and its old walls! The Emperor Maximilian — 'the last of the knights' — once spent weeks in besieging the fortress that was held by a rebellious noble named Hans Pinzenauer. Whenever one of the Emperor's cannon balls landed on the walls, Hans Pinzenauer at once had the dust that it created swept away from the spot. This made the Emperor so furious that he caused two enormous cannon to be cast in Innsbruck — the biggest of their day — and by means of these compelled the fortress to surrender.

A carriage and horse awaited us at the station at Kufstein. 'They are the village innkeeper's,' my father said bitterly. 'We can't keep them any more. The stables are empty, the carriages are in the lumber room.' It was as if a shadow had passed over me — the first warning of a change for the worse.

My depression did not last long. It was one of these days which one finds only in the Tyrol. A sky of such depth that it seemed to have no end. A sun that really, as the peasants say, gave one a glimpse of heaven. Brightly coloured flowers, fields of golden corn, softly moved by the wind, clover so green that it seemed one could use it for painting, and then the mountains — the mountains.

You big, good, brown animal in the north of the valley,

52

SCHOENWOERTH, A HUMAN FACE WITH TWO LARGE ROUND
EYES AND A LARGE KINDLY MOUTH

symbol of rural life, cow with spots and folds turned into stone. And then you in the south, Ruler, Protector of my cradle, first memory, saga-surrounded *Wilder Kaiser*; not into the Kyffhäuser, into your caves many lay the *mysterium* of the Germans, the sleeping Emperor, the Pantocrate, Bearer of the Universal Crown, which shall be Roman forever, and ever German. The gold of this crown, the peasants say, sometimes glitters between the rocks; few have seen it, and yet it is visible; no one has touched it, and still it is there.

At the feet of the Wild Emperor lies the 'Tame Emperor,' a much lower mountain. There it lies: a symbol of decay, mild and without desire to rule. The tame Emperor seems to exist only so that the High One may be still higher, still more eternal, and his majesty more exalted.

A gentle mist veiled both mountains as our carriage drove along a narrow road through the early summer landscape. The confused and confusing whirr of grasshoppers was all round us, while the sound of the horse's hoofs was full and deep. The parish church of Langkampfen came into view. A new parish priest was there now. The old priest who had baptized me was dead long since.

An eight-year-old child returning to his birthplace — what more was there to it than that? But no, it was different. I came home like one who had wandered for years, through experience and guilt.

I was fully conscious of this. Here once more I should be a child, free and unburdened with cares. I thought to myself that the change in me would be visible even to the grass and the trees and the flowers — the bluebells, the wild pinks, the yellow and white daisies. I smiled at them until all of a sudden I became very serious, almost solemn. Schoenwoerth had appeared round a turn of the road, with its thick central tower that seemed to have a human face with two large round eyes, and beneath them a wooden balcony, like a large, kindly mouth, and welded onto it the narrow, round tower that served as a fire-escape, with its pointed roof.

The top of Wotan's ash tree was motionless — the air

quivered between it and us. I did not know that I was
arriving at Schoenwoerth for the last time. But something
filled me with fear. So Adam might have felt if he had ever
been allowed to return to the Garden of Eden.

Then the banner of our house — the fusilly bendy white
and blue — appeared fluttering in the first breeze of this
summer day, and nothing was left in me but happiness,
gratitude, and fulfilment.

The weeks that followed will remain in my memory forever. I was under no compulsion, I could go wherever I
wanted to go — far into the woods or along the brook or
high up into the mountains. Once I even went as far as the
castle of Mariastein about which the peasants say that it is
connected with Schoenwoerth by a subterranean passage.
The entrance is supposed to have lain beneath the roots of
the ash tree.

At Mariastein — an hour and a half's walk for an adult
from Schoenwoerth — ended our fishing rights over the
brooks; there lay the boundary of our property, far removed
from the castle, away in a wild and unknown land. Mint and
ferns, Alpine roses and gnarled trees grow there. And if one
searches carefully many flints are to be found that smell
curiously of sulphur and will give off sparks in the dark.

The superintendent's son George had also grown up and
was my constant playmate. He taught me much. He knew
all that there was to be known about Tyrolese dwarfs and
fairies. He even knew of an ancient slab of stone that was
said to have been a pagan altar ages ago and in the neighbourhood of which (so he averred) all kinds of queer things
happened.

The astonishment of the first few days speedily vanished
to give place to these new interests. I had been surprised
to find that Schoenwoerth seemed small, the walls low and
thin, and the tower less high than I remembered them to
have been. That is only natural, I thought to myself, for
I was only a child when I last saw it. Now that I am grown
up, I am able to judge its proportion rightly.

54

One place alone remained closed to me: the balcony on the highest story of the castle that looked from a distance like a mouth. I must be much older before I could be allowed to go up there, my father said, because it was most dangerous. My entreaties were unavailing. So I had to content myself with standing below the castle, or with clambering over the steep leaden roofs and gazing upward at what symbolized for me the beginning of life. For I was resolved to date the beginning of my real, independent existence from the moment when I no longer needed to ask anyone's permission to stand upon the balcony. My first arrival there should be a symbolic act showing that at last I had achieved power.

A few days prior to the arrival of my brothers and sister I helped George to collect timber for the bonfires to be lit on the mountain peaks on June 24, the Feast of Saint John. I was, it is true, forbidden to go to the top of the mountain where the fire was to be lighted. Nevertheless I looked upon the bonfire that I could see with the naked eye upon the back of a mountain opposite Schoenwoerth as my own personal work. I had built it up stick by stick in order that it might be the largest and brightest when the great moment came.

The moment was at hand. I stood in the garden and waited for the last daylight to disappear. The air was heavy. A few fireflies flew round me, shining in their own greenish-white light. I saw others shining in the grass like crystal drops — tiny stars twinkling in the dark.

Then the moment came. On the topmost pinnacle, the 'Cow,' a flame leapt up. My bonfire was burning — the first on this festal night! The flames ran like lightning from peak to peak on both sides of the valley until the sky itself seemed to be on fire. An eventful night, at once sad and joyful, filled with an indefinable longing, a touch of pain and also — perhaps — a slight feeling of fear.

The next and the following days it rained. I remember how the drops beat against the tiny leaded panes and that it was nearly evening before the mountains stood out in a clear light. But it was not unpleasant rain, not the rain that shuts in the valley beneath a covering of clouds for weeks at a time. It was soon over, and I walked across wet shale and beneath trees that shook the drops from their leaves. (It suddenly occurs to me that I used to think as a child that it was the shaking of the trees that made the wind.) I sat down on a swing that hung from the branch of a large chestnut tree and amused myself by watching the drops that fell with every movement.

My father was standing not far from me in front of the castle talking to Joseph.

Suddenly I heard steps behind me. The superintendent was coming along the chestnut avenue. He passed by me and went straight up to my father. He looked extraordinarily upset, twisted his hat in his hand, and stuttered. As I stopped swinging, I suddenly understood what he had to say to my father:

'I beg your pardon, Your Illustrious Highness, but the Archduke Franz Ferdinand — the heir to the throne — has been murdered by the Serbians.' The next thing I heard was my father's very clear voice saying: 'Then haul down the white and blue flag and hoist the black and yellow half-mast.'

An hour later we were sitting at dinner in a small room hung round with many stag and chamois heads. In the middle of dinner my father uttered the words that were soon to be heard in prayers and curses alike: 'That is the World War.' My heart stood still, and I thought 'You are also responsible, for you said you'd be glad when it came.' I anxiously waited to see whether my father would remind me of the scene the previous winter. At that moment I would have accepted as just any punishment that could have been imposed. But my father seemed to have forgotten about it. We continued our meal in a silence broken only by occasional remarks appropriate to meal-times.

Immediately after grace had been said — I nearly forgot the words in my agitation — I went out into the park. And then I saw it: once again fires were burning, not this time on the summits — there had been no time for that — but on the Alpine meadows below the summits. Walls of fire surrounded us, far-flung, not sparkling and distant as on Saint John's Eve. Thus the people learnt and made known that the heir to all the crowns of Habsburg was dead.

On the next day but one my brothers and my sister Sophie arrived and I forgot the outside world again. We were very happy and got on well together. We could now carry on our knightly games of the Gmunden days on a far bigger scale. The superintendent's children joined in as in former years. I was very pleased that my sister also made one of us, dressed herself up in tin armour, and declared that she was not a woman but a knight like ourselves. It was therefore all the more shame to us, that we shortly afterward played her a mean trick.

One day when she was dressed, not as a knight, but in a white dress, we led her off to a woodland meadow covered with bilberries. The bilberries could do us no harm because we were wearing *Leder Hosen* that showed no stains. But my sister's white dress was a different matter. We tricked and cozened her into rolling about on the ground with us. She did not realize what would happen until she actually saw it: her white dress was entirely covered with blue stains. Then she was very angry and felt quite ashamed to have to go through the village in such a state.

A few days later she revenged herself bitterly upon me. First — and doubtless by way of preparation for what was to come — she told me a hair-raising story about a witch who hated her and whom she had met in a wood. The witch had told her with evil glee that she (the witch) knew for certain that I no longer loved her and that this would have dreadful consequences. Naturally I laughed at this nonsense, and said: 'After all I am not a baby any longer to believe such stories.' 'You'll see,' she replied. 'But I don't know whether you'll laugh or not.' And with that she disappeared, putting all the gloom she could muster into her last look.

57

A little later I was playing by myself in the garden when the superintendent's wife came running up to me. 'Quickly,' she shrieked at me. 'Come quickly, quickly, the Comtesse is dead, she's lying in our house, she's gone quite white.' Appalling — and I had refused to believe it!

I tore along to the superintendent's house. There she lay, motionless, and as dead-white as one can be only when one's face is covered with flour. But I never noticed the flour. I believed she was dead, and threw myself upon her, crying bitterly. My tears fell upon the flour. Now it was my sister's turn to cry from sheer emotion — a thick paste formed over her face. She only wanted to see, she declared, whether I really did love her.

This was the only melancholy episode during those happy weeks. Our high spirits did not leave us until we found out the plans that were being made in all seriousness to sell Schoenwoerth. We were furious with the strangers who came to look over the castle and who behaved as if they already owned it. One man even tapped my armour, believing it to be an especially valuable relic of the Middle Ages, and declared, 'Without the armour I refuse to buy that castle.'

One day a party arrived in a motor car and wanted to drive down the chestnut avenue. I shut the gate in their faces and told them they could go round by the servants' entrance. All to no purpose. Soon they were going all over the place with my father and putting on airs. They even addressed me as 'Du,' which infuriated me.

As my father was standing with them in the inner court-yard, I joined them and said: 'Don't you buy the castle! The thunderstorms here are dreadful. Just before I was born the castle was struck by lightning, and one day it will surely burn down. If you are caught upstairs, you'll never get out: the stairs are all built of wood. Papa always says the castle would burn like tinder!' The visitors stared at me in astonishment. My father was embarrassed and ordered me to be off. I should have gone in any case. As it was I ran happily to my brothers, crying: 'They'll never buy Schoenwoerth. That's certain!'

I was wrong. Either they did not fear thunderstorms or they put their trust in lightning conductors and fire insurances. Whatever the reason may have been, I was walking across the park with my brother a few days later when the 'Frenchwoman' came to meet us and called out to us from a distance: 'Ne dîtes rien que je vous l'aie dit, mais c'est vendu!' 'What?' 'Yes. Schoenwoerth is sold. We are going away in ten days, back to Gmunden.'

The parting — not that of a child but of a man about to become an exile forever. I will not write about it — how the flag was hauled down, the white-and-blue flag; how I went over the whole place once more; how I kept counting: 'There are still four hours, still three, still two, and now it is over.' And then the carriage came.

We drove to the nearest railway station at Kirchbichl where we took the train. 'There! Take a last look at Schoenwoerth!' said my father, and let us look through the carriage window. There it stood — the thick centre tower — the face with its round, kind eyes and great, broad mouth was turned away from us, the round, steep-roofed tower that served as a fire-escape, Wotan's ash. Then it was gone.

IV. *Gay Departure*

*W*E ARRIVED in Gmunden on the day on which Austria declared war on Serbia. All at once the Serbs were the most abominable people in the world, the source of all evil — the scum of the earth. It was extraordinary that we should never have realized it before. Nevertheless they remained in possession of this satanic distinction for only a few days. Then they were forced to share it with the Russians, French, Belgians, and eventually the English — until later on a number of other aspirants were added.

The peaceable population of Upper Austria became fiercely warlike. Next door to the house we had just moved into lived an Austrian cavalry officer. One day he spoke French in the street. Whereupon the mob made a united attack on his house and destroyed everything that could be destroyed.

We still had our 'French' governess. It was a good thing now that she was really Swiss. We were absolutely forbidden to speak French among ourselves. It is very curious, thought I — we used not to be allowed to talk German to her.

And when the English declared war —! At first the declaration was greeted with laughter. Ridiculous fellows, with the souls of jealous shopkeepers, what did they expect to get out of it? They couldn't hope to win the war through their traditional perfidy alone, these beefsteak-knights. My father became positively chauvinistic. 'Thanks be to Thee, O Lord, that Thou hast made an end to idle peace. The iron die is cast!' And, 'On the banks of the Thames, ye shall lie at our feet,' were the first lines of some of his poems.

'Mind you never tell anyone that your grandfather was Lord Pirbright!' he admonished us. As though we should! We were German boys, and had nothing, absolutely nothing, to do with the enemy.

Very soon war books for the young began to be published. I devoured them with avidity. The issue of the war was plainly foretold in them. Germany was going to win, of course — how could it be otherwise? Our opponents would soon see what it meant to conspire against Germany. We'll kick that out of them forever!

I began to read newspapers too, that is to say, the bulletins from the front. They confirmed exactly what I read in my story-books. 'Which fortress have we taken today?' was my daily enquiry. For the first few weeks I generally had a very clear answer. 'And when shall we be in Paris, in Belgrade, in St. Petersburg, in London?'

The whole world was concentrated in the palm of the hand of our victorious army. On the walls of our room hung maps of the battlefields. At first we were able to move the flags forward every day. It is true that we heard of the Russian invasion of East Prussia only after it was over. The name of Tannenberg and of the victor of Tannenberg, Paul von Hindenburg, assumed gigantic proportions. I possessed dozens of photographs of Hindenburg. I took a personal pride in him, as did everyone else.

That is the true secret of popularity. Everyone sees himself in the hero whom he worships. In exalting him men exalt themselves. I thought so much of Hindenburg that I often used to say that really the contest was hardly fair, seeing that we had such a great leader and the other side only ordinary ones.

At the same time I regarded it as a divine judgment. If we were not in the right, we should not have a Hindenburg. It has been forgotten now that even at that time he became a sort of legendary and mystic figure. I remember any number of stories in my war books that attributed miraculous immunity to fire and bullets to possessors of his picture, even to those who called upon his name. As far as we were concerned, the greatness of the German Emperor (and of course he was the greatest Emperor who had ever lived) consisted chiefly in his having discovered Hindenburg and given him a free hand.

None of the Austrian commanders made such a deep impression upon me, although I was living in Austria. But I liked the new heir to the throne, the Archduke Charles, who later became Emperor, after seeing him at Gmunden one day at the beginning of the war. But it may be that my feelings were roused chiefly by the military music which played him onto the boat in which he crossed the Lake of Gmunden.

The prohibition to talk French to our governess soon proved to be impracticable. She spoke such broken German that we hated to listen to it and unconsciously kept on dropping into French. As a result we were often remarked in the streets, and apparently there were even some anonymous threatening letters on the subject. A few weeks later, therefore, my father decided to make a radical change and to dismiss the 'French' lady.

Her place was taken by an appalling person, for whose existence we could see no possible justification. She was a Croat, the daughter of an officer who had just been killed, and she had no doubt been recommended on that account. I can still remember her pointed nails, her large and vicious-looking teeth, and her disproportionately high heels.

She must have been bad through and through. We soon found out that no word or gesture of hers but concealed something evil. Either she tried to vilify us to my father or to play us some other mean trick. She seemed never to have a decent impulse.

There really appeared to be no way in which she could be of use to us. She could teach us neither manners nor anything else. Her German was hideous and ungrammatical, her ideas idiotic, her education non-existent.

The one definite quality she possessed was a hatred of all things German which roused us to fury. She actually wished that the German army might suffer defeat — could anything worse be imagined! If she had her way, only the French and the Austrians would be victorious.

Inevitably the entrance of the Croat into our family involved serious complications. There was a general feeling of unrest, all manner of private alliance, intrigue, and actual personal mishandling came to pass. This was all the harder to bear since we were often left alone with her for weeks at a time when my father was obliged to go to Germany. And when he returned, we did not like to add to his worries with our troubles.

At the time all these things naturally seemed to me very important. Nowadays I realize that they all passed over me without leaving much trace. Only one episode that I can never forget must be recorded.

I had been given some guinea-pigs for Christmas, enchanting little creatures which lived in a small gaily painted chalet. True, they very soon gnawed it to bits, and once the young ones began to appear, I had to move the whole family into a wire cage where they got more air and sunshine.

Of course I looked after them myself and loved them dearly, especially one of the young ones, an adorable little beast, whose fur was one mass of small curls. The cage stood in the bathroom, and I used to let them run about loose in there sometimes.

One day there had been another violent domestic upheaval about something or other. I went into the bathroom to comfort myself by playing with the animals. They ran about, eating scraps of turnip and cabbage leaves, rolling over one another and being as happy as possible; especially the curly-haired one, who actually jumped over little hurdles.

The Croat came in and all the animals ran nervously to their cage. Only the curly-haired one seemed not to notice her.

She looked round without saying a word and ignored me completely. She knelt down beside a little box as though she were looking for something. Her left foot rested on its toe with the long spiky heel off the ground.

63

She turned half round, looked at her foot, and waited. I stood beside her as if I had been turned to stone, feeling what was about to happen, but incapable of movement.

And then the awful thing did happen. As the little guinea-pig ran under her foot, she stood up and squashed it. I saw the little animal lying on the floor, a trickle of blood flowing from its mouth. I said nothing to anyone, not even to my father.

I never even cried when I buried the little corpse. But soon afterward I gave away the rest of the guinea-pigs to a friend.

Thus I saw death for the first time, death as a result of cruelty, as a result of deliberate wrongdoing. It was a new piece added to my picture of the world, a fresh stage in my awakening.

I began to notice the casualty lists which filled the back pages of the newspapers. The front pages only told of the victories. Under the heading 'Roll of Honour' there were daily increasing lists of names. People we knew, the sons of neighbours, familiar friends, vanished. Several boys had joined up from the school my brothers attended, much envied by us all. Now their names came in the grim list. It was inconceivable, horrible.

And when the day came for our servant Joseph to go to the front, and then my father — he had joined as a volunteer — the deadly ring seemed to be close about us.

I was filled with a nameless dread for my father's life. I prayed for him for hours and hours every day. I said: 'I want to build a sure fortress round him. There are still gaps that I have to fill up.'

Every evening at six o'clock we went to the Intercession Service for the war, which was held in the chapel of the convent where my sister Sophie was educated. Nothing would have induced me to miss this Service, its prayers for the victory of the 'righteous cause,' and above all its prayers for peace. I joined in every petition, an endless litany, appealing to the patron Saints of every one of the belligerent Powers. I still remember some of them:

'HE SITS THERE LIKE A
PASHA'

IN GMUNDEN, SEVEN AND A
HALF YEARS OLD

'I WAS ALLOWED TO WEAR A
SUIT OF ARMOUR. TRUE, IT
WAS MADE OF TIN'

'I HAD VISIONS OF SMUGGLING
MYSELF IN AMONGST THE
TROOPS WEARING THIS SUIT'

'Saint Louis, patron Saint of France,
            Pray for peace!
Saint George, patron Saint of England,
            Pray for peace!
Saint Gudule, greatly honoured in Belgium,
            Pray for peace!
Saint Andrew, greatly honoured in Russia,
            Pray for peace!
Saint Henry, Emperor of the Germans,
            Pray for peace!'

Not that I was at all 'pacifist.' I yearned to go on to the field of battle myself. I prayed earnestly for peace day after day, and at the same time thought: 'The war must go on till I am at least fifteen; then I can go to the front too.'

I generally wore sailor suits or Leder Hosen. But I possessed a navy-blue suit which I imagined looked almost like a uniform. I had visions of smuggling myself in amongst the troops wearing this suit; nobody would recognize me, and so I should be able to go to the front and protect Germany.

There was no doubt whatever in my mind that we were the only righteous, the only honourable nation on earth. We were fighting for the happiness of all the rest and not merely for our own glory. (Who shall rebuke us for this faith? Did not America justify the war with the slogan that it was 'to make the world safe for democracy'?) France, of course, was our hereditary enemy, but when it came to it we were even fighting for France. For we were fighting for a principle, for the principle of monarchy against the horrors of republicanism. 'If France were to become a monarchy to-day, the Emperor would take pity on them at once and make peace!' I don't remember who first told us that bit of nonsense, but we suddenly knew it, it was a political axiom.

Our only real hatred, curiously enough, was directed towards England. 'They are our cousins,' we said in the very spirit of official war propaganda, 'and they have betrayed us. They have basely attacked us in the rear, because they are jealous of all our achievements, of our navy, of our Emperor. No quarter can be given! England must be crushed per-

65

manently.' For if this were not done, we were told, England would be forever causing disturbance, forever inciting other nations against us with loathsome hypocrisy and cunning.

In normal times we never used political catchwords at home. But 'God punish England!' and the answer: 'May it be so!' (which was later changed to: 'We'll punish Italy ourselves!') was used by us all.

Even my sister, who had been brought up in a convent, who had spoken English from her earliest childhood and had been very fond of it, suddenly became actively Anglophobe. She composed numerous verses about King George, the Tsar, Poincaré, and so on, all meeting in Satan's house to conspire against Germany. I remember one of them quite well:

> There in the devil's land,
> The name of God is banned;
> So all they could say in their infernal ring
> Was, 'Let's save the King.'

Soon also I gave way to the impulse to make rhymes on everything 'non-German.' Many of the poems I composed at that time might be published in the *Völkische Beobachter* without the slightest alteration.

The anti-English atmosphere that descended upon our family is no doubt to be explained by the deep disappointment that England had inflicted upon Germany's statesmen. Berlin had been so badly informed or so blind as not to understand the warnings uttered by England. Until the last moment everyone had hoped that England would remain neutral. England's mistake lay in her failure to realize the lack of sensitiveness of German diplomacy, so that she omitted to make her future attitude still plainer. If this had been more clearly expressed, so it is said today, war might have been avoided. I do not know if that is true. But it certainly is true for the next war. England's strength or weakness in regard to fascist aggression will decide whether or not it breaks out.

At the beginning of the year 1916 there was one memorable day — the day when we came down to breakfast and found that there was no more white bread. Instead of that we had a strangely dark kind, 'war-bread' it was called. How thrilling to have war-bread for breakfast!

Heavens, if I had had any idea of the things to which this day was the preamble! Until then the shortage of food had only been a joke to me. I used to tease the cook and say that I would tell people she was hoarding butter and sugar, and then she would be put in prison.

Otherwise our lives were still passed very quietly. My brothers went to school in the mornings and I did lessons at home. Our leisure was almost entirely occupied in playing with tin soldiers. We had been given enormous quantities of them: exact representations of the real thing, marvels of the toy industry. We had long since cast aside those of 1870–71 as no longer 'fit for active service.' We would have none but those clad in modern uniforms. We had examples of nearly all the German, Austrian, Bulgarian, and Turkish military units: Uhlans, dragoons, cuirassiers, machine-gun sections, every kind of infantry regiment, Alpine troops, and goodness only knows what besides — men marching, lying, standing, and kneeling, officers, Red-Cross men.

Almost as complete were the hostile armies under our command. We had French, English, Italian, Russian, Serbian, and Belgian regiments, Senegalese, Zouaves, Indians, Australians, Canadians. Very soon the forts, trenches, and artillery that we had been given were no longer sufficient. We made new ones and kept pace with everything that we saw in the illustrated papers. We invented much deadlier shells, with high explosives and greater penetrative power. We made drawings of the French and Russian fronts and worked out the battles in miniature. We calculated our reserves of men, road conditions, rivers and towns. It was an elementary school for future members of the General Staff.

I got a lot of fun out of all this, and I did not feel that it was in the least inconsistent with my prayers for peace. The only thing that grieved me was that my animals were being more and more pushed into the background — for, frankly, I was still much attached to them.

For the Commander-in-Chief it was after all a very sad day when my brothers declared that as far as they were concerned there would be no more games with the animals; indeed, if I wanted them, I could have their lions. Naturally I did not accept them. The lions were the symbols and embodiment of a power that had for many years meant something in my life. How could I use them now as lifeless, valueless things that had become nothing more than toys? Far from being a triumph for the Commander-in-Chief to see his former enemies thus diminished and brought low, it would have implied his own downfall, the annihilation of all the laws to which he owed his own being.

In the early spring of 1916 our home at Gmunden was suddenly broken up. Soon after the first time that we ate war-bread, a letter came from my father to say that we were to move to Würzburg. He had been stationed there for special duty for some months and wanted us to be with him. The Croat accompanied us, while the lady companion returned permanently to her parents. I said good-bye to her with feelings of complete indifference.

My father had been made commandant of a camp of French prisoners of war in Würzburg. In this connection I will give one little episode out of its turn. I happened to be in the camp with him one day when a revolt broke out among the prisoners. One of the officers was about to turn machine guns on them when my father made a witty speech in French and thus ended the revolt.

My brothers were sent to the Würzburg Gymnasium, and I passed the entrance examination for it with distinction. Whether I should actually enter the Gymnasium in the next school year was still uncertain as our plans were quite unsettled. Only one thing was clear: my eldest brother would be sent to the so-called 'Royal Bavarian Julianum for the Nobility' in the first term of the next school year. It had been founded in the beginning of the sixteenth century by the great Bishop of Würzburg, Julius Echter von Mespelbrunn, for the sons of the Catholic nobility. My father had also been a pupil there, after several years' education in an Austrian Jesuit college. My brother Leopold, on the other hand, was entered in the Cadet Corps at Munich.

For a long time I could not make up my mind where I should prefer to go. I liked very much the Julianum, which I had visited in the summer holidays, and it had an extremely nice and intelligent head master. Moreover — and this was most important — the pupils wore wonderful navy-blue uniforms with caps that were a cross between French and Austrian officers' caps. And on Sundays they were allowed to wear silver swords which were presented ceremonially by the head master.

The Cadet Corps was rougher, but it quickened your officer's career. The uniform was simpler, but — an important point — it was a real uniform. Cadets were permitted, indeed obliged, to greet officers with a military salute. Moreover, they wore bayonets.

Nevertheless I said (and was dubbed precocious and conceited for my pains): 'One should not be swayed by a uniform. If the war lasts long enough, I shall become an officer anyway, so that I should not need to go into the Cadet Corps. And afterward I'm going to be a statesman. So I'd better go to the Julianum.'

In the end circumstances decided the problem for me. If the revolution had not taken place, I should have had to be a cadet in 1918–19. We could no longer have afforded the Julianum, and as an officer's son I could have had a free education in the Cadet Corps.

Würzburg with its ninety thousand inhabitants was the first great city that I saw as a 'grown-up.' It is a beautiful place. If I wished to show a foreigner Germany, the true Germany, I should take him to Würzburg before almost any other town.

Through it flows the Main, its gentle river in which vineyards and old chapels are reflected in southern lines. It is spanned by beautiful old bridges, and passes the soaring towers of the former fortress of Marienberg, near which in 1866 a battle took place between the Bavarians and the Prussians. The Bishop's Palace — for Würzburg was for centuries a sovereign bishopric of the Holy Roman Empire — with its hall of mirrors is the finest baroque building in Germany.

There are wonderful parks in Würzburg and at the Bishop's summer palace close by at Veitshöchheim are world-famous fountains. The whole country is gentle and charming, and full of inner radiance, its people are of a sensuous piety, without hypocrisy or narrowness. The saying, 'Life is good under the crozier,' originated at Würzburg. And it was true — for its bishops were wise, art-loving, just rulers.

Our move to Würzburg had brought us into closer contact with the war. Opposite our hotel was a barracks. We could see how short was the interval now between joining up as a recruit and going out to the front. We had our first sight, too, of Zeppelins, bombers, and pursuit planes. This excited us so much that we wanted to imitate them.

At first it was all very harmless. We collected burrs, hid under the window-sill in our room, and then dropped them onto the heads of the passers-by. Though the effect was some-times quite satisfactory, we soon felt that it was too tame. So we proceeded to the manufacture of aerial darts, at first quite small ones that did no harm. They startled people and made them look up, wondering whether a hostile but somewhat childish aircraft was about. A few days later we got tired of this game too; so we made larger darts, and finally one which was quite good-sized, with steel wings and an iron tip.

When the dart was ready, we debated for a long time on whom we should drop it. At length we decided to favour a postillion (as a consequence of the shortage of motor cars, the old custom of postillions had been revived). There was one who often stopped in front of the hotel and looked very nice in his black-and-yellow suit and a tall shiny top hat.

It was probably this top hat which attracted us — it would be such fun to get it right in the middle.

As our room was on the third story, the dart fell with considerable force. Fortunately it missed him, but the effect was all that could have been desired. There was quite a panic — everyone ran about frantically, and the horses shied. The misdeed was never brought home to us. Nevertheless we stopped playing 'bomber' from that time on.

An important episode in my life was my first visit to the theatre. It must have been in June, 1916, soon after the battle of Jutland, because that had a certain importance in the play. The piece was called *Der Hias*,[1] and represented the very heroic life of our troops and the excessively depraved one of our enemies. We, of course, were victorious all along the line, despite immense difficulties. In addition there was a film showing the capture of sundry towns and fortresses.

We had arrived a quarter of an hour before the curtain rose and were sitting in one of the stage boxes. The curtain was covered with chubby cupids, houses, boats, curious animals and trees. What the play was to be about my father had more or less told me beforehand. And now I sat in front of the curtain, staring at it.

'Grown-ups really are queer,' I thought. 'They go to a theatre and look at a painted thing like this and think they're seeing a play. They must have an awful lot of imagination to turn all these lambs and angels into French and German soldiers, into taking fortresses, and into scenes in their homes and all the other things they told me about. If you know what the story is meant to be, I suppose perhaps you might imagine it, though with difficulty. But how ever did the first people who came think of it?'

At last I began to get bored and wanted to go home. My astonishment was boundless when the curtain went up, and I realized that the real performance took place behind it.

During the evening there was an amusing patriotic inci-

[1] An abbreviation for 'Matthew,' a typical name for Bavarian peasants.

dent which happened extempore. An actor wearing the mask and uniform of a French Senegalese performed savage dances on the stage, singing a song containing much abuse of Germany. Gradually the audience became steamed up — these black apes were being loosed on us; it was really a disgrace! All at once the 'nigger' danced towards our box; he continued to improvise, quite realistically, so that everyone should see how French 'niggers' kidnap German children, and jumped at me with a great roar, as if he wanted to grab me.

I took the attack seriously and landed him a hefty one on his chest. He bounced back, slipped, and fell on his back. For a moment there was complete silence. Then, while I was still looking at him, pale and indignant, a terrific storm arose. The audience burst into an intoxication of patriotism and honoured me with ovations. The unfortunate 'nigger' was given his share, too, in the end; after all, it was his good acting that had created the scene.

This happening in the theatre considerably increased my self-confidence. I felt heroic and mature. The very next day I told my father that I was old enough to go out for walks by myself. And since Würzburg did not seem to him to be a particularly dangerous place, he agreed. So I began to explore the town in all directions.

Everyone was friendly and ready to help. Perhaps the Austrian accent of my German touched them, perhaps they were amused at my appearance — a little fair-haired boy in a sailor suit armed with a map of the town and a sort of Baedeker, giving a military salute with his hand to his blue cap (S.M.S. U 9 [1] was the legend upon the ribbon): 'Please would you be so kind as to tell me how I get to the Palace, to the Cathedral, to Walther von der Vogelweide's tomb?' — and similar questions — which was a little astonishing. Gradually it came to be known who I was, but that did not altogether please me. I hated it when people jokingly returned my military salute, or put their hands to the seams of their trousers and said, 'Yes, sir.' I felt I was being treated as a small boy — which I obviously was no longer.

[1] The German form for H.M.S. Submarine 9.

This tomb of Walther von der Vogelweide, for which I searched, and, when I had found it, returned to again and again! Years before, in the South Tyrol I had come across Walther's name. And here anew, and then and now and always! The poet of the Holy Roman Empire, the super-national, Occidental community, the singer of Ghibelline Christianity: the Emperor as Protector of Europe, not of one nation only, above all not of the German nation alone, whose son he would usually be — and the Papacy fulfilling its mission only in harmony with the imperial law of the Occidental oekumene ——

How shall I, today, go on writing of 1916 and that which followed, when all I longed for as a child seems lost, and lost all the sacrifices my people brought? Crushed, profaned, sacred land that I walked in as a boy, that in spirit I shall walk in always wherever I may be.

If my sorrow were not so great, I should be shamed by the child whom I see now, who walked through the streets of a German town under a summer sun in the Great War, who entered cathedrals and churches to vow: 'I will serve the *Reich*, in justice, strength, and selflessness.'

This was the vow that closed the 'atheistical' period of my life into which I had fallen in Würzburg.

The beginning of it seemed grotesque. When my brother Leopold — who had got hold of some 'enlightening' literature somewhere — asked me: 'What would you say if somebody said to you that there is no God?' I answered: 'I wouldn't talk to an idiot at all.' Nevertheless, the idea stuck in my mind, especially as my brothers were always referring to it, and as a proof that everything proceeded 'naturally' and without any miracles, instructed me in their newly acquired knowledge concerning birth and conception.

My first reaction was an enormous disgust. I was much too undeveloped to feel anything else. When my father came in, I looked at him with horror. I had always thought so much of him, and now I knew this! He had five children, so he had — five times ——

73

My second reaction was: If things really happen like that, perhaps there is no need for there to be any God after all.

Now no one should say to me: 'But didn't you realize that conception in itself is a miracle?' No, I did not realize it, not at that time, and I am only speaking of that time. Until I was ten I had always assumed that children came into the world in some specially supernatural manner. I probably thought that God put them into a cradle all nicely dressed, but that I don't remember any more. At all events, what I had now found out must have seemed so simple that it made the need for the existence of God doubtful.

I did not let my brothers know that their information had impressed me particularly. I continued to argue with them in favour of our faith, although I was no longer fully convinced of its truth. This was a good thing because it tempted them to overplay their parts. 'I would only become a believer again,' said my eldest brother, 'if you were to be struck by lightning at your First Communion.' He could not guess what a troubled conscience he was rousing in me.

Ancient — ancient as far as I was concerned — feelings of guilt arose in me. Was sacrifice needed to purify me? I pondered for a long time. Then faith came back to me and the realization that it was a fearful thing to live without God. It would be better to die for His Name's sake. I saw again the great examples of my childhood — the boy Saint Pancras and the others. I would not be shamed by them.

I began to pray: 'Lord God, let me be struck by lightning at my First Communion, so that my brother may become a believer again.' I said this prayer daily. Every day I fought down my ever-renewed fear of death, my dread of lightning.

I said farewell to life. A bare year — no, only just over six months — remained to me. I must make the most of the time. I drew up the balance sheet: 'You have lived for ten years,' I said to myself, 'and what have you done? Is there anything for which you deserve immortality?' It was a melancholy reckoning. I could think of nothing to put on the credit side. Only my death might be of value—possibly.

74

And then I wanted to do one thing. I wanted to write something that would survive me, an epic of my fatherland, something to bear witness to its greatness, its mission. I planned to put in the experience I had had as a child with Michael: 'If the Emperor commands people to do things they don't want to, he must go!'

One curious thing happened. While I was preparing for death in the midst of the summer among the vineyards of the undulating Franconian landscape, I quite distinctly foresaw the fall of the German and Austrian monarchies. I saw their fall almost as a vision and as an absolute certainty.

My great work never materialized; not a line of it was written. It was far beyond any creative ability that I may have possessed. I was, however, incautious enough to give utterance to my forebodings as to the fate of the monarchist form of government. Imagine! In the year 1916, the son of an officer and a nobleman, in the midst of victorious battles! It was blasphemy, it was more monstrous even than the time when I had cried, 'Vive la République!' years before. It was impossible to punish me for it. What I had said was beyond the bounds of punishment. A way out of the difficulty was found by saying that I was not to be taken seriously. Small children should be seen and not heard.

There was something to be said for this. I was forced to withdraw into myself and to ponder in silence anything I observed. My sister Sophie, who came to Germany at that time to finish her education in a Bavarian convent, was the only person with whom I discussed the things that troubled me.

There were plenty of such things. As I went about the streets I noticed how the number of beggars was increasing, how many pale, hungry faces were to be seen. Children of my own age, clad in rags, would stand looking longingly at the windows of the few shops where food was still to be obtained.

A dim sense of foreboding awoke in me. How long would it be before I was in the same case? It must have been during these weeks that I first realized what was meant by the prayer: 'Give us this day our daily bread.'

V. *The Great Reality*

*W*HEN fatless and meatless days were introduced, which we could not avoid any more than anyone else, I was almost glad. The deprivation was easier to bear than the shame by which I had often been assailed.

Only the fact that it was increasingly obvious that this was not the end of it, but that much worse lay before us, caused me to regard the new regulations with less complacency.

The newspapers, it is true, said: 'The harvest is splendid. We are well provided for the coming winter, and there are enough raw materials to last for many years yet.' But bread rations grew smaller, cloth and boots became rare. On the other hand, prices went up, as we soon felt very strongly.

In this connection I heard for the first time words like 'inflation' and 'depreciation of the German currency.' Our income came from England through our mother, who was living in Austria. (Of course! I also had a mother! I wondered what she looked like. I could not remember her, nor was there any portrait of her about the house to remind me.) A bank advanced us the money, which meant that it was all reckoned at the nominal exchange value of the English pound. And we had to pay heavy interest on it.

Reckoned in terms of prices, the paper mark of 1916 fell very considerably. Sums which shortly before had seemed large to me — fifty pfennig, a mark, or two or five — turned out now to be very small when it came to buying anything. 'It will end by being like the assignats after the French Revolution,' I said one day. But I was strictly forbidden to make such remarks.

76

My father's pay as an officer soon came to be an important factor in our budget, after having been at first merely a supplement. He had volunteered as a second lieutenant; later on he became first lieutenant, and then captain. What can he have received at that!

So we must economize. Economize in every way, especially in regard to food. Even at that time the point where a good appetite merges into real hunger was sometimes reached. Dare I speak of it? Is it not petty, to make such a remark about a time when there were plenty of people already approaching real starvation?

Everything is relative. Life had been easy for us; to live well had been a matter of course. The very fact that there was doubt of its continuance was a shock. And it was clear that a great deal else was going to happen. This certainty of uncertainty was the most oppressive circumstance, even for us children. We also knew that we were living on the money obtained from the sale of Schoenwoerth. It was a comparatively small sum, for Schoenwoerth had been sold for a song. Once this money came to an end we should have no more. And that moment could not be very far off, for the money had been invested in Government stock, the value of which was steadily declining.

There was already a very gloomy atmosphere when our sojourn in Würzburg came to an end in September, 1916. My eldest brother, as had been planned, went to the Julianum, Leopold into the Cadet Corps. My father, the Croat, and I proceeded to Bamberg in Upper Franconia. My father was to put in a few months' service there with the reserve squadron of the First Uhlan Regiment, and I entered the lowest form in the so-called New Gymnasium.

Unfortunately my rank was the highest of anyone's in the school, and furthermore I was a Löwenstein, that is to say, as every Bavarian boy knew, a member of the House of Wittelsbach, with a hereditary right to the throne. At the beginning this was a great nuisance and made it very difficult for me to make friends. The biggest and oldest boys, whom everyone else looked up to with awe and respect, were quite ready to allow themselves to be ordered about by me. Very soon this got on my nerves to such an extent that, simply in order to prove that I was a boy like any other, I became the worst-behaved rowdy in the place. I'd show them that I was worth something apart from my title! I achieved my aim. My reputation among the boys went up week by week, in proportion as it went down among the teachers.

In Bamberg I met the true spirit of Germany even more clearly than at Würzburg. Anyone who has ever gone up the steps to its Gothic-Romanesque Cathedral will know what I mean. Bamberg is a coronation city of no less dignity than the cities on the Rhine; it should some day be made the residence of a prince primate of Germany.

There the Eternal Image of the German Spirit can be found. It is the equestrian statue that stands in the cathedral, a wise, noble and serene, a human and truly royal figure.

I know only one other statue that equals this one, or possibly is even superior to it. It is the equestrian statue of the Emperor Otto the Great, the founder of the Reich, in Magdeburg, the city of his burial. I said 'superior,' because this one includes a touch of sorrow and a noble grief, the wisdom and the power of renunciation that distinguish the true ruler.

Bamberg, like Würzburg, was also for centuries an imperial bishopric, spiritually and politically an autonomous State, subject only to the Emperor. Not until the year 1803 was it incorporated in Bavaria. This long independent history has not passed without leaving its trace on town and population. The cultural independence, the love of civic freedom can still be felt chafing against the monotonous uniformity of State administration. Only the war atmosphere has influenced this attitude. It was noticeable at school.

With the exception of myself — I had my own rights and privileges — the 'rank' of the boys in the classes went

78

according to the military rank of their fathers. It was a serious blow to the upholders of this order when I chose two of my friends from the 'lowest' ranks. The father of one of them was a sergeant-major; the father of the other one was, it is true, one of the most respected lawyers in Bamberg. But what did that signify? He held no military rank of any description. This boy became my first real friend.

Among my other friends were the two sons of another lawyer (who, however, was a captain). They were twins, so much alike that it was almost impossible to tell them apart, and were the most delightful couple of rascals, up to any mischief. One of them wore his hair parted on the right side and the other on the left. Every now and then they used to change over and drive the teacher nearly distracted.

The school was almost entirely Catholic. In my form we only had one Jew and one Protestant. We marvelled at them as though they had been some kind of fabulous monster, or exotic animals whose rarity made them attractive and noteworthy. When we discovered after some weeks' careful observation that they talked, wrote, sat, and disturbed the classes exactly like all the rest of us, our interest waned and we forgot their religious peculiarity. Anti-Semitism as a principle was unknown. Moreover, the Jewish boy's father was the first of all the fathers of the class to win the Iron Cross of the First Class, and he was duly envied for it. Anything to do with the war interested us, and the important thing as far as we were concerned was the Iron Cross and not the religious views of the recipient.

Gradually the war had come to be such a matter of course that the idea of the restoration of peace never entered into our calculations. The world divided itself into two armed camps for us, as though this were part of the natural order of things. Never having heard any differently, we were proud of the fact that the enemy camp was so much larger than our own. It did not occur to us to worry about what the consequences of this might be.

So much we knew for certain (I too had regained my faith in it): we shall win the war whatever happens, even if it

79

takes thirty years. I myself supported this point of view most ardently, and after every fresh battle made appropriate orations. The other boys listened to me willingly, for in matters military I was looked up to as the highest authority. Was I not the 'child of the regiment' of the First Uhlans, with more opportunity for seeing and hearing things than almost any of the others?

In Bamberg we had no house of our own; we lived in the Hotel Bamberger Hof, which had been called the Bellevue before the war and renamed on patriotic grounds. The hotel was occupied almost entirely by officers, and I was allowed to come down to luncheon and dinner — the only male civilian among all the uniforms. The insignia of the different ranks were already perfectly familiar to me, and I knew that only commoners were addressed by their military rank, but titled officers, from Counts upwards, by their titles.

The two youngest lieutenants, neither of them more than eighteen, a Count Pappenheim (the name recalled certain memories) and a Count Castell, were my best friends. One of them, I forget which, sometimes gave me glasses of liqueur in secret. I cannot say I enjoyed them very much, but I was flattered at being given them, regarding it as a proof that I was accepted as one of themselves.

This increased my longing to get into a uniform and go to the front. I planned to run away, to smuggle myself into a military train, a thousand ideas, and all of them absurd. My feeling of inferiority increased when my brother came home for Christmas from the Cadet Corps. He was only thirteen and a half, but he carried a bayonet and was obliged to give the military salute. Younger cadets had to stand to attention when he spoke to them. When my father wished to be specially impressive, he used to say, 'I'm not speaking as your father now, but as your superior officer.'

My first literary effort was completed in time for this Christmas. It was a fairy tale, the scene of which was laid in two stars at the same time. I stood beside the Christmas tree and read it aloud, and was delighted when everyone applauded it. This work for the first time reflected the shortage that was now beginning to be felt seriously. So far as I can remember, the struggle to obtain food played a considerable part in it.

Cards were issued for all kind of foodstuffs, even for the substitutes for certain articles of food. It is true, we had found a cheap and secret source from whence still flowed sausages, bread, and butter. It was a smuggling trade and outrageously unpatriotic. I felt that very strongly. One day my friend, the son of the civilian lawyer, came to see us and was given a real 'peace-time' tea. He talked about it at school and I was horribly ashamed.

Very soon the signs of the incipient collapse became even clearer. Soon after Christmas there was great excitement one day. Wild rumours were current, officially suppressed, secretly whispered from one to another. I saw disturbed faces at the officers' mess at the Bamberger Hof. Then I heard the truth. Part of the Fifth Bavarian Infantry Regiment, I think it was, which was being sent back to the front after a short spell of leave, had mutinied. A few soldiers had begun shooting in the station; when they were in the train things got worse. Rifles were pointed out of every window; anyone with officer's shoulder straps was fired at. The train was run through all the stations without stopping, but everywhere the soldiers fired. Not until they were at Frankfurt on the Main were they overpowered and disarmed.

A short time later satisfied faces were again seen in the officers' mess.

'None of those fellows is alive any more.'

'Executed?' I enquired in matter-of-fact tones.

'Lord, no! Just put in the front line, the whole gang of 'em — that's much quicker.'

Oh, thought I, so they were given a hero's death by way of punishment? Odd. I had always thought it was a distinction to lie in the first trenches. There was nothing about this affair in the newspapers (nor did I ever discuss it with anyone). Nevertheless the story gradually filtered through.

It also became known that the major — he sat at our table every day —who was in charge the night the troops left, had not gone to the station. Possibly he had guessed that the men would not be as joyful as officially they were supposed to be, and so like a wise man he had excused himself in time.

It was plain that all was not quite what it had been at the beginning. After all, the third wartime Christmas lay behind us, and there was still no end in sight. The army bulletins of course sounded as cheerful as ever. And none of us doubted that victory would be ours.

But want increased and the people began to waver. My form at school showed it. The slices of bread the boys brought to school with them grew steadily smaller, and more and more we talked about food. It also startled us, that an official bureau was opened at the school to collect waste material. We were no longer allowed to throw away our old exercise books; we were enjoined to collect used tea leaves and similar things and to hand them in. The classrooms became more and more poorly heated.

The great event that drove all this into the background was our First Holy Communion. (Had I not prayed to be struck by lightning on this occasion? That was a long while ago!) We resolved among ourselves not to talk any more about our privations. This was to be our sacrifice and a further preparation.

A short time after the First Communion we were confirmed. On a brilliant day in May we drove up the steep hill to St. Michael's Church. I knew a very beautiful legend about its foundation.

Saint Cunigunda, the wife of Saint Henry, the Emperor Henry II, had herself overseen the construction. Whenever she went up the doors opened before her, even if they had been fast locked and bolted. One day the Empress was very tired, so she picked up a staff that was lying in a vineyard to support her. She supposed that, as always, the doors would fly open — but they remained shut. She fell on her knees and cried: 'Why dost Thou punish me, Lord God?

Tell me wherein I have sinned.' A voice replied, 'God does not choose that the least wrongfully acquired property shall be in the hands of His elect.' The Empress, so the story continues, stood up and went back the long way. She put back the staff where she had found it, and when once again she stood before the church with empty hands, the doors opened to her as they had done before.

A few days after my confirmation we left Bamberg. Before returning to the front, my father had been ordered to do a few weeks' garrison duty in the neighbourhood of Munich. I was sent to the Gymnasium at Pasing, a small place near Munich, which has almost become a suburb now. I lived in a school boarding-house in which there were about fifteen boys besides myself. One of the masters, a great beer-drinker, looked after our work.

In Pasing real misery began. The woman who ran the boarding-house, a very nice, kind-hearted soul, did her best for us, but there was simply nothing to be had. We walked the long way to school with aching hunger, generally finishing our 'elevenses' — two thin little slices of bread with turnip jam — before arriving. At half-past one we came back, and our lunches satisfied our cravings for half an hour. We used to sit together, talking and dreaming of all kinds of good dishes — or, really, simply of having enough to eat.

All at once the phrase 'in the old days, in peace-time' came to mean a sort of indefinite romantic vision of plenty of food — plenty of bread and butter and meat.

These conversations were the only thing in common between my school-fellows in the boarding-house and myself. They were all oppressed, full of guilt, shy, and gave obscure hints: 'We must be quiet and obedient. Dr. X [the beer-drinking teacher] has us in the hollow of his hand. If he says anything, we shall all be expelled from the school.'

'What's the matter?' I enquired. They did not altogether trust me, and I only got half answers. But gradually I found it out. Something had happened once among the boys that probably happens in all boarding and public schools.

The master had found it out, and was using his knowledge to bring pressure to bear upon the boys. Other methods of education he did not seem to possess. It was an uncomfortable, depressing atmosphere. I was glad when I was told that I should not return to Pasing for the next school year.

My father was ordered to the western front. My eldest brother, my sister Sophie, the Croat, and I were to go back to Gmunden. My brother Leopold remained in the Cadet Corps. I was delighted at the news. Why, it may be asked. Because at all ages the unpleasant is easier to forget than the pleasant.

Gmunden suddenly appeared to me as a kind of substitute for Schoenwoerth. At all events we had lived in nice houses there, with gardens which to me as a child appeared large. Besides, when we had left there had been plenty to eat. Why should it be any different now?

I comforted myself at leaving Germany by saying that there was really no difference between it and Austria — we were on German soil in either case.

We saw my father off at the station. The next day we started off ourselves, but the train only went as far as Salzburg, where we had to spend the night. We did not arrive in Gmunden until late the next morning, after taking twenty hours over a journey that needed five in times of peace.

Already in Salzburg we had realized that conditions were actually worse in Austria than in Germany. There could be no question of beginning again where we had left off in the spring of 1916. We had hardly put our feet on Austrian soil before we found out how difficult it was to get anything at all to eat. And we were told in Salzburg that things were still worse at Gmunden.

The villa to which I had been looking forward did not materialize. Our income was only sufficient for a flat, though the house was pleasantly situated on the banks of the lake and had a pretty garden. But it was cold and damp, and the windows of the bedroom allotted to my brother and me looked north and east.

84

At this time I had no friends of my own age in Gmunden. So I got very bored during the rest of the summer and longed for school to begin again. At last the time came. It was the middle of September, the holidays were over, and I was able to take stock of my new surroundings. The first thing I did was to find out the name and rank of every single boy. I discovered that almost one third of the boys in my form belonged to the nobility, but only those whose fathers were big landowners were still well off. All the other aristo-cratic families who in the old days had possessed a sufficient income were in exactly the same case as ourselves.

None the less the peace-time custom of mutual invitations was continued, at which tea made of strawberry leaves was drunk, and everybody declared they were not hungry. I still remember the delight with which my sister told us one day, when she came home after visiting the mother of one of her school-fellows, that she had been given a potato for tea as a mark of particular friendship.

We children copied the example of our elders. We too were continually extending invitations to one another. If a particularly dear friend was coming, we used to save up a piece of our breakfast bread for him. Commoners of course were only invited in very special instances. Either their parents must show a very high social standing, or they must be good at lessons and therefore useful for one's homework, or else — and in the course of time this became the most important of all — they must have sources of food.

I was lucky at the first stroke. I noticed a fat, vulgar boy, infuriatingly fat for those days. His nose always wanted blowing, his speech was inconceivably common. Between lessons and sometimes also during them he wolfed moun-tains of sausages and cheese. That's the fellow for me, thought I. I made friends with him, went for walks with him, treated him as an equal. The 'nobility' was horrified.

'Fancy making friends with a chap like that! With Alois Fürstinger, whose father is a village shopkeeper!'

'Just you wait,' I replied. 'I have my own reasons for making friends with Alois Fürstinger.'

85

I became still friendlier with him, made him tell me about his father's shop, and pretended to be interested. In reality I had difficulty in concealing my arrogance, and also to some degree my disgust of myself. 'One can make use of fellows like that,' my father would have said, I thought, 'but not make friends with them.' Well, my father was at the front and knew nothing about what things were like at home. Otherwise he would have realized that one had to make friends with Alois Fürstinger if one wanted to make use of him.

Events proved me right. I had soon made a pact with him. I would do his German compositions for him, in return for which he would provide me with a given number of 'elevenses.' Everything went swimmingly. His essays and mine were the best in the form, and I had my middle-morning lunches. Unfortunately the good time did not last long, because the other boys found out what I was up to, and so one of them took over his mathematics, another his French, and so on, with the result that my rations were sadly diminished. I was obliged to extend the field of my operations, and so I concluded agreements with all the boys who came in from the country. It was hard work, because it was essential that the master should not find out that anything up to twelve essays came from my pen every time. I turned out those essays as if I were working by machinery. The boys came to me and I dictated their essays to them one after another. Not, by the by, only in return for snacks. One of them did my drawing for me and another one my arithmetic.

When my pact with Alois Fürstinger became less productive, I had to introduce fresh currency units. I appointed him 'Minister for Food Supply,' which made him liable to a special tribute over and above what he provided in return for the essays. Unfortunately the 'Cabinet Fürstinger' was not a long-lived one. It gave in its resignation when he said to me one day, 'If you want me to keep on feeding you, you'll have to stop being a count,' a proposition which I turned down.

86

Another boy, who also came of a very low class, I made field marshal. As a matter of fact he was a very nice boy, and I was soon great friends with him. Franzl Dertlgruber was his name, and he, too, was the son of a small shopkeeper. At that time to be a shopkeeper made one into a Great Power, because it meant that one was connected with the sale of tobacco — a monopoly in Austria. And tobacco was now of incalculable worth. It was needed in bargaining with the peasants for foodstuffs. Actually the quota of tobacco was subject to strict regulations. But anyone who was on good terms with his supplier could get more.

Franzl Dertlgruber took his duties very seriously and raised a small army for me, composed of bakers' boys, cobblers' boys, apprentices, and young mechanics. They were all made to take a solemn oath, which I am quite sure contained the words 'Faithful unto death.'

In certain respects our realization of the distinction between *mine* and *thine* grew dim in those days. Fruit, for instance, was regarded as anyone's property, as the spoils of war (not that the peasants agreed with this view). Dertlgruber's band was firmly convinced of the rightness of this attitude. They wandered merrily through the countryside and always returned laden with booty. But they would have considered it a gross dereliction of duty to eat it without bringing me tribute.

It should be mentioned that Upper Austrian fruit is not of the best. Most of it is intended for making cider. It has to be cooked before it is worth eating. But the fact that it was edible at all was what counted.

I myself was unfortunately quite unsuited to the occupation of apple-stealing. That is a fact that I do not propose to deny. But as regards the additions which my brothers, in particular, make to this statement, I have banished them long since to the realm of legend. One day, for example, they aver, we lay concealed near an apple tree to which we had crept up stealthily. Some peasants were walking across the field, among them no doubt the owner of the apple tree; whereupon I emerged from my hiding-place, put up an umbrella to shield me from the view of the peasants, and made straight for the apple tree. Only hasty flight saved us from the wrath of the honest country folk. However, I have always contested the truth of this story, nor do I admit it today.

A new idea swam into our ken, and soon became the alpha and omega of our conversation: 'foraging'; that is to say, going to the peasants to try to buy food. My good opinion of the peasants was somewhat shaken in the process. With very few exceptions they proved hard-hearted, grasping, unfeeling, and selfish. Provided with a rucksack, and wearing shoes the leather of which was cracking, my brothers and I started out — in winter it meant going knee-deep through snow by paths, the existence of which we could only guess — to walk for hours across country, fit to drop with weariness, hungry, and frozen to the marrow. We felt like beggars, and as beggars we were treated — despite the fact that we were charged fantastic prices.

The procedure was always the same. We came to a farmhouse and knocked at the door. They were delightful carved doors with texts on them. After we had knocked three or four times, a gruff voice would be heard behind the door, which remained shut:

'Got any tobacco?'

'No, we've got no tobacco, but we wanted to ask ——'

The voice became still gruffer:

'Oh, no tobacco? Well, what have you got? Tea? Candles? Underclothes? Nothing at all? Well, then, you may as well go away at once.' And the door stayed shut. For in addition to the high prices one was expected to give them all kinds of things that were supposed to be easier to obtain in the towns. Later on candles were not asked for, as most of the peasants had installed electric light.

Naturally we proceeded to employ all manner of ruses. For weeks we brought packets of tea to one peasant woman who was specially fond of it, containing tea leaves that had been used two or three times. She enjoyed it just the same, and we obtained in return eggs and butter and all kinds of things. Until one day apparently another campaigner who wanted to sneak our source of supply for himself went and told her that we were giving her second-hand tea. The next time we went there she set two great dogs on us, whereupon we departed hastily and never went near her again.

Nevertheless, in the course of time we succeeded in discovering some kind people — blessings on their memory. But it was not very much use any more, because at about this time we found ourselves hardly able to pay for anything at all. However, it meant that we could have a slice of bread and a glass of milk, and if necessary we would gladly walk for half a day to get that.

The worst concomitant to hunger is envy. People began to watch their friends suspiciously to see whether anyone had more than they themselves. If so, they got indignant about it and said to each other that 'really the authorities should step in.' Then again one made attempts to rise above it, to defy one's wretchedness.

'One ought to have so much to eat that one does not have to think continually about food,' I said. At that time, however, one thought of little else. It was not so bad in the summer. We got to know a great deal about edible wild plants. We collected herbs and berries which in normal times no one would even have noticed. And if one could lie in the sun for hours, one somehow was able to forget one's hunger for the time being.

In winter time it was worse. In 1917–18 there was no more wood or coal and, as I said, the house was damp. It got so cold that my brother and I were often unable to do our homework because the ink froze in the inkstand, and by the time it thawed our hands were too numb to hold a pen.

Then I found a wonderful source of strength. One of our teachers had told us about Shakespeare, about *Julius Caesar*, and Mark Antony's speech. In the worst days, when I could hardly turn the pages, the Shakespearean verse spoke to me, fortified me, gave me hope. I still remember what I felt the first time I read:

89

> 'But I am constant as the northern star,
> Of whose true-fix'd and resting quality
> There is no fellow in the firmament.
> The skies are painted with unnumb'red sparks,
> They are all fire and every one doth shine;
> But there's but one in all doth hold his place.
> So in the world; ...

To become great beyond the temporal confines, to create, to be an active force, to be a shining light, to be unforgotten, immortal — what was hunger, what was cold, what was any suffering? Was it fitting that a man should complain of it? I was not slain in my mother's womb when the lightning struck through the window; I was not drowned on the night of the storm when Messina was destroyed; I was not crushed by the mill wheels, the venomous snake did not bite me — and was all this to go for nothing, did it imply nothing, was it not to be taken as a pledge of the future? Twelve emperors and twenty kings were among my ancestors, a mountain of legends, Wotan's ash, watched over my cradle. And should I now die miserably of hunger and consumption? No, never! God could not intend that.

I thought of lesser things too. (Oh, the standards of childhood!) What would my army do if I were to die? Could I show myself weaker than my men, seeing that I was their leader? Unconsciously I did the right thing for myself. I sought heroes and exemplars, whose lives and deeds could wing my thoughts.

How, I wonder, did I light on the Emperor Tiberius? The history book we used at school had nothing good to say of him — 'the bloody tyrant,' 'the debauché on Capri,' and so forth. But somewhere I had read: 'He kept the provinces in exemplary order, he punished injustice and oppression, he maintained peace, security, and justice in the whole Empire. The people honoured him, the nobility hated him. The distortion of his character is typical of the biased aristocratic view of history taken by Tacitus.'

Perhaps this passage induced me to investigate him further. An emperor who punished oppressors, whom the people loved and the nobles hated — had not the vision of such a one come to me once before? Had I not, indeed, spoken of it — 'A republic with an emperor at its head'? I obtained Suetonius' *Lives of the Caesars* and whatever else I could lay hands on about Roman history under the emperors, and read and read and read. In feverish excitement — Roman Empire, imperial glory, one Empire, one Law, one Ruler, to include all Europe. And Germany is the heir to the Caesars. Its kings needed the Roman crown, and the Roman crown came to Germans alone.

Eternally alternating currents, mystical union that lasted for a thousand years — should it cease now? Can one to whom a duty has been entrusted cast it aside, as though it were a thing of nought, as though it had never been? Never. Then how was it that we were waging war in Europe, and talking of nations and individual rights?

Oh, Lord, since 1914 there has been a Civil War. Has nobody realized that? There must be peace so that Europe may be built up, a single Occidental Realm, a sacred confraternity of all its peoples.

The first result of my new historical concepts was a drama — *Tiberius*. I have lost the manuscript, but I still remember its form and content. It was written in heroic iambics, a drama on the antique model, but concerned with modern problems! The first newly established organization of the vast empire — which contained no fewer races and languages and cults than present-day Europe — was to be secured. The essential thing was to prevent its dissolving into its component parts, to prevent the Barbarians from destroying Greek and Roman culture.

One man is in Italy, first on the Palatine Hill, then at Capri, who plans and wills it, who perhaps foresees already that the spiritual heritage of Rome must be preserved for the successors to the Roman Empire, the Germans, whom he has come to know during his campaigns, even if they are as yet immature.

Tiberius fought for the well-being and peace of the Roman Empire, not from personal ambition but with his mind concentrated upon the future — thousands of years ahead.

I was capable of thinking these thoughts, but had not the artistic power to give them expression. The verse must have been childish, just as the manner in which I set about the creation of the work was childish. I could not write in our gloomy room. If I was to forget the world I lived in, I must make another one for myself. So I picked leaves from a laurel bush that stood in the garden and wove them into a wreath. A blue cape with a red lining I turned inside out, and wearing the laurel wreath on my head, I hid and wrote the drama of *Tiberius* in secret. No one realized what I had been doing when I was late at table, a table on which a few turnips were the whole meal.

VI. *Kalvarienberg*[1]

*A*T CHRISTMAS time in 1917 my brother came home from the Cadet Corps for a fortnight's holiday. What a Christmas! Once again we sat together in the dark as in former years — this time, however, in order to save light. My sister told no more fairy tales; perhaps she was the most unhappy of us. Only one hope in life was left to her: to become a nun like my father's sisters, who lived and died as nuns in the Convent of the Sacred Heart. She had offered herself as a novice in Vienna and was now awaiting an answer. The hours of Christmas Eve, dearest to me in all the year, seemed endless and depressing. There was nothing holy in them. My brother told us stories of his life in the Cadet Corps, the same tale of hunger and misery that we already knew by heart. Slowly it grew late; we were chilled, depressed, and yet somehow filled with expectancy. We knew that our grandmother had sent money for us, a fairly large sum, so anyway there should be something.

At long last the moment came. The door of the Croat's room opened — a well-heated room into which we were sometimes allowed in the evening, where the warmth used to send me to sleep. She appeared and spoke — I shall never forget her words as long as I live! — words that replaced the customary wishes for a happy Christmas, and peace on earth. She said: 'Come in! The rubbish is alight!'

The 'rubbish' was the Christmas tree. There it stood, lit up by a few candles. My poor Christmas tree, still sacred, still symbolizing the Light that shineth in the Darkness — although the Darkness comprehended it not.

[1] Mount Calvary.

Now many years have gone by, but I still see the touching sight of your tiny branches, your slender trunk. You might have grown tall and big and seen the coming of brighter days. But you died in childhood to carry Christmas candles for us, for me. You thought too well of me; you believed that in your light I should see the promise that night is not eternal.

On this evening I did not see it; I saw only with the eyes of an eleven-year-old boy, that there were no presents for me, except one or two tiny things, and that there was nothing to eat — no nuts, no cakes. Four big rosy apples alone stood at the four corners of the table which bore the Christmas tree. Those four apples — we rejoiced over them for days until first one, then a second, then a third, and finally the fourth disappeared. None of us children got a single one of them.

Should I reproach myself for my want of stoicism? Have I any right whatever to speak about these things, seeing that I had at any rate a roof over my head?

Laughter and tears, seriousness and high spirits, often mingled in those days. It could happen that I would speak or discuss things like a grown-up only to run off immediately and play at Red Indians with Franzl Dertlgruber, or join with five other boys in smoking two cigarettes in secret.

I often think now that one should try to keep something of this child's inconsequence throughout life. People inspired by an 'animal seriousness,' as a clever man [1] once called it, who never dare to leave their work for a single moment, are incomprehensible and deeply repugnant to me. They are not really more serious-minded; they are only less honest. Their faith in themselves and their mission is so weak that they are always fearful of losing it. And especially, they are perpetually worried lest others should discover their insincerity. Hence their constant zealous look, and their inability to laugh at themselves.

As regards the roof over our heads, in many ways it was actually a burden. We had to go on keeping up appearances,

[1] Karl Kraus.

94

and the façade had to be preserved at the cost of the content. And this was still thought to be essential even when the lowest depths had been reached.

The great German offensive against France in the spring of 1918, in which my father was also engaged, once more roused my enthusiasm to fever pitch. Let this be understood: neither the gloomy forebodings which I had entertained since 1916 nor the obvious collapse of the hinterland had prevented the continuance of my passionate belief in victory, just as my prayers for peace did not stand in the way of my hoping that the war would last long enough to enable me to take part in it.

Up to the very end I indignantly refused even to discuss the possibility of our defeat. It also seemed to me impossible to conclude peace on terms that would not give us possession of Belgium and parts of France and Serbia. When we defeated Russia, Rumania, and Serbia, it served only to strengthen me in my conviction, if indeed that were necessary.

The dogma was: 'Germany is unconquerable, so something is bound to happen. And if we starve in the course of it, what does that matter?' It is not therefore, the resurgence of shattered hopes — they never were shattered — that I mean when I write of the fresh hopes aroused by the spring offensive of 1918. The offensive restored our cheerfulness and strengthened our belief in a brilliant victory. It did not merely restore belief; that was always present.

My sister, the one we called the 'Berliner,' arrived on a visit about this time. Her presence was like a breath of the strong, invigorating wind that blows over the Mark of Brandenburg swirling through Gmunden, that unhappy corner of suffering Austria.

We were very fond of her, despite the fact that she had been brought up quite differently from ourselves in our grandmother's house in Berlin, where the foremost interest was in art, music, and the theatre. We, on the other hand, as I mentioned before, were surrounded by abysmal ignorance and cultural darkness.

My sister had been brought up to be very 'Prussian.' Her North German accent alone distinguished her from us. All this aroused the greatest astonishment in me — this feeling of something foreign, something bigger than we had known. It impressed me immensely. My sister was not indeed more 'patriotic' — that would have been impossible — than I was. But she was patriotic in a different, more aggressive and more active, sense. She knew more of what had actually taken place.

As long as she was with us we never cared what we had to eat. She could tell us far more about events at the front than we could learn for ourselves in Austria. Her motto was: 'Be worthy of the times in every thought and every word!' I owe a great deal to her, and through her I learnt much about literature and art which became precious to me. It is to her that I owe above all else my earliest faith in my task and my work.

This was the last time of glamour in the Great War. The retreat I could not understand, and probably heard little about it. First came the news that the offensive had come to a standstill. What did that matter? We should start again somewhere else. There followed the news of the retreat. I saw from my atlas that the towns that were abandoned lay far behind the former German front. Doubtless we were retreating for strategic reasons.

I did not become alarmed until towns were evacuated that had been German as long as man could remember — that is to say, since 1914. But then came the announcement in the newspapers that we had retreated to a new Siegfried line in order to await the result of the peace with the Ukraine.

The Ukraine! The magic word on which all hopes were centred. The granary of Europe was now opened to us! Soon we should have everything again — bread, meat, eggs, butter — and be able to hold out for years.

The Austrian capacity for irony at one's own expense found vent in the stories that were soon circulating. I still remember one of them. A man enters a café and orders a piece of cake. The waiter takes the order and disappears.

When ten minutes have passed by and the waiter has not returned, the customer begins to get impatient, calls the waiter, and asks why he has not brought his cake. 'It will be here any minute now, sir,' the waiter politely replies. 'I have just telephoned the Ukraine again.'

In the late autumn of 1918 my eldest brother and I were allowed to move into a smaller room that could be heated to some extent by means of wood which we fetched from the forest. We went out collecting sticks several times a week. It tired us, and took up much of the time that should have been given to our school work. In those days, however, school work seemed less important than that the room should at least be above freezing point. Each time we went to the forest we also brought back acorns to be ground up for the breakfast 'coffee.' The taste of it may be left to the imagination.

There was hardly any sugar. If it was procurable, or if we managed to get a pound, it had to last for a few weeks. We were so starved for sugar that I usually ate up my allowance in two days. Fortunately I had a friend whose father was a chemist, and from him I got saccharine. If one crushed it into a fine powder, so I discovered, it could even be eaten without tasting bitter.

The bread ration sank to a loaf a week, which we usually finished in two days. Also the composition of the bread (had I not once rejoiced over it?) became stranger and stranger. At times it crumbled like sand — that was when it was made of maize meal; at other times it was damp and soggy like clay — which was worse, and meant that there were horse chestnuts in it.

The days grew gloomier and gloomier. My twelfth birthday in October passed as if it had been a day like any other. This was sad, as I loved my birthday. But what was there to celebrate this time, and how could it have been done?

The town lay in darkness. A cold mist from the lake and the mountains hung over it. It was seldom light enough to read before nine or half-past nine in the mornings. School hours were shortened to save light. Rumours were already

97

circulating of mutinies at the front. The fathers of some of the boys suddenly returned home. On leave? Yes, self-accorded leave. The proportion of officers among those on 'leave' was specially great . . .

Slovenly uniforms appeared on the streets. To my indignation I noticed that soldiers ceased to salute properly. The air was filled with a sense of the approaching end. So strong was this feeling that my hitherto unwavering faith crumbled. Its final disappearance came with a crash. Suddenly I seemed to be standing on the edge of an abyss into which everything fell which I had known as everlasting values. 'We cannot win any more,' I said aloud to myself as I walked alone on the shore of the lake. 'We cannot win any more.' Did I really know what that meant?

My second thought was: 'If we are defeated, we must be defeated with honour. No collapse through weakness, no sudden failing, no throwing away of our arms, no begging for mercy!'

A third thought came: 'Only a miracle can save us. But miracles do not happen while men look on motionless. Perhaps I can do something. Perhaps I can save my country. It must be tried.'

I turned on my heel and ran up steep streets to the house in which Franzl Dertlgruber lived. In a few words I told him what I was planning to do. I speedily overcame his doubts: 'You have given me your word. You must keep faith with me!' His question was childlike, though I did not feel it as such:

'And will you really make me a field marshal?'

'I will — if you prove yourself worthy.'

At home I said nothing. I behaved as usual and nobody suspected anything. On the next day I invented an excuse for leaving the house and went up again to Dertlgruber's. I had summoned a meeting of my friends — Dertlgruber's bakers' boys and shoemakers' apprentices, mechanics, and learners of all kinds. Eight or ten boys belonging to my own form at school had joined us.

It was a misty afternoon. Darkness had almost fallen by

98

the time we met behind an isolated waterworks that stood on a hill known as the Kalvarienberg. Boys came from every direction, none of them over fifteen. I was the youngest, twelve years old. Altogether there must have been between thirty and forty boys present, of whom not a single one was an aristocrat or an officer's son or the child of an academic family. All of them were the children of lower middle and working class families or peasants' sons, mainly strong, healthy boys, carefree, trustworthy, and loyal. A few who had come across the hills that were covered with thin patches of mist had brought pocket lamps with them. Two carried torches that burnt slowly and with a smoky red light in the damp air.

I can still see all their faces clearly. A secret society, a conspiracy, a band of children and adolescents who had come prepared to obey any order I might give them. Many of them had lost their fathers or brothers in the war and were suffering as I was under the threat of the coming collapse.

They were waiting for me to speak. A superhuman task confronted me, a task too great for adults, too great for entire nations. But the call was there, an imperative 'You must!' I climbed up on to the waterworks; beside me stood the torch-bearers, Dertlgruber one pace behind me.

I made a sign. A deadly silence fell. Then I began to speak. It was my first public speech. I uttered the words as I felt them, without rhetoric, impelled by all I had lived through for years.

'The Fatherland is in danger,' I said. 'Bulgaria, Turkey, and Hungary have collapsed; Austria falls to pieces. But the German Reich still fights — and we are Germans here in this German cradle of Austria. Those who are still fighting are fighting for us, we must help them. Do not tell me that we are too young. We can help if only we have faith and courage. At school we have been taught about the Children's Crusade. We will organize a Crusade of Youth: someone must make a start, and then everyone will join us, the whole country, the weary soldiers, the despairing people. It is we who must begin! We owe it to God and our country,

99

for our cause is righteous. Nobody shall be able to say to us in later years, "You took advantage of your youth in order to stand aside." When a nation is engaged in a life-and-death struggle, then even the children must play their part! You boys from my form know how the Carthaginian children gathered stones and sharpened arrows, how they joined in the fight armed with knives and daggers. Besides — we are children no more!

'I propose, therefore: we will meet tomorrow outside the town, we will march through the villages and summon all the boys to join us. I will organize several companies and appoint their leaders. Where we will meet again, I shall announce later. The goal of our march is the Tyrol, where German troops have just arrived to defend it against the Italians. We need not be afraid of the police. They will not fetch us back. They're no good any more, and besides our fathers aren't there to ask them to do it. Will you come?'

Then the boys all shouted 'Yes! We'll come!' — 'Hurrah!' 'Bravo!' and God knows what else, until one boy suddenly called out:

'How are we going to know who belongs to us? We haven't got uniforms!'

A curious thing then happened — to my own surprise I said: 'We'll wear black-red-gold bands!'

An outburst of enthusiasm followed. Black-red-gold, colours that I named publicly for the first time at this moment, were the Symbol of Greater Germany in Austria, and specially loved and revered by the youth of the middle and lower classes. From the standpoint of the Habsburg dynastic interests these colours were tantamount to high treason. But now that we were about to offer ourselves to serve Germany, and not some dynasty on the verge of dissolution, there could only be one flag for us: the thousand year old symbol of the Occidental Realm — the black-red-gold colours under which the German revolutionaries of 1848 had fought, and which kept alive in Austria the consciousness that we are one people and want to become one Reich again.

The fact that I chose these colours to be the badge of us

Crusaders revealed no less clearly than did my speech what had to happen: An uprising of youth with a new aim — a common destiny for all Germans no longer severed from the fatherland.

This was a great and solemn hour to us, though a grown-up watching might have mocked us. We believed in our mission; we believed that we should sacrifice our lives and our blood. The faint tremor that passed over us bore witness to our willingness but also to our secret fear of horrors to come. Of that none spoke. The fear had no sooner seized upon us than it was overcome.

Dusk had turned into night and the torches had burnt low when I continued my speech. My followers had become one — one will, one faith, one host. I felt the strength that emanated from them. They urged me on to thoughts and words which I should otherwise never have uttered. For there was still an Emperor of Austria, and I had been brought up to believe that the rulers and princes came first and the country only second. The ideal of Greater Germany was looked upon at home as high treason, not because of Austria, but because it was turned against the super-national fatherland of the High Nobility. No ruling prince must be reduced in his rights, I had always been told, if the nobility were to prosper. (And then came the facile conclusion: If the nobility is prosperous, the people will also be prosperous.)

All this passed through my mind, in this moment, when for the first time I turned against the laws of my class. It was a break with the traditions of generations and at the same time a return to those who were the born enemies of the nobility — the Emperors of the Roman-German Reich. And dimly, unconsciously, in the visions of my blood I saw once again this fight waged by the Nobles' International — this worst enemy of the people — against the Emperors.

All of a sudden I realized something that nobody had ever told me — that the 'natural alliance' between Monarchy and Nobility was only invented much later, that it was hypocritical and mendacious. Whenever the nobles lent the Emperor their support, they did so as wolves in sheep's clothing, treacherously, merely in order to turn the situation to their own account by disuniting the Empire and the people and holding them in subjection.

At this moment, when I was wise and mature — truly only for a moment since I did not possess the strength to grasp and retain all this — the words hammered so loudly and insistently upon my brain that I was compelled to give them utterance:

'And herewith I release you from every allegiance to the Emperor of Austria. There is one alone whom we must still serve because he represents us as well as the whole Reich and its last struggle in which we are now going to take part — the German Emperor! He alone shall lead us. He will march to victory at our head, or will die beside us for Germany. To him we swear loyalty——'

Suddenly Dertlgruber stood beside me. It occurred to me that he looked much older than usual, but his voice interrupted my thoughts:

'Why to the German Emperor in Berlin——? It is you to whom we swear loyalty!'

'No!' I called out as loudly as I could, but my voice was almost drowned by the cheers that answered Dertlgruber's words. For an instant I hesitated — oh! the kingdom of this world. Your first — behold — your first temptation! But it would be madness, folly, to yield; I should destroy my own work — all that it might lead to. That must not happen? Again — still louder — I cried 'No!' and this time it must have rung out clearly and decidedly.

'Swear loyalty to the German Emperor and the German Reich!'

Purer now and stronger because more worthy the voices came back:

'We swear it! We swear it! We swear it!'

I no longer heard boys alone, no — a multitude, an army, a whole nation. As the voices echoed into the damp evening air on this wet hill-top outside a little town in a famine-stricken, dissolving country, voices of boys who became men because they remained boys — a second revelation pierced

my soul like the prophecy of things to come and the tearing
asunder of the veil that hid the sufferings of my people for a
thousand years:

'The Emperor must be a republican!'

I passed it on — this unheard-of, unintelligible, monstrous
thought — in the midst of the crowd and thus let it fall into
the hearts of these boys in their credulity and devotion.

'But if he fails you — this Emperor — if he does not keep
faith, then you are freed from the oath which you have just
sworn. Another loyalty will be found until our revelation is
fulfilled and the legend becomes reality:

'Long live the German Republic!'

Not singly and by twos and threes, but all together and
again and again, they took up the cry that none of them had
dared openly to think of and each of them had thought of in
his secret heart:

'Long live the German Republic!'

Perhaps the words echoed over the hills and the houses
from which people were at this moment pouring forth into
the streets to hear the latest news. As I entered the town
with Dertlgruber I heard it — printed and proclaimed, greeted
with tears and rejoicings, the end, the incomprehensible,
disgraceful end. Revolution, peace at any price, princes chased
from their thrones, powerless through their own miserable
weakness — and the German Emperor fled from his people!

I saw officers and soldiers run together, they cheered
(shame upon them!), dancing and shouting. The middle
classes joined them (who became so 'patriotic' again, when
everything was over): 'France is sending us food!' 'We'll be
an English colony!' — these and more abominable treacher-
ies rang in my ears as I ran home. Subsequently it occurred
to me that I had not seen a single worker amongst this undignified chorus.

I could only think of one thing: 'We are too late!' For the
first time in years I was not hungry — I went to bed the
moment I got home. I did not sleep that night, only wept and
prayed, but my prayers were also weeping.

VII. *Two Shades of Red*

*T*HE men returned from the front ragged and hungry. They sold or bartered everything they could lay hands on — horses, cloaks, motor cars. Anyone could have obtained great possessions for a small amount of money. At Gmunden the more responsible of those who returned were formed into a Red Guard, who had to secure order and to prevent the continued wastage of State property. Nevertheless they were abused. It was considered good form to abuse them. True, it was done secretly, because everyone was afraid of the Revolution — this mildest and most passive revolution there had ever been.

A fortnight after the collapse, my brother Leopold suddenly came back from the Cadet Corps early one morning. He was wearing a most appalling suit of civilian clothes, having been obliged to leave his cadet's uniform at school. I ought to have been pleased at his return, for he might very well have been killed in Munich. Instead I was horrified, for we had to turn out of the smaller room which we had been able to heat to some degree, and go back into the icy-cold, sunless, big one. Also it meant one more to be fed, which was a further ground for complaint.

But to consider my father's return from the front in the same light never came in my mind. My heart was filled with happiness, which was mingled, though, with indignation against the Republic — as in the meantime the whitewashing of the Emperor and the other deserting German Princes already showed its result in me.

'So for that,' I thought, 'my poor father has spent years

at the front — just to have Socialist traitors smash up everything in the end.'

The legend of the 'stab in the back of the unconquered army' was already current. My father repeated it as if he believed it, so it must be true. Hatred of the new State and longing for a war of revenge were the result. Everything would come right again once the Republic was abolished and the shameful peace at an end. That came to be the basic axiom of my political views. The fact that I myself, when there was no republic and as the result of a war, had already been starving for three years, and was likely to go on starving for several more, made not the smallest difference.

Millions of Germans shared my credulous acceptance of the theory that the Republic and the peace were the cause of all misery, and that the end of both was the necessary prelude to all good things. The war, for which the Republic could certainly not be blamed; the collapse, for which either no one or else the old system, but certainly not the new, was responsible; and all other losses were purposely ignored and forgotten — and by those who had a very short time ago lived through them all.

Most of the boys at school thought as I did. We were talking already of the next war, with this one hardly over. And we wondered when the confounded Republic would collapse, at a time when it was only just coming into existence.

The most abusive, of course, were the aristocratic members of my form, whom a republican law (valid only for Austrians and therefore not applicable to our family) had denuded of their titles. They were imitated by those of the untitled who did not wish to be thought to lag behind the nobility.

Dertlgruber and his friends, on the other hand, were much more ready to fall in with the new order, although actual events had long since invalidated the hour on the Kalvarienberg. The revolutionary current swept through our school as it did through the whole country, and those of my form who went with it based their acceptance upon the speech I had made there. Amongst other things, it was no longer compulsory to attend Divine Service. In the old days boys who missed going to Mass were expelled from the school.

Moreover, pupils' councils were established, which were intended to promote fruitful co-operation between teachers and pupils and to represent their rights — an inconceivably revolutionary idea for those days.

With the exception of the history and mathematics masters none of our teachers were well disposed to the new régime. I was much surprised at these two, having always regarded them as 'decent fellows'! 'Decent' meant being a monarchist, and so long as the contrary was not proved, I preferred to assume the best about everyone. I judged all events from this standpoint — hostility to the new State seemed to me such an excellent end that all means must be permissible.

When Kurt Eisner, the Prime Minister of the Bavarian revolutionary government, was shot by a murderer of the extreme Right, I at once hailed the deed as a great and truly patriotic act. This seemed to me so obvious that I took no trouble to conceal my joy when I was walking home with the mathematics master later in the day.

'Don't you agree,' I said to him, 'that it is splendid that Eisner has been killed?'

The answer I received was unexpected; so much so that I simply did not understand it. It took me some moments to realize what he had said. His reply had been:

'You ought to be ashamed of yourself to be pleased about a murder!'

Now I knew for certain, this man was really a Red. There was no further doubt of it. But, curiously enough, I could not make up my mind that he wasn't 'decent' on that account. I walked further with him, and did so as often as possible. I never told any of the other boys anything about this conversation, for fear they should play tricks on him.

The history master, who should, strictly speaking, also have been reckoned among 'not decent' people, became of even greater importance. Just at this time he was giving us

106

lectures on the French Revolution, from quite a different point of view to the one I knew from the books which my convent-bred sister had brought home. My childish exclamation of 'Vive la Liberté!' an isolated episode in my life, a spontaneous outburst and an appalling blasphemy, appeared to be the foundation of all modern life. If the French Revolution had not taken place, he told us, the revolution that had seemed to me to be no more than a single long-drawn-out crime, there would be no new Europe. We owed to it all we possessed of the rights of man and of liberty.

I got no chance to contradict him. Anything that I could think of in the way of argument seemed so flimsy even to myself that I had not the courage to advance it. I was forced to listen to the statement that we owed the German and Austrian Republics to the French Revolution, and that we had at last developed sufficiently to be abreast of the times. We were no longer subjects, but citizens, free democratic youths in a democratic community.

Even if all this were true, and even if the beheading of Louis XVI had been necessary for mankind, one thing really went too far for us: it was said that our history teacher would march with the workers on May 1, carrying a red flag. I contradicted it. 'It's absolutely impossible,' I said. 'After all, he is an educated man and knows how to behave.'

I grew less certain as May 1 approached. I wanted to know how far the rumours were true and how far they were a base libel. Hence I decided upon a bold venture — to go myself to the Socialist demonstration on May 1. I took a few of my friends with me, and the more impressed I was by the parade of the workers, the more sarcastic became the remarks I made.

Then came the great moment, the dreaded, suspected, denied moment: our history master appeared carrying a red flag and stood close beside the speaker's platform! He was a young man still. He looked so serious and so full of enthusiasm that all of a sudden I did not feel that it was ridiculous any longer, but rather frightening; and more than that, it made me feel ashamed of myself. From that day on I constituted myself his champion whenever my school fellows made jokes at his expense.

At this time my personal influence among my school fellows became very great. I represented their demands to the teaching staff — most of the demands were only too just. At a time when the boys had chilly homes and were not allowed to burn lights, when they had practically nothing to eat either at home or at school, they should not have been overburdened with work. Interesting lessons should have taken the place of what they were supposed to cram out of books. This seems very obvious. Nevertheless it met with the strongest opposition. Day after day I stood at the master's desk before school opened to lay my school fellows' case before him.

At last I could go on no longer. A slight cold developed into a serious attack of tuberculosis as a result of the debilitating effects of the privations I had suffered, and I was in bed for nearly three months. What I needed was plenty of good food, and that was simply unobtainable. My temperature was no lower during the third month than during the first.

My cure was finally accomplished in quite a different way. After I had been ill for a long time, a delegation came from my form at school and informed me with due ceremony that I had been elected chairman of the Pupils' Council. No one had opposed the election except a few of the aristocrats. A week later I was back at school and was received with a great ovation, while the aristocratic Opposition tacked the word 'Red' onto my title.

I took my new office very seriously. I made laws by pinning them to the blackboard — laws about how leisure should be spent, about mutual help between classmates, about the distribution of food, and the loan of rooms in such houses as were still able to afford fuel. After all, there was still a good deal of revolutionary feeling in the whole country, and so my regulations carried a not inconsiderable weight.

The sons of the aristocratic landowners were those who

108

felt my rules to be most irksome. They could not do very much against them, for they were the worst scholars and dependent upon the help of others. But they made clandestine opposition. They introduced opposition into the council itself by bribing one of my fellow-members.

I stood it for several weeks, then I made a kind of *coup d'état*. I called a meeting of the whole form, explained the situation to them, and tendered my resignation. I was at once re-elected, but refused to accept office if anyone else were put at my side. I proposed choosing my colleagues for myself. Hence I was elected alone, as 'Consul sine collega,' as I called it. In addition they agreed that the election was to be for life, that is to say for all the rest of my schooldays. I arrogated to myself the right to deal with '*saboteurs*' and 'wreckers' according to the means customary among us.

I used the power of my office without hesitation. I could send 'anti-democratic' elements in the form to Coventry for anything from three days to a month. This meant the complete severance of all relations, and especially of all help with homework — quite an unpleasant measure. The opposition forces among the aristocracy tried to intrigue against me among some of the masters. After a grim fight in which Franzl Dertlgruber's men gave my opponents a very rough handling, that also ceased.

As a result I was treated with greater respect, not only by the majority of my form but also among both younger and older boys. At the same time I became still more unpopular among the sons of the big landowners: I had mobilized the proletariat against them, was their reproach. By way of reprisals a sort of social boycott was declared against me, which troubled me very little. Even less did it trouble me that my opponents began to talk of the 'Bolshevik monarchy' that I had introduced into school.

It was at this time that I was 'kept in' for the only occasion during my schooldays. It happened in this way. There was a boy in my class, a very clever, intelligent fellow, who was likely to be hounded to death by part of the teaching staff because he had turned Protestant. I was a good Catholic, and had no particular use for Protestantism as such. But this went against the grain.

As a protest, I organized a general strike against the Scripture teacher who was the boy's chief persecutor. In consequence I was to be expelled from the school. Upon my threatening to appeal to the Minister of Culture and Education in Vienna, however, a compromise was reached. I agreed to two hours' detention, during which I was allowed to do my homework, and in return promised to say nothing about the affair. From that the Protestant boy was unmolested.

All these events made my position at home very difficult. The way I was behaving was considered to be simply disgraceful. My father and my brothers demanded over and over again that I should resign my post on the Pupils' Council. I steadily resisted.

It was all most important to me. I began to consider very seriously what I should do in future. It seemed to me specially important to train for public speaking. I let no opportunity pass for developing my oratorical powers. Then I read a great deal, and especially historical books. My surroundings, limited and youthful though they were, thus became my political preparatory school.

Meanwhile my position on the Pupils' Council did not change my political convictions in general. Soon after the death of the Emperor Charles of Austria I organized a monarchist demonstration. I had no feelings whatsoever about the Emperor Charles himself, and still less for his dynasty. But I wished to make a demonstration in favour of the monarchical principle. I was filled with the deepest contempt when I heard that all the aristocracy in my form regarded the proposal with great anxiety. They were afraid of the few Republicans among the masters. Not more than two or three aristocratic boys were present at the culminating scene of the demonstration, the memorial Mass for the dead man.

At this ceremony a farcical episode occurred. Our Scripture teacher, who was to celebrate the Mass, spent his time as a rule in making veiled attacks upon the Republic. But now that it came to making a public demonstration he was afraid. When it came to the place where he had to pray for the dead: 'Let us pray for our dead Emperor,' he stuttered and hesitated. At last he brought out the words: ' . . . for our dead, dead, dead — Charles.' He almost fainted with fright when I stood up at the end of the service and began to sing the Austrian imperial anthem, in which everyone joined.

Social distinctions at school became even more sharply defined after the end of the war. When gradually a small amount of food came into the country, those who had enough money were able to still their hunger. The rest continued to starve. Among these latter were ourselves. Actually we had nothing at all left. We were living on what my father earned by writing short stories and novels, which he did with indefatigable industry, always copying them out fair so that the publishers should have a clean manuscript. Everything that he had written for his own amusement in former days he now tried to reconstitute into something salable. It was a hard-earned, scanty living, and produced nothing like a sufficiency. Hence more and more things vanished from our flat, things with which we had been familiar from our earliest childhood: old prints, silver candlesticks, china figures, table silver, clocks, furniture.

The flat — we had meanwhile moved to another one which afforded us more light and air — grew steadily barer. It was very wretched, for even these sacrifices did not suffice for our needs. We had hardly enough clothes to cover us; my shoes were mended with the lead foil from old cigarette boxes.

One day, just after several more things had vanished, our footman Joseph came back and settled down to our service again just as if nothing had changed. He wore the same blue livery with silver-crested buttons; he set Meissner china dishes on the table and announced to my father, 'Your Illustrious Highness, dinner is served.' Then we came to table, Joseph adjusted our chairs with ceremony, and served the meal — a few turnips, a few potatoes.

And I must confess that it was a good thing. In preserving the formalities, it saved me from becoming a complete sav-

III

age, from sinking into absolute barbarism — a phenomenon not infrequent among the nobility once they have got below a certain point. Much the same was happening to a large part of the aristocratic families in Gmunden. Those of their sons who were in my form at school were in consequence driven more and more on to my side and against the well-to-do.

This was clearly shown on the occasion of a piece of news that turned out to be most important and joyful for us. At first we could hardly believe it, but it proved to be true, none the less. An American relief organization — I think it was the Quakers — organized mid-morning lunches for needy children at our school. A medical inspection was to take place, and according to its findings those who most required the meal were to be selected. This implied something of incredible importance. We should be given things at those lunches that we had only known by hearsay for as long as one could remember — things like milk, rice and chocolate, bread and butter, and so on.

When the news was first made public, one of the well-to-do aristocrats called us together and said it would be undignified for members of the nobility to accept these lunches. Nor were any of us to attend the medical inspection. He was shouted down, and we entered the race for the Food Stakes — successfully too, for not one of us was turned down as a result of the medical inspection.

These American lunches became the main element in our nourishment. They probably saved us from complete starvation, even though they could not altogether still our cravings. I can remember many hours during which my brothers and I discussed — jokingly, it is true, but these things are not really funny — whether a man would be acquitted if he committed theft because he was hungry. Yes, but from whom could one steal? Possibly a few grocers' shops. Some of them were beginning to have small stocks again. Old packets of chocolate, American ship's biscuit, bully-beef, and corned beef had turned up from some army depôt — all priceless treasures.

112

No one will therefore be surprised to hear me say that I take a very mild view of crimes committed out of social need. I myself escaped committing them only by a hair's breadth. And that I did so escape is perhaps due only to chance.

For one day a most astonishing thing happened — a parcel of food came by post from my mother. A fortnight later there was a second one.

These parcels were the first sign of life that we had had from her for ten years. During this time she had passed completely from our ken. We only knew without realizing it that she was still alive. And for years already we had had a half-brother, Werner von Alvensleben, the son of my mother's second husband who had died at the beginning of the war. Up till this time the war and a number of personal reasons had prevented our meeting again, but now, in the summer of 1920, the meeting was to take place.

At that time my mother was living at Graz in Styria, which seemed to us to be a very long way away. My eldest brother went first; a short time afterwards my brother Leopold and I followed.

I should not have recognized my mother if I had met her in the street. I was shy and embarrassed when we met.

And then I saw one of the wonders of the world — a well-laid breakfast table. I sat down and found myself confronted by an egg in an egg cup. I picked it up and looked at it, I turned it over and tapped it, then I put it back in the egg cup. I noticed that my brother Leopold was doing the same. He too was looking at the egg with great interest, or what appeared to be interest. Actually we were both at our wits' end. We had long since forgotten how to eat soft-boiled eggs.

Before breakfast was over I got to know my little half-brother. He came to the door wearing a long white night-shirt; he had fair curls, and talked German with a faint English accent. I could hardly realize that this eight-year-old boy was my brother. He had been brought up quite differently from the rest of us, and was not in the least like us in appearance.

Things had not been easy for my mother during the past years either. She had kept her head above water for several years by giving English lessons. It was a most remarkable achievement when one considers her upbringing and the demands she had previously made of life.

Then came a sudden turn of fortune such as usually only occurs in films. She fell ill, and was no longer able to give lessons. When her last savings had gone, the postman arrived bringing her a sum of money in English notes that represented untold wealth in those days of inflation, and she was told that her whole income would soon be released. Hence the parcels of food; hence all the meals that were a continually renewed feast to me all through the summer of 1920.

I had been so long in the little town of Gmunden that Graz seemed to me like a mighty metropolis — though it is really only a pleasant little place of medium size. But it is charming and pretty. In the middle of it stands the castle hill, with bastions dating from Napoleonic days. Beside it rises an old tower, called 'Liesl' (Lizzie), containing a bell whose clear, deep tones are much beloved by all the inhabitants of Graz. My new little brother and I spent a lot of time climbing about the castle hill, or else sitting in the municipal park and behaving in a very grown-up manner.

My joy knew no bounds when I was given a new suit, some grey breeches, and several new shirts. I also received some pocket money. Most of this I spent on tram fares. There was one line that ran all the way round the town and then across the river. I used always to stand beside the driver and pretend that I was driving the tram; or else that I was in a brand-new car of the future, which was not running round the town, but was going from one town to another at a speed of a thousand miles an hour.

Occasionally I went to a picture house, where the first super-dimensional post-war films were just beginning to be shown, usually as eight-part serials. Or else I lay on a sofa at home, ordered tea and cake, and smoked a clandestine cigarette. All through this summer I never stopped eating, so much so that I developed jaundice.

114

During this time I had the opportunity of reading a certain amount — Dostoievsky, Tolstoi, and Thomas Mann, and in addition my little brother's adventure stories. I also began to write again — a play called 'The Black Outrage,' which was to describe the negroes in the Rhineland. But I did not get very far with it, because as soon as I had recovered from the jaundice I began eating again. And so I spent the rest of the summer.

Unfortunately these weeks that had begun so paradisiacally were overshadowed by a severe emotional conflict. We were faced with the problem of whether or not to ask my father to allow us to stay in Graz with my mother. The impression that we had now got of her was very different from that which we had for years believed to be true.

My brothers were very soon agreeable to the proposed change, but I hesitated for a long time. It seemed to me like disloyalty to my father, who had cared for us all through the time of the worst troubles, who was sitting at his typewriter for twelve hours a day working for us, and who had for years denied himself the least enjoyment. My mother mistakenly attributed this hesitation to want of affection. It was years before she revised her opinion.

At the end of the summer we all returned to Gmunden. Then, not without much sadness and depression, we came to an agreement whereby my brothers were to return to Graz, but I was to spend another two years in Gmunden.

VIII. *The Grown-Ups and Ourselves*

A NEW epoch set in with the departure of my brothers. Its outward expression consisted in the fact that I now had our large room all to myself, in which I might spread out my books and papers just as I chose without being restricted any more.

The room was on the ground floor, so that I could even go out at night — though with great trepidation. But what could I do? As Commander-in-Chief of the Dertlgruber Troop I had a number of responsibilities which I could not evade. One of these was regular attendance at the meetings of the General Staff, which usually took place on a hill outside the town, opposite the Kalvarienberg. Franzl Dertlgruber, together with several others, had built a wonderful snow hut there which made us feel as if we were on a polar expedition. It was even possible to light a little stove inside without fear that the 'house' would begin to melt.

It contained two rooms, which were comfortably furnished with skins and rugs. The larger of the two was used as a general committee room; the smaller was reserved to me and to such of the others as were specially invited. Only Franzl Dertlgruber had the right to go in and out as he wished. For a time he shared this privilege with another boy called Fritz Jäger, because we depended upon his room when the weather was too bad for us to use the snow hut.

Dertlgruber did not like this arrangement at all. He said Fritz would not be loyal to us — he would certainly betray all our plans one day. I did not believe him, and said that he just wanted to get rid of him out of jealousy; that I did not hold with that sort of attitude; and that in any case there was no reason for jealousy. Who had been with me on the Kalvarienberg, Fritz or himself? And who was, whatever happened, going to be field marshal?

For a time I succeeded in pacifying him, until something else happened. Fritz Jäger suddenly said one day that he had a girl cousin whom he would like to invite, as she had wanted to see the snow hut for a long time. 'There you are,' said Dertlgruber to me. 'Now he even wants to bring in girls! I don't believe for a moment that she's his cousin.'

This application was therefore unanimously rejected, and Fritz accepted our decision—so far as we could judge, at least.

A few days later when Dertlgruber and I came to the snow hut at an unexpected moment we saw that a light was burning inside. 'That's Fritz and his cousin,' said Dertlgruber, and looked in through the window: there they were, sitting side by side, apparently very pleased with life, and never noticed that they were observed!

The next day there were two bloody noses, Franzl Dertlgruber's and Fritz Jäger's — though I was unable personally to confirm Dertlgruber's assertion that the two had been kissing in the snow hut and had, moreover, laughed at our plans. But I realized that Fritz must be kept at a certain distance, for if you are discussing a prospective war with France and Italy, you cannot have anyone present who may pass it all on to an almost certainly talkative girl. Furthermore, this girl had black hair, so that she might very well be French or Italian or Jewish.

Just at that time the seeds of National Socialism were sown in our school. It was not long before one or another amongst us announced himself to be an adherent of the new party, without really having very much idea of what it was all about. So far as we could gather, however, it was chiefly occupied with revenge for the collapse, both without and within the country. That meant on the one hand war with France and Italy (which therefore coincided with the aims of our group), and on the other a campaign against the Jews, who were said to be the cause of the collapse.

Every one of us discussed politics in those days, and I was amongst those who professed themselves National Socialists for a certain time; if only out of opposition to the extreme clericalism of some of our masters.[1] The war years had destroyed our material foundations to such an extent that the idea of Socialism attracted rather than repelled me — and of course it must be a 'national' Socialism.

In practice our National Socialism expressed itself in sticking labels bearing swastikas and various slogans onto walls and houses, and on our textbooks and exercise books. I suppose this form of amusement must have continued for several weeks or months. When we got tired of it, our interest in National Socialism also evaporated.

While it lasted, however, it played an important part at our nightly meetings.

'It is disgraceful that the Government doesn't simply say that we take no further interest in the Peace Treaties,' I declared. 'If the French and the Italians and the English don't like it, let them come and say so. But they daren't!'

Dertlgruber agreed with me, but pointed out that in order to achieve anything it was necessary to be armed. We actually succeeded in the course of time in collecting five or six rifles, a number of revolvers, and quantities of ammunition from old war depôts. The next problem was how to use them without anyone's hearing. And this difficulty finally put an end to our manoeuvres. When spring came we patched up a derelict woodcutter's shanty in the forest, and with great precautions transferred our armoury thither under cover of darkness. So there it lay, awaiting the moment when a war of retaliation should bring it into use again — unless, of course, some earlier occasion should present itself.

For, as a result of the May Day demonstration which we had once again attended, our thoughts now turned from foreign policy towards internal politics.

'What will you do,' Dertlgruber asked me, 'when you

[1] I am told that this is again the main reason why National Socialism nowadays finds so many adherents among the young in Austria.

have some control over affairs? Will you allow the nobility to come to power again?'

'I shouldn't dream of it,' said I. 'They will always be the same, just as now they were opposed to the Pupils' Council — at least the rich ones amongst them. And the poor ones are only different so long as they stay poor.'

'What about yourself?' enquired Dertlgruber.

'I should have thought you might have known,' was my reply. 'When I am in power I shall be able to be as "Red" as I like — though of course I shan't be a "Sozi."' [1]

'Neither shall I. All the same, I nearly joined in the "Internationale" the other day, simply because so many people were singing it. When I told my father that, he whacked me!'

'If I told my father anything like that,' I said, 'he'd simply send me to a lunatic asylum.'

'I know,' Dertlgruber nodded, 'you have to be frightfully careful what you say to parents. Since they've come back, they never seem to see reason at all.'

'No — they say, "Be quiet; you weren't at the front," or else, "You're really too old to behave like a child." Now, what I should like to know is, are we too young or too old? Or both at the same time?'

'I don't know,' said Dertlgruber. 'I never thought about it. But it's mean of them to rub it in that we weren't at the front. Firstly, we couldn't help it, and secondly, things have not been easy for us either.'

'They'll never see that. And because I say sometimes that we ought to make a completely fresh start now, my father calls me a Bolshevik, and says he supposes I imagine I could do everything better than other people.'

'As if the grown-ups had made such a good job of it! After all, it's to them that we owe all this mess!'

'Franzl,' I said, 'it's no use crying over spilt milk. The great thing now is that you and I should back each other up.'

'Well, if you do, I will, of course.'

[1] An abusive term for 'Social Democrat.'

Neither of us said any more for several minutes, until I suddenly got up. 'We shall go all sentimental in a minute and start kissing each other if we aren't jolly careful!' And we parted rather more abruptly than usual.

A few days later I brought the conversation round to Fritz Jäger and his 'cousin.'

'You know,' I said to Dertlgruber, 'perhaps we are being unfair in not inviting him any more. We don't even really know whether he talked about our plans to that girl.'

'It doesn't make any difference. It's always dangerous to let girls in on anything. If they find another boy they always talk, and then what a fool you look!'

'But there are girls who think the same as we do, and who are good fellows too. Like Trautl,[1] for instance.'

'Yes, that's true, Trautl is a nice girl, she's always been a friend of ours.'

'Oughtn't we to take a bit more notice of her?'

'What for? Are you in love with her?'

'You're a fool, and it's impossible to have a sensible conversation with you,' I said, and flung off in a temper.

The fact was that I was not quite sure myself. Trautl and we had been sitting on the same school bench for four years. She was a good sport, and behaved no differently from us boys. So I had been sorry to hear that she was to be sent to Cologne in the following year to stay with some relations; but there was no more to it than that.

Now, it had happened not long since that she had forgotten her book one day in the Latin lesson and had to sit next to me and share mine. Our heads were close together, and I suddenly realized that she had very soft fair hair. The next day she had forgotten her book again. When this happened several more times I began to get anxious lest our Latin master should notice it. Already he growled at her in his deepest bass when she went to him before the lesson to apologize about the book. It was inevitable that he should at last say, as he did, 'This isn't Latin any more, this is flirtation!' Of course the whole class laughed, and not merely

[1] An Austrian abbreviation for Gertrud.

because he pronounced 'flirtation' as though it were a German word.

In the interval I took Trautl aside. 'Look here,' I said. 'This won't do. They'll be saying next that we're lovers!' She made no reply, but during the next lesson she sent me a note: 'After what you said just now, we must discuss whether we can still remain friends.' 'Yes,' I wrote back, 'between three and five tomorrow'; and I decided to cut the Greek lesson.

The next afternoon I set along the path that runs past the foot of the Kalvarienberg, then beside the river that flows through the lake, and quite a long way farther across a small wooded hill. Beyond the hill lay the village of which Trautl's father was mayor, and where he owned an amusing shop where you could buy everything — coloured shawls, suits of clothes, scythes, oil stoves, exercise books and so on.

I went straight across country along narrow footpaths, through fields in their fresh spring green, where the winter wheat was already standing a foot and a half high. I saw a few overblown anemones, and some buttercups and cowslips. I wondered whether to pick any. At the edge of the wood was some mezereon in full bloom. I can take that, I thought; she must be pleased with that.

At last I saw the house that Trautl had described to me. The shutters were painted green, and there was a big verandah in front covered with flowering creepers. The house stood so high up that one could see the lake from it.

The door was open, and I went inside without meeting anyone. Nor did there seem to be anybody in the rooms. Then I saw Trautl without her seeing me. Her pale gold hair gleamed with a curious sheen; she was wearing a white dress with a black patent leather belt, and a narrow gold bracelet. I went out onto the glass verandah, and before either of us could say a word we were in each other's arms. We kissed as children kiss, abruptly and with closed lips, in front of a window through which came the sunshine, tinged red by the flowers through which it passed.

Soon afterwards her parents came in, a rather noisy father with a broad kindly face, and a mother whom I liked no less.

While Trautl went to get coffee I heard something of the life of the family — of the little sister and of the brothers, who helped in the shop, since the father took his position as mayor very seriously. I asked if it was quite certain that Trautl was going to Cologne next year. Yes, quite; the mother was from the Rhineland, and wanted to send her to her relations for a few years.

Trautl came part of the way home with me, but somehow conversation didn't flow very easily. At last I urged her to tell me the reason.

'It's because of school,' she said; 'supposing anyone finds out that we kissed ——'

'But I don't see how they could find out.'

'I suppose you'll tell Dertlgruber! And once he knows everyone will know it too.'

'I swear to you,' I said, 'that I won't tell Dertlgruber or anyone else. There, now, does that satisfy you?'

'Yes,' she said; but I could see that there was still something on her mind.

When we came to the edge of the woods, to the place where I had picked the mezereon, she stood still and said: 'Well, if you must know, it isn't anything to do with school; it's because I'm going away next year, and by the time I get back you'll have forgotten all about me.'

'I shall still be thinking of you in ten or twenty years' time,' I answered, 'but you'll go and marry somebody in the Rhineland, and then it'll all be over between us.'

'Oh,' she said, 'have I got to ask your permission before I marry anyone?"

'I don't want you to marry anyone else at all,' said I.

We had gone a few steps into the wood and came to a small clearing.

'Have you got to go yet?' I asked.

'Soon,' she answered, and then we sat down silently side by side.

Ought one to conjure up feelings so long past? Is it fair to look back at the two, the boy and the girl — I can hardly realize that one was myself — with the eyes of an adult?

They are in each other's arms, looking at one another as though there were nothing else in the whole wide world, while evening falls and the lake gleams between the trees, a coppery red that turns almost to violet. Beyond are mountains, grey up to the point where the last rays of the sun still catch the summits. And breezes of gentle evening air pass over the countryside, each one a quiver that is like laughter before it turns to tears.

Across all this and through the veil of many years I hear the girl's voice. She says words — often said before by others — they transform her, they are shock, intoxication, fulfilment: 'I love you,' she says. And 'I love you,' answers the boy.

The spell is broken. I see the girl releasing herself. 'I've been dreaming,' she says, 'and so have you. And it's late. I must go home.'

They say farewell and each goes his own way, never once looking back.

Next day at school everything was as it had always been. Trautl had even brought her own Latin book, and she behaved no differently to me than to the other boys. I was almost beginning to get anxious, and thought something had happened. But during the interval as I was going out I heard her breathe very softly as I passed, 'Dear.'

In the next few weeks I often went to the little house with the green shutters and the flowers growing over the verandah. If Trautl was late I used to sit with her parents, to whom I became more and more attached. Her father knew a great deal about local history, about the peasants' wars of which I had heard as a child.

All sorts of early visions awoke in me again — the peasants' grave at Pinsdorf, my dream of a republic with an emperor at its head. Trautl's ancestors had fought at the time when the peasants rose in the Emperor's name to drive

Count Herberstorff, the Bavarian Governor, out of the country. Perhaps one of them lay buried on the other side of the valley under the mound that had been shown me when I was a child — in 1913, just when it had become flat enough for a cart and horse to drive over it.

To think that this Count Herberstorff who oppressed the peasants and called upon Pappenheim's cavalry to help was a 'nobleman.' He invited the leaders of the peasantry to discuss the peace, and when they were gathered together he killed them all.

I often felt ashamed of myself as I sat there listening. Was I not in opposition to the Republic that had given the people its liberty? And for how long had I not possessed other knowledge without making proper use of it? From Michael to the walk to Pinsdorf, the French Revolution and its 'Vive la Liberté,' the privations of the war, the Kalvarienberg and the cheer for the German Republic, possibly the first cheer that had been given for it.

When I went down again into the valley after these visits I used to think: 'What could I not do now! How strong my will is, the strength of thousands: When, in years to come, they speak of my people's fight for freedom, then my name shall be found in their ranks.'

It was on such an occasion that I returned to the town one summerlike evening, and nothing warned me that I was about to experience one of the worst moments I had so far gone through in my life.

Hardly had I arrived home before my father summoned me.

'Where have you been?' he enquired.

'Out for a walk,' I said. 'It's lovely out.'

'Out for a walk, eh? I'll tell you where you've been. Aren't you ashamed of yourself to be running after a huckster's daughter?'

'No,' I said. 'I'm not in the least ashamed of myself. Besides, Trautl isn't a huckster's daughter, and I love her.'

'Love her?' said my father. 'Have you gone completely off your head? A nobleman may possibly have a liaison with someone like that, but he cannot love her!'

'Papa,' I said, 'I won't have you speak of Trautl in that way!'

'You won't, won't you? But you will carry on an affair with a wench who expects to be made a countess, will you? Not so long as you live in my house. Do you understand?'

'No,' I said. 'I think it is far more worthy of a nobleman to love a peasant girl than some idiotic little comtesse, or to marry for money.'

'Very good, sonny,' said my father. 'Then go on loving and leave the rest to me.'

'For heaven's sake, Papa,' I said then. 'What are you going to do?'

'Only what I am driven to do. I've written to your head master to tell him what sort of a good-for-nothing your Trautl is, and I shall also write to her father. And if all this proves unavailing — well, there are laws to punish people who act as panders to their children.'

'Are you really going to do that?'

'Unless within an hour I have your word that you will give up seeing her ——'

An hour! I went to my room and thought it over; no, I did not think it over, I raged, wept, despaired. I made a thousand plans, all of them impossible. I'd run away with Trautl, go to Germany — I had no money and no passport. I'd fetch Dertlgruber's band — what use would that be? It would be ridiculous. Should I go to my father again and speak to him? Quite useless; I knew what his answer would be. Simply say no, and let things take their course? What would happen to Trautl then?

Meanwhile time was passing — another forty minutes, thirty, twenty. Why were my thoughts suddenly with the past instead of with what was to come? With my ancestor Frederick the Victorious, who had married the beautiful Clara Dett, the mother of Ludwig of Bavaria, the first Count of Loewenstein? Had not my father written poetry eulogizing her?

Clara Dett was the daughter of an Augsburg patrician, so perhaps even related to the merchant class. Trautl was

of peasant ancestry. Was it not always said that the aristocracy and the peasantry were of the same origin? But that
seemed no longer to hold good. 'A liaison perhaps, but not
love!' he had said.

So that kind of thing is permitted to a nobleman, is it?
I thought I knew better what was permissible and what was
not. Before the hour was over I went to my father.

'Don't post those letters. I've thought it all over.'

'Your word of honour?' he said.

'Yes, my word of honour.'

How I got through the rest of that day and the weeks that
followed I cannot remember. I could only hint, I could not
explain: I was ashamed, though if I had been frank I am
sure everything would have been all right. Possibly Trautl
guessed the truth, and for that reason alone did not utterly
despise me.

Once more we met alone outside the town, by accident
— or possibly by Providence. I found my tongue again,
but by then both of us knew that it was too late.

On the following day, while the farewell seemed to be
still burning on my lips, her place was empty at school.
Later on we heard that she had gone to her relations in
Germany sooner than had been anticipated. I never saw
her again.

The summer holidays began soon afterwards. I informed
Dertlgruber that I should be taking part in the life of the
troop again regularly — to his great joy; he had been wondering what was the matter. For quite a month I had never
had time for him and had given him unfriendly evasive
answers.

Many of the boys were not in Gmunden now, so that our
community life was necessarily restricted to 'private'
meetings. One of those who remained behind was solemnly
admitted to the troop at the very beginning of the summer,
a fair-haired North German called Waldemar Claus. Soon
he was becoming of an ever greater importance in the circle
of my friends.

He soon took a very prominent part in the games which replaced every other form of activity during the summer. There was one in particular at which he distinguished himself, and which demanded skill and a certain amount of daring. It was called 'Fighting prairie fires,' and was played in this way:

Two sides were formed; each lit a fire, and that side won whose fire advanced the more rapidly. Once I very nearly caused a really serious conflagration. I fired some grass at the foot of a slope — and in a moment the flames had run up to the top, as far as the woods, which were dry after weeks of sunshine. Without Waldemar Claus, who kept cool while I lost my head, there might have been a very bad accident.

From this time onward I preferred water games. We used to take small tree trunks down to the lake and use them as warships for our battles. 'You must never be conquered,' said the fair-haired boy, and fought so valiantly that once we had considerable trouble in fishing him out of the water. It was the more difficult because this happened near a swan's nest: the old swans came sailing up like avenging angels, and drove us to flight over and over again.

In reward of his bravery in battle I soon afterwards entered into 'blood brotherhood' with Waldemar Claus, according to the old custom of our band. The ceremony of course took place on the Kalvarienberg at our sacramental place, although he had not been present on that first occasion. Nevertheless I had by means of a special retroactive 'decree' made him of the number of my Old Guard. We decided on this occasion to pitch a joint camp which should be ours alone, where we would live all through the summer by ourselves.

The camp was pitched on the extreme end of a peninsula. It was protected on the lake side by a thick bed of reeds, and on the landward side by thorn bushes and undergrowth. We alone knew the way to it.

Here we discussed our future, which we intended to spend together. We lay on our backs with our eyes on the shimmering sky, often not speaking a word — I can still hear the gentle lap of the waves among the reeds, the occasional splash as a fish leapt out of the water, and the whirr of brightly coloured dragon-flies as they passed.

Summer days, boyhood's days, full of hopes and faith. The world is still full of mystery; one does not yet know of the valley behind each mountain, a valley and beyond that again a mountain; the unknown surrounds every path, but one can penetrate it if one's longing is strong enough. A sword and a friend — what else does one need? But the friend, like the sword, one must keep for oneself.

One episode occurred during my last year at school at Gmunden which would certainly have meant my expulsion if it had ever been found out.

A new girl had come into our form after the summer holidays who, I imagined, was rather like Trautl. At all events I noticed her immediately, and for the time being thought myself very much in love again. But since I never managed to see her out of school hours, I was obliged to do what I could during the classes and in the intervals. I helped her in every possible way, and used to pass notes to her in lesson time.

Possibly on this account, possibly also because she was not much used to boys, and we had been accustomed by Trautl to good fellowship between girls and boys, she enjoyed no great popularity. This feeling was for a long time merely latent, until suddenly it burst out all the more stormily for its suppression.

She was called up to the blackboard by one of the masters to be examined. He seemed to be very fond of her too, and his questions were therefore not very difficult ones. And she did answer them; it was not true, as some of the boys maintained, that she had failed altogether and had only been given a good report by sheer favouritism.

When the master declared that her examination was at an end, there was a tumultuous scene: some of the boys were rioting and shouting that they would complain to the head master. The master, who must have had a bad conscience, meekly agreed to examine the girl over again. She was meanwhile sitting at her desk crying.

That roused me. I stood up and protested as chairman of the Pupils' Council that the master was allowing himself to be terrorized and forced to act unjustly. The master accepted this calmly, too, especially as the majority of the class suddenly came over to my side.

That should really have meant the end of the episode. I could have brought my opponents into line. But something in me revolted from applying my official power in this case. I had the feeling that I ought to finish the affair in a more personal way. Hence I sent Franzl Dertlgruber to carry a challenge to the noisiest of my opponents, a huge boy, two heads taller than myself.

For a long time we discussed what the weapons were to be. I was for pistols — what, after all, was our armoury for? But then someone said that the one who received the challenge had the right to the choice of weapons, and he chose swords. Moreover, he decided that we were only to hit above the waist, and that our heads were to be protected with wire masks.

An exciting time began. I cut innumerable lessons in order to learn fencing in the short time at my disposal. At last the great day came. One wet afternoon, with rather anxious feelings, I went to the memorable spot behind the waterworks on the Kalvarienberg with Franzl Dertlgruber, instead of attending my Greek lesson.

My opponent's seconds had already arrived. One boy who had once read some medical book played the part of doctor. From his satchel he produced a packet containing cotton wool, several bandages, and some sticking-plaster, also a bottle of lysoform. I could not resist saying softly to Franzl Dertlgruber:

'If I fall, give my love to Käthe.'

Käthe was the name of the girl, the innocent cause of the duel.

I did not fall, but we went for one another hammer and

tongs, finally with both hands, I believe. We shed no inconsiderable amount of blood, I rather more than my opponent. I was unanimously declared to be the loser, and the verdict appeared to me to be eminently correct. We shook hands, and then I was treated by the 'doctor.' The lysoform on the open wounds stung considerably, but everything passed off quite well. Only I had to be very careful at home not to give myself away by exclamations of pain. For weeks I trembled lest the affair should become public, so that I never had even dared to say anything to the girl. This was hardest to bear of all.

In the summer of 1922 I left Gmunden for good. I said good-bye to many friends there, with whom I had shared the most difficult years.

Except for Waldemar Claus, the fair-haired boy — at the very end we climbed a mountain, standing on which I divided up our 'provinces' — I have never seen any of them again. Of Dertlgruber himself I heard later that he had entered the Austrian army as soon as he left school and has since become an excellent officer. I am firmly convinced that it was the games of our boyhood that made him choose this career.

IX. *A School for Politics*

IN THE summer after I had left Gmunden, and while I was still in ignorance of my future place of abode, I made my first long journey alone.

I spent a month in Munich and then returned to Graz. Meanwhile my mother had left for England, and my eldest brother was in charge of the house — an occupation he regarded as so important that he did not want to be disturbed. Therefore he sent me away again with such an absurdly small sum of money that I had spent it all by the time I got back to Munich. After a lengthy correspondence I eventually extracted a cheque from him for exactly six English shillings.

These were the days of the inflation in Germany, and six shillings were worth more than today. Nevertheless they did not spell riches. I was unable to stay on in the hotel in which I had hitherto been living, and transferred myself and my belongings to a fifth-rate hotel called the Golden Goose. This time I did not enjoy Munich nearly so much, especially as a friend of mine, an historian, was away on holiday.

At luncheon and dinner I sat alone at a corner table in the dining-room of my hotel and ate my meals on credit. They were neither good nor sufficient. All kinds of people from the working and middle classes came there. Although I never talked to them, I noticed that they were observing me with growing interest.

This lasted for about three weeks, before I finally received a little money to pay for my ticket back to Graz. The schools were about to open again. But it was still undecided where I was to go.

On my last evening in Munich a curious episode occurred. I was again seated at my corner table, and eating various sour dishes such as chopped liver and lights in vinegar, when suddenly a man stood before me. He bowed deeply and gave me his name: 'Engineer Weber.' Before I had time to give him my own name he again bowed deeply and said:

'Will Your Royal Highness allow me to invite you to join us at our table?'

'I am not a Royal Highness,' I replied.

'I know, I know,' he said. 'Your Royal Highness is not Your Royal Highness, but nevertheless Your Royal Highness is Your Royal Highness.'

'Won't you sit down?' I said; I was certain that he must be drunk. He evidently perceived what was passing in my mind, because he began to defend himself.

'I am not drunk, not at all. Your Royal Highness will hurt my feelings very much if Your Royal Highness thinks that. The truth is that my friends and I know who Your Royal Highness is: a Loewenstein, and that the Loewensteins are the heirs to the Bavarian throne, and we believe that Your Royal Highness is the man for us. Now will you come over to our table?'

'Yes,' I replied. 'I'll come if you really are sober.'

They all jumped up, and refused to sit down again before I was seated. A moment's silence followed. Then Engineer Weber ordered a fresh round of beer for all of us and gave a signal to one of his friends.

'Your Majesty,' he said, 'up till now we have spoken of you as His Royal Highness. But now that we have at last talked to you personally I address you as Your Majesty, and my friends will agree.'

Now they have gone completely mad, I thought to myself; but I merely said:

'I am still less a Majesty than a Royal Highness.'

But the speaker, to the accompaniment of a murmur of applause, not only from those at our table but from the whole room, refused to listen to my objection.

'You are "Your Majesty" for us. Do you understand?

132

Your family are the rightful heirs. We don't know your family, but we do know you. Are you prepared to take up your duties — "Yes" or "No"? Answer me!'

There was nothing I could say except 'Yes — if the people call me.'

I felt a perfect fool. After all, this formula had been used by everybody in similar situations for more than two thousand years, and the effect had invariably been the same. Everybody in the room suddenly stood up. The speaker sprang onto a table and shouted:

'Three cheers for Hubertus the First, King of Bavaria!'

My God, they all cheered not three but four or five times, and again and again! I thanked them, and promised to make good use of the coming years in the fulfilment of the duty they had laid upon me.

With triumphal ovations the incident was brought to its close. Long before the departure of my train next morning Engineer Weber stood at my door and asked permission to carry my luggage to the station. I had barely enough money to pay my hotel bill and my ticket. There was not enough left to pay our fares on the tram: hence we had to walk to the station. He took leave of me in a properly ceremonial manner. I have never set eyes on any of the 'Kingmakers' again.

On my return to Graz there were more pressing problems than that of the Bavarian throne. Shortly before the schools opened again we found a boarding-school belonging to Herr Rudolf Koenig at Klagenfurt in Carinthia — now the southernmost town on German soil. An exchange of telegrams between Herr Koenig and my brother settled the matter.

I arrived at Klagenfurt on a glorious autumn day. I wore an appalling yellow suit made of wartime material. Two years before it had belonged to my brother Leopold, and had created a sensation.

The school was situated at some distance beyond the town on the slope of the so-called Kreuzberg — a pretty wooded hill. The boys were housed in two pleasant villas; the one had blue, the other red, balconies. A large garden surrounded the houses, and there was a football field across the road.

I arrived to find the football field crowded with shouting boys. It was the five o'clock play hour. I was uncomfortable — I felt as if I had fallen among robbers.

Rather nervously I walked through the garden towards the house. A nice-looking man with a fine forehead and grey hair was descending the steps as I came up. He was carrying two watering-cans, and in my confused state of mind I took him for the gardener.

But it was my future head master, Rudolf Koenig, himself. His greeting was not too friendly, and he asked me in a strong North German accent if I had not brought at least a letter from my mother or father — even if I did arrive by myself. I replied that I only had a letter from my brother asking that he should defray all my expenses for the time being.

Koenig shook his head and told me to come into his study. There I at once felt more at home. In the first place, the walls were covered with books, and in the second a book on theosophy lay in the middle of the table. Koenig was not himself a theosophist, but he was interested in theosophy, and when I told him of my own interest in it he said:

'You can look upon it as a dispensation of Providence that you found such a book in this dreadful house. It is not the place for you. I don't want you. You won't like the boys here; you will think the food awful and me a very disagreeable person.'

Thereupon he handed me a list of addresses. But before I left he showed me the room which he had intended me to have in his own house. It was a nice room, furnished in white, very light and with a small balcony.

Then I stood in the street again and spent several hours in toiling round Klagenfurt to visit all the addresses he had given to me.

I found nothing to suit me, and came back tired and hungry to find that supper was over. I was sitting on a seat as the fifty boys belonging to the school came out from their meal. They stood around me gazing at me with awe and curiosity. Their awe was due to the gold-tipped cigarette that I was smoking. I had brought some with me from Germany, where they were not uncommon, though in Austria at that time only the dearest cigarettes had gold tips. But the boys could not have known this.

'If you cannot find anything endurable,' Koenig said, 'you'll have to come and stay with me.'

I went to my room, and for a short time observed how the house grew gradually silent. Then I went to bed, and before I fell asleep I was as happy as I have ever been in my life.

Rudolf Koenig became of the greatest importance for me. There was nothing insincere in him, nothing artificial, no malice, no meanness.

Before he came to Klagenfurt and founded his school, Koenig had been a Protestant missionary in Asia Minor for many years. His aim had been to establish a modern type of school. But his attempt was defeated by the narrow-mindedness of the townsfolk, and not least by the enmity of the Protestant clergy, who found his Christianity too unorthodox for their liking.

He was one of the truest Christians I have ever known. All his savings disappeared during the summer holidays, as he kept open house for all comers. Once when I ventured to remonstrate with him he said casually and as if it were a matter of course:

'In that case I couldn't let my boys say the grace: "Come, Lord Jesus, and be our guest." How am I to know? Perhaps one of those who wants a meal is the Lord Jesus.'

Koenig's nearest assistant was a very young man named Wilhelm Zuffar. He was not much to look at. He had high Mongolian cheek-bones and a long, pointed nose. He was highly intelligent, and often so caustic as to give offence. Whatever could not stand the strictest examination — feelings, thoughts or words — broke down under his criticism. I was often furious with him. I thought myself misunderstood and ill-used; and yet I owe a great deal to him.

The majority of the boys at Koenig's school had already been there for several years. Hence I was regarded as something of an interloper.

What I wanted were friends, as I had had them at Gmunden. The first I found — and all others sprang from them — were two fourteen-year-old boys named Oscar and Erwin. They differered greatly from each other. Oscar was silent and gentle, slight and lithe. He was one of the best boys in the school at games, and had a strong influence over all the others.

On the other hand, Erwin was dark and lively, a great rascal and comedian, somewhat frivolous, superficial, and very clever. He was nicknamed "the Blue Boy" by the others, as he usually wore blue sailor suits.

I met him on one of my first days at the school, as he was coming up the steps leading from the garden to a covered-in playground in front of the house.

'Blue Boy,' I said to him, 'I may be a new, but you might at least say "Good morning" to me.'

'How do you know already that I am called "Blue Boy"?'

'That's easy. Someone told me that the worst rowdy here was the Blue Boy, and then I saw you and knew at once that you were the Blue Boy.'

A little later I learnt that he was one of the boys who had been specially impressed by my gold-tipped cigarette. Naturally he looked upon me as being very wealthy.

'I can't understand why you don't do something sensible with all the money you've got,' he said. 'For example, organize theatricals with proper costumes and scenery, or something like that. We could all take part instead of always going for walks on Sundays.'

'Is that so dreadful?'

'You'll soon know! We walk all day. The Head thinks it's healthy.'

'He's probably right, seeing that one never gets out the whole week. Besides, first of all I can't organize theatricals if there are no costumes and scenery in the school; secondly,

136

you've never acted; and thirdly, there won't be anything doing before next Sunday anyway.'

I should not have brought forward so many reasons, for now he let loose on me. I could do it if I liked, but I didn't want to; he had already acted, and acted very well, for everyone had said so, including his mother; and in any case one could at least make a beginning next Sunday, which would certainly be an awful day otherwise — that went without saying now. Thereupon he left me in high dudgeon, and was not to be seen the next day.

Sunday came. With a hat and stick but no coat Rudolf Koenig went ahead, and we followed him. Zuffar and I walked immediately behind him. We wandered through woods rich in their autumnal dress and across meadows from which the last crop of hay was being cut. Our objective was a mountain towering above the neighbouring lake.

Next came mountain meadows, little rivulets confined in wooden runnels, wind-blown cottages and stunted trees. On looking back into the valley below one saw the fires where the peasants were burning leaves and decayed vegetation. Long, pointed streamers of smoke rose perpendicularly into the still air.

I was overcome by a sense of freedom such as I had never experienced before. I have grown up, I thought to myself; I'll soon be leaving school and then life will begin. I felt I must communicate my feeling to somebody, and to make an opportunity of doing so I turned to my companion.

'What are you going to do with yourself?' I asked. 'I'm going to be a statesman.'

In those days I did now know Zuffar well enough, or I should have guessed what his reply would be.

'So that you may be hailed as a king in every Golden Goose, eh?'

'I shouldn't have told you about it.' I said indignantly.

'Why not? I thought it a very funny story. But don't get excited — I am not going to dissuade you. Personally I have other ideas. I am going to be a writer. First of all, a book about Van Gogh.'

'Van Gogh?'

'He was a painter. Things like that are just as important as your politics. In any case, do you really know what politics are?'

'Politics? Of course. Mainly that the Republic must be got rid of.'

'Ah! So that's the most important thing, is it? The best revolutions are made by Archdukes.'

'Why ask me if you are not going to take me seriously?'

'I am taking you very seriously. Only I am not sure if you take yourself seriously.'

I sat down and began to write a play. It was a satirical play parodying life in the school. Zuffar promised to help in its production, a cast was collected among the boys, and I assigned everyone a part, ten altogether. The very first rehearsal showed that Erwin was in truth the most gifted actor among them.

The Christmas holidays interrupted our preparations. Of all the boys Erwin and I alone remained in Klagenfurt. The others went home.

The holidays came to an end a few days later, and school life resumed its usual round. We rose at half-past six, breakfasted at a quarter past seven, and then went to school until twelve or one o'clock. After luncheon we were free until three, when we resumed our work till half-past four; then came an hour for games, after which we went on working until half-past seven. We were free again from suppertime until nine-thirty.

When the play was finally produced it was a tremendous success. Visitors came from the town, and everybody agreed that Erwin was the best actor of all. Mention was even made of him in the local newspapers.

We produced a special gazette ourselves for this one day. Zuffar did the illustrations. The best one was a drawing of one of our Sunday walks, at the head of it Rudolf Koenig, very alert with hat and stick, and behind him milestone after milestone — ten and twenty and fifty miles — and at the last

138

one he was followed by the remnants of his pupils — on stretchers! At Carnival time no one takes anything amiss. Besides, Koenig was the last man to have done so anyway.

'You know,' he said, laughing, 'I am really a bad German. Good Germans lack a sense of humour. They think it proves their national pride.'

One day there was great excitement in the town. General Ludendorff was about to visit it. I was tremendously pleased, because I looked upon Ludendorff's visit as an expression of the intellectual unity of Germany and Austria, that was to be followed one day by political union.

My school fellows both in Koenig's school and in the Gymnasium to which we went shared in my enthusiasm for Ludendorff, at any rate the older ones. Lively discussions took place, however, with some of the younger boys on this subject.

'Who's Ludendorff, anyway?' they asked me.

Who's Ludendorff? Ludendorff!! Everybody knows that: the great general of the World War, and one of the greatest men in history. Do you mean to say you really didn't know who he was? No? But Ludendorff was Hindenburg's right-hand man! Or don't you know who Hindenburg is either? Oh! Yes, Hindenburg, naturally, a great general in that war. Is that all?

These boys were ten years of age — born in 1913, one year old at the outbreak of the war and five at the time of the armistice. Could a mere seven years really make such difference? Ideas with which I had grown up, war, generals, battles — a whole world, the only world that existed, the end and fulfilment of all history — and these ten year olds calmly say, 'I don't know anything about it,' or 'Ah! of course, during the war...'

'That's a nice thing,' I said to Zuffar. 'The children who are being born today will look upon the Great War as we used to look upon the war of 1870.'

'Of course,' he replied. 'And so when they're grown up

there will be another war. It only needs someone to get hold over them!'

'So it's going to be a long time before the hour of freedom strikes?'

'Not so long! But to make sure that it really does come, mind you don't tell the youngsters about abdominal wounds. You must say: "When a man is hit, he is always shot in the head and feels nothing . . ."'

He walked off. But after he had gone a few steps he turned round and called out to me:

'The fact that the kids know nothing about Ludendorff and Hindenburg, and all the other heroes down to the lieutenants, needn't excite you. They'll learn soon enough. Where's one going to find examples for them otherwise?'

On the evening of Ludendorff's arrival I stationed myself at the end of the street leading to the railway station, just where it opens into a big square in front of the station itself. Both sides of the street were lined by men belonging to Right Wing associations. The square itself was full of people — Socialist workers — as was soon to appear.

At last the train came into the station. A movement passed through the crowd, at first softly, then increasing steadily until one could hear isolated words, sentences, refrains. It was not long before I could make out what was being shouted. The words were quite unmistakable: 'Bloodhound! Who prolonged the war? Down with war! Three cheers for Socialism! Three cheers for the working classes! Three cheers for the Republic!'

A storm of protest broke loose that soon became a veritable hurricane. But in the very middle of it I saw an open space in which a solitary man was walking. He walked towards us and the silence walked with him, surrounded by the menacing roars of the workers and overshadowed by the red flags that grew out of the crowd.

The solitary man was Ludendorff. Now he was standing by the first of the men lining the street, then he was already in the street — he walked on steadily, quite alone, followed at an interval of several paces by two or three men, behind whom came a motor car that soon got struck in the crowd, which poured forth like a flood. It overflowed into the narrow street, swept away the men lining the sides, broke their ranks, and carried them along in its mad rush.

I too was swept forward by the pressure of the crowd from behind me. Suddenly I was able to breathe again. I found myself standing in the centre of what seemed to be a magic circle that nobody could penetrate next to Ludendorff. He walked on — no! he strode on — completely undisturbed, immovable, superior to those around him, as if he neither heard nor saw anything, or as if he knew himself to be accompanied by tens of thousands of his troops — an endless procession, each individual only part of a single whole commanded by him and animated by his mind.

I went too. But only for a few steps. For then I was overcome by an awe, a power that told me what I had to do. And as the first notes of the 'Internationale' rang from the throats of thousands I cried out in a voice that I did not recognize as my own:

'Long live Ludendorff!' and then, 'Long live Germany!'

I do not know what happened after that — but the 'Internationale' must have come to a sudden end. Along a street that opened up before us we entered the inner town. From the balcony of his hotel Ludendorff delivered a speech, which I did not wait to hear him finish. What he said was transitory compared with what he had been when he went alone, when his enemies could not subdue him.

A meeting was held on the following day in the largest hall in Klagenfurt — the Musikvereinshaus. Even while Ludendorff was speaking a medley of voices could be heard from outside. Gradually they grew louder until the speaker was hardly able to make himself heard. When he had finished speaking, it was announced that everyone was to remain in his seat except for a few volunteers.

I and my friends went to the doors. There was a small garden in front of the hall, filled with bushes between which the path led out to the road. Across the road lay a field covered with piles of wooden stakes. It had snowed heavily during the day. But one could not see the snow, for in rows upon rows, stretching from the bushes across the road and far into the field at the back of it, stood Socialist workers.

One of our company, a boy belonging to the form above mine, called out, 'Onward!' and we followed. We burst through the first rows and were joined by others coming from the hall. Right and left I saw hands holding sticks and knives, and knuckle-dusters, similar to those I had myself. I saw others picking up the stakes piled in the field. I did not notice that my left hand was bleeding, that my coat, my clothes, and my face were covered with blood, until the police whistles grew louder and louder and the battle came to an end.

One thing more. Beside me lay the boy who had given the order for the attack. I saw a red hole where his left eye had been. On the ground beside him lay a worker several years older. Blood and brains were oozing out from his split skull. The whole field had become a mass of red ice.

Feeling that I had lived through something tremendous I reached home to find Koenig and Zuffar waiting. As soon as I had told them the barest details, I said: 'I must go to Germany as soon as possible; I must find out what is happening there, now that fighting has started even in Klagenfurt.'

'I can tell you what is happening,' said Zuffar. 'In Germany the workers are in and Ludendorff is out, so you must change your direction if you don't want to attack in the wrong one.'

'You shouldn't be so sarcastic,' said Koenig. 'After all, Ludendorff shouldn't have been received here in this fashion — although I can understand the bitterness of the workers.'

'Understand?' I said. 'Socialists, guilty of the collapse ——?'

'They were probably men who had been four years at the front, including the one whom your school friend killed.'

'He'd lost an eye, and acted in self-defence.'

'In self-defence? You yourself told me that he gave the signal for the attack. Why couldn't you wait for the police?

Violence and lawlessness, from whatever side they come, mean the end of the State. Have you for a moment thought of the dead man's family?'

'Something must be done for them, of course,' I replied, 'by the State, or else we will make a collection in school.'

'And perhaps you will have your own knuckle-dusters melted as a contribution,' said Zuffar, in a voice that sounded different.

I wanted to answer him. But all of a sudden I could not find the words. My pride in the fight vanished. I felt an immense void, which soon turned into shame. Then I left to have my hand bandaged, while I laid aside the knuckle-dusters that had been my constant companions for a fort-night.

X. *Germany in 1923*

*M*Y trip to Germany took place at Easter. It was to
include Munich, Jena, and Weimar, where there was a man
to whom I had a letter of introduction. The journey was a
great adventure, because for the first time in my life I was
going to see Germany beyond the Main and to hear German
spoken in another dialect than my southern one.

While the Austrian currency had already been stabilized
for several months, Germany was just reaching the height
of the inflationary period. As a result I was able to pay for
the whole of my fortnight's journey in Austrian crowns, the
equivalent of thirty gold marks.[1] This is significant of the
condition of misery the country was in at the time, which
has so often been described since. Political unrest had increased proportionately.

I became aware of this when I arrived at Munich. The
city, which had a few months earlier presented a rather
peaceful aspect, seemed to have been turned topsy-turvy.
The station and the square in front of it, all the streets that
abutted onto it, almost every tree, were covered with placards
and small bills. In addition there were inscriptions in chalk
or paint. The swastika and the import of the words were
common to all. Most of them said: 'The inflation is due to
Jewish rule in Berlin. Its aim is to destroy the German
nation.' Or else: 'The Jewish Government in Berlin is trying to stop the struggle in the Ruhr. It has been bought by
France.'

In some places, lost amid the flood of the others, I dis-

[1] At par $7.50.

144

covered smaller notices. It was necessary to go close in order to decipher them. 'Germans!' they said, 'the inflation is the price that we are paying for the struggle in the Ruhr. It is our national duty to hold out and not to lose our nerve.'

Which was the truth? Quantity was in favour of the swastika; reason of the others. Then I saw more. A band of men wearing a peculiar shade of brown, curious in appearance. Their heavy boots crashed on the pavement; they wore straps under their chins and fierce expressions on their faces. Boys of my own age also were marching with them, in a kind of semi-uniform.

In the middle of the town I saw another procession, Socialist Workers' Youth, boys and girls. They were carrying red flags and were singing — a strange and forceful song loaded with sincerity in every word. I had never heard any workers' songs apart from the Internationale. I suppose I imagined that from people of this kind one would only hear words like blood and revenge and revolution.

The song they were now singing was different. It was a song of battle and wrath, of self-sacrifice and faith.

'Brothers, with hands now together...' I could understand. Yes, they were brothers, these whom I saw marching. They were not marching to order, they did not form a mechanical unity, they were no mercenaries.

> 'Brothers, make laughter of death;
> Holy this last of our battle,
> That slaves may have freedom of breath.'

I watched the procession long after it had passed. In the far distance I could still hear the song — it was like an end and a beginning:

> 'Endless the marching of millions
> Pours from the dark into sight,
> Till our hearts' irresistible passion
> Shall break through the heavens and night.'

How many had I seen? A hundred, perhaps a hundred and fifty. And still it seemed to me as if the millions of whom they sang had been in their train.

In the afternoon I asked my learned old friend the historian:

'What about the German Republic? There are good elements in it, aren't there? Like the "Workers' Youth," for instance.'

'I don't know,' he said. 'I'm an old Liberal and don't like the Reds. They are not national enough.'

'What could they do that is more "national"?' I enquired. 'The whole nation is suffering for the sake of the struggle in the Ruhr.'

'None the less,' said he, 'don't let yourself be bamboozled into anything.'

On the following day I proceeded to Weimar. It was Good Friday, but the spring seemed to be late in coming. There was no more than a faint green shimmer over the landscape, still mingled with the silvery grey of the first buds. The people one met looked pale and shivery, and seemed to have no joy in life, no feeling that Easter was near.

In the evening I met the man to whom I had the letter of introduction. Almost the first thing I had to do was to ask his wife to bandage my hand, which was still suppurating. 'That was because of Ludendorff,' I said in answer to her enquiries, 'a few weeks ago when he was at Klagenfurt.'

'Oh, I'm glad to hear it,' he said; 'it must have been a very difficult decision for you to make. Which group do you belong to? The Socialist Workers' Youth?'

'Oh no,' I said, suddenly feeling terribly ashamed of myself. 'It wasn't that at all.'

I remained for five days in Weimar with the family of my new acquaintance. It seemed so obvious to him not to belong to the political Right that he simply ignored my opinions.

'Stab in the back of the unconquered army?' said he. 'But, my dear boy, the army had already collapsed, and whatever was still holding together was destroyed by Ludendorff. After all, it was he who demanded an armistice within twenty-four hours.'

'And the Treaty of Versailles? The policy of fulfilment?'

'Could the hunger blockade be allowed to go on? Germany's position today is stronger than ever. Unarmed, it will in a short time become the greatest intellectual power in Europe.'

Nevertheless, I ventured to ask him how soon he thought we should be ready for the next war. There could be no liberation without war. And the majority of young people were in favor of it and against the Republic...

That was a mistake, he said, even if the Republic had committed many sins of omission. Did I know anything at all about the boys of my age from the working classes?

Yes, I knew little about the Austrian ones; and of the German what I had seen recently in Munich, and that seemed to be good.

Yes, and their groups in other parts of Germany were even better. Would I not like to join them? The Republic was a State of Liberty, and Liberty the need of youth.

'Quite impossible,' I said; 'I could never show my face in Klagenfurt again. 'When I think of it — I, a Red!'

True, it would take courage, what was called moral courage; and sooner or later everyone had to take his stand. If I disliked red so much, there were other groups — Democratic and Catholic Democratic Youth, but perhaps I had never heard of those?

I had, but without going into the matter at all. So far as I could tell, all of them were merely different varieties of red, and there the matter had rested so far as I was concerned. However, I did not say all this; the other man was such a much better talker than I that there would have been no point in it. I dared to ask only one other question:

'What do you think of Adolf Hitler? There are numbers of people in Munich who believe in him.'

'You'll have to make up your own mind about him. Go to one of his meetings if you are interested. You'll hear plenty there about a war of revenge.'

When I returned to Munich I followed his advice, if only out of opposition, for Hitler could surely not be as bad as his opponents made him out. After all, Ludendorff believed in him, and I had seen and admired and defended Ludendorff.

I went to a Hitler demonstration in company with a young student. He had been in the Cadet Corps with my brother, and now he occupied some post in the National Socialist Youth group, but was on leave for the evening.

'Hitler will manage it,' he said, 'this very year. He is a splendid hero, the only true patriot in Germany. If possible I'll introduce you to him later on.'

The meeting took place in a beer hall — I believed it was the *Bürgerbräu* — that a few months later was to become famous as the starting-point of the unsuccessful *Putsch*.

Long before the meeting was due to begin the place was full to overflowing. My first impressions were of the rattling of glasses, of the sound of mugs being set down on the tables, of the squeak of chairs being moved across the floor, of a confused babel of voices, and of an almost impenetrable atmosphere, a mingling of tobacco smoke and the fumes of beer. Standing along the walls was a row of young men with swastika armlets. Some of them were wearing Bavarian hats with chamois brushes.

My companion and I had with some difficulty worked our way up to the very front, where there were a lot more men with swastikas. It struck me that they were not drawn up in any sort of order, that there seemed to be none of the stern military discipline that I had expected.

Then the noise stopped suddenly. Not a sound was heard, only the smoke still drifted over the tables. Hitler had appeared from somewhere. Now he was standing behind the men with his hand raised. In his hand was a mug of beer, so he cannot have been a total abstainer in those days. At intervals in his speech, if the applause had lasted long enough, he raised the mug and took a draught. This appeared to exercise a powerful and favourable impression upon his audience.

This, however, is to anticipate. The mug was still being waved aloft and the people were still cheering and raising their right hands in greeting. Some raised their arms vertically, some bent them, others waved their hands. There did not yet seem to be unanimity about the salute.

When Hitler put down his mug silence fell again. He began to speak, jerkily, with his words falling over each other, with sudden bursts of rage. He was talking about Germany's internal and external liberation; some of the first lines he spoke have remained in my memory:

'The internal enemy has combined with the external foe to twine like a serpent about the backbone of the people. Its poison fangs must be stamped out. A strong arm is needed to do this, an arm which cannot be formed of parliamentary resolutions but only and solely of a single ruthlessly determined will.

'The army would have held out but for the revolution that was fostered by Marxists and Jews, who had failed to destroy Germany by war alone — which they had also fostered. Only when Germany is capable of fighting for its own freedom will it learn and receive it again. Until France and world Jewry are laid upon the ground incapable for all time of acting or moving, Germany cannot live. To gain this end, we must have a will of steel, which will beget arms, a ruthless national government, and above all no parliament.'

If I remember rightly he also made something like an offer of alliance to the Bavarian monarchists and the House of Wittelsbach.

I admit that I was impressed by the speech until it was well advanced, if only on account of the elemental passion with which it was delivered. I saw, while the speaker fumed, banged his fists on the table, clutched at his heart, and stretched his hand in the air with the fingers passionately spread, all the pictures that he called up — Germany trodden in the mire, its weak government, the country surrounded by foes bristling with weapons and ready to hurl themselves on us afresh, the people led astray by maundering about peace and the policy of 'fulfilment.'

I saw the people starving and perishing through the fault of the Government, which certainly consisted of scoundrels and wretches — otherwise how could it act as it did? A single word, a single act, would suffice, and the whole net that bound us to the ground would be rent asunder. But

149

this was not to be expected from these men, from Berlin. Only a new army, a new form of heroism, such as had come into being at the beginning of the war, with banners and standards, could save us. 'Victorious shall we beat the French' — the marching tune for a reawakened Germany — and the world of enemies would collapse.

Then suddenly something seemed to snap in me as I looked more closely at the man who was speaking to us. Was he really our destined leader into such a future? Could it be he who would give us a new Germany? There seemed to me to be an unreality about his words, as though he were speaking from a stage, the effect of every phrase calculated, with great technical skill — nearly the truth, but only nearly, not fulfilling it.

The contact between the speaker and myself was broken. His words slipped off me; they no longer moved me; there was nothing in me that responded while his gesture swept the rest of his listeners with him.

From now on I was able to watch the intoxicated audience. I remembered a fairy tale of a man who possessed a magic wand that had the property of making any whom he touched with it appear in their true colours: donkey's ears or the claws of wild beasts became visible underneath the masks and the clothes they were wearing.

I saw bony men staring at the speaker with wide open, distorted mouths — murderers, I thought; and others, pale, desperate, hollow-eyed, in ragged uniforms. From them nothing new could come; they would follow anyone who made them promises.

And others again — their weighty forms filled up whole rows, their heavy hands were clasped round their beer mugs as though they were sacred relics. Their pendant moustaches, dripping with the froth of the beer, quivered with emotion. Some of them had thick gold chains across their paunches or were wearing heavy rings. Many had taken off their coats, sweating with excitement. One thing distinguished them all: they all bore the unmistakable stamp of abysmal, grossly arrogant commonness.

150

The speaker was now giving his views on trade and industry; the stout men all moved interestedly nearer, leaned
over their mugs, and nodded approval. 'And then there will
be an end to Jewish speculators and department-store Jews'
— or words to that effect. What they took this to imply
was obvious, and how superior they felt was also clear, because they certainly were not Jews nor did they own department stores; hence they stood to win whatever happened.

I saw young people too, most of them only a few years
older than myself. They must have been the sons of middle-
class families, students, black-coated workers, and men who
did not follow any profession. The man on the rostrum was
speaking of socialism. But he said that there was no need
to become proletarianized to achieve it. Everyone might
stay as he was, including his bourgeois class consciousness,
and still be a revolutionary. This was an immensely attractive formula, as could be judged by its effect.

Not all were moved by such arguments, it is true. The
younger ones — and now I discovered a whole series of boys
of my own age — fastened onto other words of the speaker
which I admit caught me again.

He had changed his theme. Now he was speaking of
national liberation, of the revolt of youth, the necessary
rebellion against tradition, against schools, against the
grown-ups. This Republic calls itself free, but it is ruled by
the aged, by the conventional, by bureaucrats . . . Of course,
if such a thing were possible — a youthful Reich, a great
national community such as I had had in miniature at
Gmunden — then there would be no German boy who would
not join in.

It seemed odd to me, nevertheless, that the speaker should
say so many different things that all contradicted one another,
while everyone heard in the speech only what pleased him.
The boys of my own age were still raving with enthusiasm
long after he had passed on to talking about the patriarchal
virtues and stricter authority. What had we to do with
them?

For years we had struggled through life without our

fathers and elder friends; and, taken all in all, we had not done too badly. Were we to reinstitute of our own free will something that we had never missed?

The meeting came to an end without my having been able to sort out my ideas. There was a mighty clamour, a confused throng of people among whom one could hardly find one's bearings.

At length my companion succeeded in pushing his way through and giving Hitler some message or report. He also found time to say that from now on I would organize the Party Youth movement in Austria and join the work in Munich in the following year.

It was a scene to which I can only look back with painful feelings. I will compare it to the condition of a man who is the only one sober among a number of intoxicated people, and who suddenly realizes that the individual who seems more Bacchanalian than any is only pretending to be drunk.

Hitler was this individual. The impression was so repulsive that without saying a word, without any leave-taking, I stepped back into the crowd. Not until I was outside the hall did it occur to me that this might have been a historic occasion; nevertheless, I did not feel that I had missed anything.

On the following day I returned to Austria, and met with a small difficulty on the way. When I arrived at Salzburg I discovered that I had miscalculated my thirty gold marks and had nothing left for my ticket to Klagenfurt. All I had was several hundred cigarettes that I had bought in Munich. So I unpacked my handbag, put the boxes of cigarettes in it, and began to sell them on the station platforms and in the restaurant. I must have caught the intonation of the other cigarette boys properly, for nobody was astonished, and in a short time I had collected enough money for the fare.

As I was afraid of being laughed at by Zuffar, I told him of my experience at Munich with greater enthusiasm than was warranted by my real feelings. I was thus led into making assertions of which I hardly knew myself whether or not they were true; until I had almost persuaded myself that I had left the Hitler meeting as an enthusiastic National Socialist — a misstatement which had its consequences a whole year later.

At the beginning of the summer holidays I caught typhus, as a result of which I had another attack of the old lung trouble from which I had suffered at Gmunden. Instead of going back to Klagenfurt, I was obliged to spend the next few months in the deadly atmosphere of two sanatoria.

Thereby Klagenfurt became an ideal, just as Schoenwoerth had been in the days of my childhood. Klagenfurt held liberty, friendship, and youth, everything that was beautiful and desirable.

Not until February, 1924, was I able to return. I count this day — it was the seventh of the month — as one of the happiest of my life. My journey through the mountains on a day that seemed to have been stolen from spring, with little tatters of white cloud scurrying across the blue sky, was like the return after a long imprisonment, almost a new birth.

In Klagenfurt I was greeted by Koenig: 'So there you are again. I never thought you'd be longing to get back here!'

The one thing that remained steadfast throughout this second school year was my friendship with Rudolf Koenig. This was the more important, as about this time I was confronted with a great crisis in my religious life.

After having been a Catholic as a matter of course in my childhood, I had settled down after the critical days in Würzburg and Bamberg to a period of calm, and had finally come to be comparatively indifferent to the external forms of the Church. This was to a great extent the result of the events of war and post-war years and our altered material circumstances. At Gmunden, before the war, it had been part of the duties pertaining to rank to go to church, especially to what was called the 'Nobles' Mass.' But as everyone gradually declined to the proletarian level this became an anachronism.

153

The step from such an equation of social circumstances with religion to turning away from the Church completely was a short one. The identification of clericalism with Catholicism and the nationalistic influences of post-war times had also had their effect upon us youngsters.

All this grew to be acute when I came to know a form of Protestantism in Carinthia, the history of which impressed me very deeply.

After the Reformation, Carinthia, led by its nobles, had to a great extent turned Protestant. The Counter-Reformation was the more ruthless. Carinthia was one of the classic instances of 'dragooning.' That is to say, the reconversion of Protestants was put in the hands of regiments of dragoons. They fulfilled their task with notable success, though only, it is true, up to a certain height in the mountains. Any place that was impossible for the dragoons to reach on their horses remained Protestant.

Even in some parts of the valleys, however, the Lutheran faith was preserved. Numbers of parishes adopted Catholicism formally, but remained secretly true to their convictions and continued to practise the Protestant rites. This was done amid tremendous danger, and often meant the forfeiture of life and property.

The congregations that held out were finally victorious. When the Emperor Joseph II published his edict of Toleration for Protestants in 1781, the Carinthian Lutheran congregations brought their Church books out into the light of day to prove how long they had practised their faith. From that time onwards they were able to do so publicly.

The pastors whom I met seemed all to have preserved a breath of the old fighting spirit. In the Catholic camp, on the other hand, I observed things that revolted me intensely. I mention them here in order to show the dangers to which the Church is exposed even by isolated phenomena, especially when a foolish politico-clerical mentality believes itself to be doing the Church a favour by suppressing and concealing facts.

In addition to Koenig's school, there was one in Klagenfurt which was in charge of the Catholic Scripture teacher at our Gymnasium. The pupils there came from poorer homes, and most of them were paid by subscriptions from congregations or by some other charitable association.

For a long time all kinds of rumours had been current about this boarding-school. It was said quite openly that the year before I came to Klagenfurt several of the boys there had caught dysentery at about Christmas time. The illness was kept a secret for fear that the appalling sanitary conditions of the house should become known. The boys were either not looked after at all or only very badly. Their letters home were never delivered.

The most heart-breaking scenes are said to have taken place. Boys lay in their dormitories feverish and crying for their parents. On Christmas Eve, when the unfortunate children were feeling most wretched of all, several of them died.

A little while later a local author wrote a play about the affair and produced it at the Municipal Theatre at Klagenfurt. There was no possible doubt at whom it was aimed. Nevertheless, nothing was done; not even a charge of libel followed. Meanwhile the head of the Catholic boarding-school continued to lecture us on Christian morality.

Not until further most deplorable facts were brought to light, into details of which I will not enter, was he dismissed from his post and confined to a monastery.

After hearing all this and thinking the matter well over, I determined to leave the Catholic Church and to become a Protestant.

There were some sad weeks at the end of my second year at Klagenfurt. It was not the summer holidays that lay before me, but 'life.' This was, in fact, the great moment of which we had been hearing for years: 'Once you've left school ...' and 'Then life will begin in earnest,' and so on.

For eight years we had been looking forward to it; once we were grown up and had a say in the world, how different everything would be! All the things we would do! No more rules and regulations, no more silly essays to write; to be able to learn and to research into whatever we were interested in; no more masters to punish us, nobody to tell us what to do.

And this glorious time was coming now, soon. A whole long period was coming to an end, eight years: war, post-war, inflation, a thousand small troubles, problems and duties, none of those things would count any longer. What would come next? So it happened that I began to be afraid of this 'afterwards' to which I had looked forward for so long, and which now lay inevitably before me. I began to cling to my status as a schoolboy, a status which was hardly mine any longer. 'They are still your school-fellows — for the moment,' I thought. 'Your friends, the same age as yourself.'

That was it: the same age as myself. Once I had left school I should belong to another generation; my age would be determined by that of the oldest university student. Now I was still taking part in the life of the youngest of my school-fellows, ten-year-olds, seven and a half years younger than myself, the new generation whom the war had not weighed down because they had been too young.

I became a prey to further anxieties. Ahead of me, among the upper students in the universities, I should find men who had been in the trenches. Would it not be the same thing over again as it had been years ago when the soldiers first came home? 'You are too young to have an opinion; you weren't at the front.'

It was always the same problem: too old for those who came after us, too young for those who were already occupying their position in life.

A new order would have to be created in which such things did not count. But what form should it have? I did not know, I could hardly make up my mind what to study. Ancient ideas revived in me when it came to choosing a career. 'A gentleman is either a diplomatist or an army officer, or merely himself. He passes his time; only the plebs follow professions.'

But it would surely be absurd to go into the army now;

and for the diplomatic service money was needed, even under the new régime. In addition to which I did not want to serve under the new régime.

A number of us discussed the situation: 'What are you going to do when you leave school?' It all sounded very simple. 'I'm going to be a doctor,' said one. A doctor? You call one when you're ill, my father said, but you don't become one! 'And I an engineer'; I was no good at mechanics. 'And I a lawyer'; to conduct cases for other people? But is not jurisprudence needed also for other ends? One must know the law in order to be able to make better laws, to find out first which is good and which is bad. I decided to study law.

I could not tear myself away. I stayed in Klagenfurt all through that summer and the following autumn, in the room that I had lived in as a schoolboy. When Zuffar came we talked about the future. We did not get very far. I used words like justice, freedom, national honour often enough, but I certainly implied hostility to the republican form of government rather than anything else.

At the time I was not a legitimist. With the best will in the world I could not have said to which candidate for the throne I would offer my allegiance.

'For the principle of monarchy,' I therefore said.

'Which will disintegrate for ever, if you don't succeed in combining it with a new social order,' said Zuffar; and I was just where I was before.

So I decided to leave the answer to the future. I should find out in Munich what there was to do. It was nearly a year and a half since I had heard Hitler speak, and almost a year since his unsuccessful *Putsch* had taken place. Who could tell how things had developed meanwhile?

XI. *Inheritance or Freedom?*

I ARRIVED in Munich on November 14, 1924, early in the morning. It was foggy and gloomy. I stood at the main railway station, not knowing what to do next. Finally I put my luggage into the cloakroom and went to the university. I was no more at home here. So I waited until some students came and a bell rang, and followed them to the nearest lecture-room, where a lecture was announced upon some legal subject.

I had just time to sit down when an old man who seemed to be the professor entered. I was preparing to stand up when I noticed that this was not the custom; the students stamped their feet by way of salutation, so I did the same. The old man nodded, went to the desk, and began to speak. The fact that no one paid any attention did not disturb him in the least. He seemed to be used to it.

I understood nothing at all of the lecture, not so much as the actual words, let alone their sense. Only after the lecture was over — it concluded with a further burst of stamping — did I ascertain that it had been on German legal history.

On the following day I looked for living quarters, and at last found a room at a pension called 'Palace of Triumph,' which was kept by the widow of an officer. She and her stepdaughter, a girl of twenty, and her brother, a captain in the Reserve, ran it jointly.

Among the lodgers were two university students, a music teacher and her young man, a girl who painted, another young man who had no occupation beyond writing poetry, and a girl from Koenigsberg who was a sculptress. In addition there was a singer from North Germany who, apart from the officer's widow, was the oldest of any of us. She was thirty-five.

Manners in the pension were most informal. On the very first day everyone talked to me at lunch, and gave me good advice about what I was to do and what not. The elder of the two university men was a medical student and advised me to take up his subject. He was twenty-five and had been at the front, and had a low opinion of legal science. His friend who was studying architecture thought nothing of it either, while the poetic young man had no use for the university at all.

Finally the pianist, the sculptress, and the singer also joined in, and we got down to first principles. The discussion grew more and more animated. I do not know where it would have ended if there had not suddenly come a loud and ominous ring at the bell.

A man appeared in the dining-room who kept his hat on and said: 'I am the Law!' (and he turned over the lapel of his coat). 'Either you pay or I'll seize your goods.'

Payment was not made, so he seized the goods. A label was affixed to every chair. 'How mean!' I said when the man had gone again, 'Just when one is at lunch!' 'Why not? Then he knows at all events that people are at home!' Nobody seemed in the least perturbed. From that day on for the next fortnight our breakfast eggs were served with our names written on them, in order, so they said, to prevent their being seized out of the kitchen by the bailiffs.

Meals at the Palace of Triumph were altogether a curious institution. I can best describe them by quoting the kind of conversation that took place. At lunch time, for instance, the stepdaughter would suddenly exclaim, 'Mummy *dear*, how wonderfully you have done the potatoes again!' And in the evening the captain of reserve would praise the spinach up to the skies. On the following day it would be the turn of the officer's widow to say to her stepdaughter in front of the guests: 'Well, anyone could tell that it was you who roasted the meat today. Isn't it delicious?' until finally they all combined to sing the praises of soup, spinach, potatoes, and the rest of it. How did the visitors respond to this? Who joined in the hymns of praise? The poetic young man did it once, was regarded as a strikebreaker by all of us, and never dared to do it again.

In the Palace of Triumph the principle of complete liberty was advocated. No one cared what anyone else did, until one day there was a terrible mix up and each believed his rights to have been assailed. This happened soon after my arrival and was fully discussed during dinner. 'Immorality,' and 'adultery' were the mildest accusations made by the contending parties. And there were as many parties as there were hotel guests.

The situation was as follows: the student and the pianist, her young man and the painting girl, and the poet, actually with the officer's widow; but this was already unbelievable — she burst into tears at the bare mention of it.

'It isn't because of that,' she said. 'But suppose the police hear all this talk and close down my pension!'

The cause of all the trouble was a rather daring poem that the poetic young man had read to the pianist and left in her room. Later in the night the elder of the two students found it and also left it there, whereupon it came into the hands of her legitimate young man, from whom the painter girl heard about it. She told the architect, of whom it was said that he had an Oedipus complex about the officer's widow. *Hinc illae lacrimae.*

Affairs at the Palace of Triumph might have grown still more complicated and have turned into serious quarrels had not the officer's widow had a son and a daughter, twins, beautiful children, just sixteen years of age. Although they were strictly brought up and only came home at the weekends, they always succeeded in reconciling the various belligerents, and thus saved the peace of the house.

The sculptress, the singer, and I were outside all the gossip. The evidently friendly relationship between the sculptress and myself was regarded as particular proof of our innocence. This girl was, indeed, a most curious personality,

160

and entirely unburdened by mundane wisdom. The fact that water was required for boiling potatoes no more entered into her scheme of things than did the ordinary laws of morality. She would have gone out for walks with no clothes on quite calmly if the climate had been suitable.

She was a savage who had been accidentally born to European parents. Everyone knew that faithfulness was not to be expected of her — and yet, despite all, it was not altogether wrong to call her 'innocent.' In a sublime sense she really was.

The Palace of Triumph was not much help to me as regards serious study. True, I had by now discovered which lectures I was supposed to be attending, but what they meant was still something of a puzzle to me. When I looked at the other students I almost felt uncomfortable at being in the same room with them. They all seemed so stiff and reserved and unyouthful.

The only contacts that appeared to exist were between those who wore the same colours. I watched two with different colours for weeks. They sat on the same bench day after day and were obviously longing to make each other's acquaintance. But they never managed it.

At first I could not understand why. After all, we were not so much older than the boys at the gymnasium. But that did not seem to matter. The tone was not set here by the boys of eighteen or nineteen but by the men, those who had been in the war, who filled all the lecture-rooms. It was simply not the custom among them to talk to anyone as one felt inclined; it was looked upon as childish, schoolboyish, bad form. It was a stern law, and whether one agreed with it or not, it was impossible to break it.

Though I had been much surprised at the others, it really could not be done. I felt it myself when I found a boy of my own age and wanted to talk to him: there was a barrier between us that could not be broken down. A few days later I noticed that he was wearing the colours of some student's association, and I thought of enquiring what they were.

Then I hesitated again; I wanted, for the time being at all events, not to be bound in any way.

It was at this time that I first saw real duellists. They turned up at every lecture, and seemed to be very proud of their wounds. But why they found it necessary to use carbolic in such quantities that the whole lecture-room stank of it, I failed to understand. Many of them wore decorations, so that they must have been combatants in the war; and again it seemed to me incomprehensible that they should still take any pleasure in knocking each other about in this fashion.

Other groups of students whom I discovered in the course of time pleased me better. They looked as if they might still be schoolboys. 'Those aren't real students,' the medical student from the Palace of Triumph told me, 'they're *Wandervögel* and Boy Scouts, some of them Catholics and in favour of democracy. Quite impossible fellows.'

'And those over there?'

'Worse. "Republican students," or something of that sort. They believe in Weimar,[1] black-red-gold, loyalty to the Constitution, and God knows what besides.'

'Black-red-gold?' I said. 'But I thought that students had always fought for that!'

'Yes I dare say they did — in the old days. But nobody decent does now. They're the colours of the Republic, of the Jews, of the Social Democrats. Also the students' song of 1848: "The band is cut, that was black-red-gold," has been changed, and now we sing "black-white-red" instead. You won't get out of it. You'll have to make up your mind one of these days.'

He was quite right: it was impossible to avoid making a decision, if only because life was too complicated otherwise. How could one find one's way in the lectures without a sure guide? Above all when it came to constitutional law. Most of them shuffled their feet on the floor when the lecturer

[1] As the National Assembly, which in 1919 accepted the Constitution of the German Republic, met in Weimar, both friends and enemies of the Republic used the name of this town as synonymous with 'democracy' or 'republic.'

mentioned the Constitution of the Republic, the President of the Reich (Ebert was still living), or worst of all the Revolution of 1918. There was always a shuffling of feet when such things were spoken of. This indicated disapproval and disagreement, and was a preliminary to whistling.

There was one professor, only one, who was not put out by this; he reminded me of our history master at Gmunden. He spoke quite calmly about socialism and democracy and the fact that they were guaranteed in the Constitution. He said it was 'the freest in the world'; yes, it was even the 'Magna Carta of German youth,' so long as we were prepared to carry it out and defend it.

He must have known what he was doing, and can hardly have been surprised when there was whistling in his lectures, which lasted until our lips were cramped. Then there was silence, and one became aware of a small group which had been consistently stamping their approval; they must be the ones, I thought, with extreme Left sympathies, who stood for internationalism rather than loyalty to Germany. So I preferred to scrape my feet and whistle, and stamped with the majority when words such as 'Bismarck,' 'the old Germany,' and 'the Army' fell from other lecturers. Nevertheless I scraped or stamped as an outsider, not quite sure of my feelings or the expression of them.

It was really essential that I should make up my mind. So I fell back on the association the colours of which I had noticed a little while before. I wrote a letter of enquiry, and as a result was visited by one of the older members. That very afternoon I was able to wear the band and cap of the association.

My visitor had made short work of my lingering doubts. The association's sympathies were well over towards the Right, he said, but it exercised no political compulsion; after all, nobody would want to belong to any party left of the German Nationals anyway! I should find pleasant companions, learn to work, and be given political instruction.

But I'm not going to allow my face to be hacked about, said I. Nor was it necessary, was the reply, because this was not a duelling corps, though of course, if a really serious case should come up — an insult to the nation or anything like that — one would have to resign for the time being and re-join after the duel. Sixteen 'freshers' joined in the same term, so there was no lack of companions of my own age, and at first I was very pleased with life. For days at a time we played at manoeuvres in the country, and with a little care one need never be drunk.

If only there had not been such a terrible amount of 'side' among the students. Even the nicest boys succumbed to it — they wanted to be 'grown-up' and not be thought to lag behind their elders. They indulged freely in esoteric expressions (mainly connected with beer and the drinking of beer); we were lectured about what was 'academic' and 'worthy of one's colours': use only the front platform of the trams; never jump on or off them; go only to certain places of amusement; don't mix with Republicans, and so on and so on. All of which reminded me forcibly of the conversations at Gmunden about the *Almanach de Gotha*.

At all events, I was now told officially what I was to stamp or scrape my feet for, although there was not perfect unanimity on the points. The National Socialist wing applied stricter rules; even negative things, such as failure to mention Hitler's *Putsch* when it might have been mentioned, were to be taken as occasion for scraping. Those who were of this opinion, however, did not succeed in gaining the day. It was pointed out that one could not, after all, scrape unceasingly. 'He ran away when the shooting had hardly begun,' said the students from Munich. 'The less said about it the better.'

One representative of the National Socialist minority (a 'non-Aryan,' by the way) whose father had been killed in the Hitler *Putsch* soon introduced me to one of the earliest members of the association. This man was called Georg Schott and had written 'Das Volksbuch vom Hitler,'[1] that was to explain to the masses Hitler's simplicity, patriotism, and significance.

[1] 'The people's book about the Hitler.'

To my queries, 'Is Hitler the Fuehrer? Can a leader look like *that*? Does he mean it all honestly?' and so on, he listened with the gentle indulgence with which a father confessor receives the religious doubts of young people. What did my doubts show but that Hitler was a master of psychology, a patriot, a hero, a genius who shunned no means to save Germany?

If I wished to know *how* necessary it was for Germany to be saved, I had only to study the power of the Jews more closely — it was so great that it was impossible to talk about it fully in public. People would either be terrified or they would laugh. What Hitler and the other leaders imparted was only a small, careful selection from all that was known.

Then I was given various books to study, amongst others a volume of German fairy tales with a National Socialist interpretation, which explained everything very clearly. Little Red Riding Hood — she is the symbol of the German nation; the wolf who eats her up is the 'Jew' (the very fact that he was called 'Wolf' showed this; the quotation is literally true). The huntsman, on the other hand, is a brilliant prophetic vision of National Socialism. He kills the 'wolf' and thus saves Germany. There remains the grandmother: she symbolizes the indolence of the German people, which is the cause of the whole misfortune (and incidentally makes possible the miraculous rescue).

But why these parables? Our ancestors were obliged to be very cautious. In their desire to hand on their higher wisdom they were hindered by the Church, which had always been in league with 'the Jew.' Only the fact that a means of expression had been discovered that remained incomprehensible to the Church prevented this heritage from being destroyed. All through the centuries no one had been able to interpret the tales, until Doctor Schott was — as a party official — illuminated.

These books of fairy tales — and all the stories were interpreted in a similar manner — gave rise to a tumultuous debate in the association. The National Socialists threatened to resign if works published by the National Socialist Party

Press were held up to ridicule again. Whereupon someone suddenly rose — a youth, the boy whom I had noticed first of all — and made a great speech, totally unprepared, arising simply from the feelings of the moment.

I listened, at first in surprise, and then completely swept away, growing more and more enthusiastic; he was saying exactly what we all felt, all sixteen of us, despite our pertness and 'academic side'; how clear it was that we were all of one mind. The speaker spoke for us, through us; it was as though he were the single mouthpiece for all the sixteen.

What possessed us, he said, to allow our elders to force their party divisions upon us? Had we, the children of the World War, been gathered from all classes to become friends and fellow students for that? Had we become brothers, to allow our elders to separate us again? We were united by common experience, different from that of older people, different again from that of the children of today. We were the bridge with tomorrow, could we allow the stones of this bridge to be torn asunder? Who should tell us what 'youth' meant? National Socialism? The greatest fraud that had ever been perpetrated. For who was behind it? The old — who refused to admit that we got on quite well without them.

National? We were that ourselves. Social — socialistic, if one preferred the word — we were made that by the war years. A united people? Could we be more united than we were, coming as we did from Austria, Bavaria, Berlin, the whole of Germany?

It needed no party uniforms to achieve that: once we put them on we ceased to be a community, we became a machine, a soulless company of men, led by outsiders, obeying them, subject to them. God Almighty! I should really like to go to the young workers and find out how they feel about it! I am sure that they, like us, must have had enough of the party quarrels of their elders. One of our members has recently been expelled because he joined the Reichsbanner Black-Red-Gold! Were we to go on discriminating between Red and Black and Brown and Blue, between 'academic' and 'worthiness of the colours'? To the devil with the lot of them!

This was rebellion, open and undisguised rebellion against sacred tradition, against an order that not even the war and all the resultant misery had been able to break down. It was a most serious threat to everything which the older men represented, everything that gave them dignity and power.

We did not realize all this at the time; we only realized that something tremendous had happened, something that concerned us all. Hence our immense and enthusiastic applause, against which no other voice was able to make itself heard.

He continued. Once again our breath was taken away; he broke through what had been accounted an axiom: Here Germany, and beyond it the enemy.

In other countries things must surely be the same, only we didn't know about them. We had only heard wartime propaganda, and today, six years after the conclusion of peace, it was no different from what it had been before 1918. We had no say when the war broke out; now we had. If we made up our minds we could *insist* on peace — in defiance of all the older people in every country, who form the most deadly of all *Internationales*. It must be done soon: we must first send over ambassadors, and then make alliances with all the young people in England and France and America; with all who suffered as we had suffered without being accounted heroes; with all whose world had been destroyed by the war and who wanted to build up a new one.

As a practical suggestion, therefore, let anyone who was able to do so study abroad for one or two terms, in Geneva, Grenoble, Oxford, or wherever it might be. And let the same number of foreign students come to us. If this idea were only carried out consistently, we should win, and we *must* win if we were not all of us to go to the dogs again.

It was a wonderfully mild spring evening when I walked home with the student who had made the speech. Until then I had hardly known more than his name, and had only occasionally remembered that he had been the original cause of my joining the association.

Now I felt as if I had known him for years. Had he not always been with us? In Dertlgruber and Waldemar Claus, and the other Gmunden boys, even in Zuffar — in every single one of my friends? No longer speaking as the students spoke, but as though we had gone back many years and were discussing some new project, some plan that we were going to carry out together, I said:

'I say, what about resigning from this idiotic association? We shall never get them to see reason. Then we can go abroad together next year as you suggested — perhaps to Geneva ——'

He made no answer, and we walked silently down long avenues, through which came a breeze that bore us along and raised our spirits, that made us happy and again sad. I felt as if it had carried my words away. I had no desire to repeat them.

A bench stood by the wayside. We undid our coats and sat down, still in silence. He cupped his chin in his left hand and reflected. And as I watched him I knew that his friendship would mean much to me — the first friendship since school.

He began to speak, and I knew that he had understood everything:

'I can't,' he said. 'You must understand. My father is an old member of the association, a parson, you know — it would be terrible for him. And besides, there are eight of us in my family, so you may imagine the size of my monthly allowance — forty marks.'

'But we can share; we can manage it if we save up. I want us to remain together; perhaps we might then make a good job of life.'

'You overrate me. What I said tonight may have been the most important task I had to do. You will have to carry it through. You are free or can make yourself free; I have not got time left.'

The breeze had grown still warmer and more nostalgic

168

— it may have been the wind which almost made me weep as if I were still a child. When I glanced at my companion once, it seemed to me as if he felt the same.

As we were parting I said to him, 'Will you stay friends with me even if I alone resign from the association?' 'While I live,' he replied — an answer the meaning of which I did not altogether grasp. I only understood it rightly when I heard a few months later of his suicide. The external circumstances were clear enough: months of starvation at another university, theft of food, and finally the continual fear of being caught. I believed I saw further. He was the first of us to fall in a great and good fight, a fight in which he had borne himself with knightly valour.

My resignation from the association had taken place in a perfectly friendly spirit. Nevertheless it seemed to me wiser to go to some other university for the winter term in order to avoid unnecessary discussion. Moreover, there was no doubt that I had hitherto done very little work, and that it was essential that I should get into a stricter atmosphere.

Meanwhile the North German singer and I had made friends as soon as the naïve damsel left. She advised me to go to Hamburg for the winter, and this seemed to me a very sound idea — I should certainly never find anything that differed more completely from the South German softness and gaiety.

For the moment, however, it was impossible to see how I was to continue studying at all, in Hamburg, Munich, or anywhere else. It was July, and nearly all my friends had gone away. I was left alone in the Palace of Triumph with my rent in arrears and not a halfpenny in my pocket. Nor did there appear to be any prospect of my ever receiving money again, because I had fallen out with my mother about something and she had cut off supplies. She had sent me fifty marks with a note saying, 'This is the very last you get from me.'

I took it seriously, and considered how I might find some way out of my difficulties. I decided to apply to the head of the entire family, my father's old cousin, the Prince Ernest zu Loewenstein, the one who had deprived him of his claims to inheritance and had worked against him in every possible way.

Now that I had been abandoned by everyone, by my parents, my brothers and sisters, now that I was entirely without means of subsistence, he must surely be willing to help me. I was, when all was said and done, the youngest member of the family, eighteen and a half years old; I would not ask him for money, only for hospitality somewhere until I had made new arrangements.

And then I would ask him to bury the old feud, and not to carry on hostility from one generation to another. I said to myself, 'He cannot rebuff me unless he is a complete barbarian.' Nevertheless my heart contracted with apprehension when I thought of the interview.

At last I took the plunge and wrote him a short letter, saying that I proposed to visit him at his castle of Kreuzwertheim on the Main, in Lower Franconia. Without waiting for an answer I set off with a friend. We travelled fourth class in a slow train to Würzburg — the dear little town in which I had lived as a child. From there we intended to continue our journey on bicycles that we had borrowed in Munich.

I spent an hour recalling old scenes: here was the hotel from the windows of which we had thrown aerial darts; there the church containing the tomb of Walther von der Vogelweide; there the barracks (part of it had been turned into a travel agency now), the streets where I had stood at attention. The field-grey uniforms of those days had disappeared; business men were going about their affairs; I was too disreputable to show myself, my clothes were shabby and dusty. Just as it was at Gmunden, I thought; history repeats itself.

Then we rode into the night, alongside the Main, towards Wertheim.

Very soon we came to the first Loewenstein boundary stones, stone lions with the fusilly shield of our arms in their

SCHLOSS NEUMATZEN IN THE TYROL, FIRST STATION OF OUR EXILE

THE RIVER AT THE CASTLE OF THE COUNT OF WERTHEIM

paws — my country, the land of my fathers, unlimited forests, farms, the first corn in the fields. Really my land? I went to it poor and homeless. Not an inch of it belonged to me, not a tree, not a bush. Even to break off a twig would be theft, taking another man's property. I got wearily off my bicycle when I reached the boundary stones; I was hungry, and felt my hunger and the fact that I was a stranger on my own soil.

Nevertheless I kissed the ground. Who would not have done it, however much reason might call it foolish and theatrical? Earth is strong; it is stronger than reason. (How I shall fall to my knees once I tread on German soil again! How I shall kiss it!)

It was very late when we reached Wertheim. I saw the silhouette of the old castle ruins. There the Counts of Wertheim had ruled and misruled, including the one who had betrayed and massacred the peasants. His heiress, the Countess Anna of Stolberg, had married the great-grandson-of Frederic the Victorious, Ludwig II, Count of Loewenstein-Scharffeneck, later Count of Loewenstein-Wertheim, Chancellor of the Holy Roman Empire under three emperors.

Beyond the Main I saw the lights of the castle of Kreuz-wertheim, partly hidden by houses. There lived my uncle, the fierce old antagonist whom I was to face tomorrow.

We rode past the good hotels in the town, the 'Loewen-steiner Hof' and all the rest of them. We dismounted at a very small inn called, if I remember rightly, 'The Golden Ox.' We left our bicycles outside and enquired for rooms. We must have looked awful, with no collars, dusty and dirty, and with uncombed hair. Our luggage consisted of two rucksacks. The innkeeper looked at us with suspicion.

'No rooms here for you, but if your papers are in order you can always enquire at the Town Hall.' At the Town Hall? Oh, of course, he probably meant the shelter for tramps and homeless men.

'We shall have to put on collars,' my friend whispered; 'then we shall certainly get rooms.'

'I'm damned if I will,' said I in a towering fury. 'The

171

fellow will jolly soon laugh on the other side of his face when he finds out who I am.'

I pushed the innkeeper aside and we went into the dining-room. An oil lamp was burning there, and three men were sitting in a corner playing cards. They seemed to be so used to playing together that speech had become unnecessary. All one heard was their fists banging on the table.

I ordered a meal. There were various Loewenstein wines on the list. The bottle that the innkeeper showed me with a somewhat sardonic grin bore our coat of arms. I said I never drank wine.

While we were eating the man brought our bicycles into the house, no doubt as pledges in case we proved unable to pay the account. The bill came to barely two marks. We added a tip of fifty pfennig, and suddenly rooms were found to be at liberty.

'Don't register your name until we've paid the bill for our rooms,' said my friend.

But that was impossible, because the visitor's book was already being produced. I entered my name. The innkeeper stared at it for a moment; then he called his wife, his children, his servants, and I was surrounded by a sea of bent backs.

'That's enough!' I said. 'I'm only sorry I didn't really go to the Town Hall when you wanted to send me there.'

The landlady stammered:'Your Serene Highness, Your Serene Highness[1] — please forgive us. My husband only meant it as a silly and certainly most disrespectful joke; he saw at once whom we had the honour of entertaining. We intended from the very first to give you the best room in the house. Please don't go!' Then she turned on her husband with simulated indignation: 'Will you kindly make your apologies, you oaf? Then the young gentleman may perhaps excuse you. But it would serve you right if he didn't. To bring such a disgrace on us, when we've always been good Loewensteiners!'

Depressed, speechless, I ignored their servility. I was ashamed — not of the innkeeper and his wife, but of my ancestors. How they must have ground down the people to

---

[1] 'Serene Highness' (Durchlaucht in German) is the title of mediatized Princes.

bring them to such a state of servility, even towards myself, the most powerless member of my House.

I lay awake for a long time during the first night I spent in our old capital. The fact that it was our capital, I thought, was because no emperor stopped the dissensions, and protected the people. The disgrace had gone on, the exploitation, to this very day ——

Then a word came into my head which I did not often use: 'Liberty.' We had a Constitution that guaranteed it now, so I had heard in Munich. 'Democracy,' the professor had said, in whose classes we dutifully whistled till our mouths ached, and 'overcoming mediaevalism.' What did we whistle for? Poor fool, he was only telling us fairy tales, beautiful dreams; why interfere with him?

And then another thought came to me from the past (oh, peasant graves at Pinsdorf! Oh, Kalvarienberg!). For the first time it came to me as a clear concept, with a shudder of longing:

German Republic! True German Republic!

On the following day I took a little ferry across the river and knocked at the gate of my uncle's castle. An oleaginous footman opened to me and took me through a long series of rooms. The same pictures hung on their walls as had hung in the Great Hall at Schoenwoerth; the same eyes followed me; my looks had been their looks; my blood was their blood. But at home everything had seemed more alive. Here I had the feeling that the dead were envious of me because I was living and they were dead.

It is said that the laws of inheritance sometimes miss a generation; in this instance they must have skipped centuries. The counts of Loewenstein and Wertheim, little tyrants, oppressors of the people — my ancestors? Never! The last from whom I felt myself to be directly descended were not among the portraits here. Not in the vaults around Wertheim did their bodies lie, but in the cathedrals of Magdeburg, of Speyer, of Palermo . . .[2]

[2] Burying-places of the Roman-German Emperors.

With these feelings in my heart I approached my uncle. I no longer felt nervous because he was the head of the family, an ancient and powerful foe, while I was homeless and a stranger on my outward inheritance. I felt only the oppression with which great age always affects extreme youth. I sat opposite to him, to this old man, whose two marriages had both been childless, who was ill and bitter and weary. In his voice was a rough tenderness that gave me assurance.

I said I had come to see him only in order to make his acquaintance, and to tell him that I proposed to spend the next few weeks with one of his head gamekeepers, who was a friend of mine, and who lived at Freudenberg on the Main. I almost wondered whether he had not understood what I said to him. Because suddenly, without any transition, he said painfully and helplessly:

'If you were my son — oh, if only you were my son! Then I should know for what I have lived; and tell me, you would not leave me alone? I am very lonely,' he continued, 'and you probably thought that I was happy?'

His voice dropped. He stared straight in front of him and then at me. I tried to comfort him — I who had come to be comforted.

But I did not say what I really thought: 'If you had the courage to take me to live with you, I could soon tell you what you must do to be happy and to be loved, there where love is worth having among your people.'

It was not shyness that kept me from saying it, but fear lest he should really do it, lest I should be bound to this house, this life, lest I should be obliged to give up my existence to something from which I had to escape if I wanted to become myself. There was a voice within me that drove me away:

'Away from here. Take as your inheritance only the duty to do better, and your responsibility. All else is worthless. Do not bind yourself to what is dead, to something that has outlived its accomplished task, when it had passed down to you through the generations the blood which must pulse for all Germany, not for the interests of one single family alone and its little country — though this country is still big enough to bring misery upon its inhabitants.'

When I closed the castle gates behind me — I never passed them again — I walked out into a brilliant summer's day. The air was warm, and I was surrounded by the scent of new grass and masses of flowers. The ferry took me back to the other shore. I felt as if I were recrossing the Styx, back to life. Things that had weighed on me since my childhood had dissolved; everything which in my father had become a constriction, all his bitterness at the slights he had suffered. I felt as if I were reborn in my separation from kith and kin; I no longer needed them.

The next few weeks strengthened this experience. I stayed with the head gamekeeper in the little town of Freudenberg, not far from Wertheim. It was the house of a friend. He shared his meagre pay with me as if I were his brother. He took me out when he went hunting, but I never used a gun myself. I spent days in wandering through the woods with him; they seemed to be endless. Once they had been common property of the peasants. The Counts of Wertheim and their successors the Counts of Loewenstein were the sovereign rulers, and so the forest had eventually passed into their hands.

In this glorious country — and in two continents I hardly know any that is more beautiful — I saw the population crowded in between the forest-clad hills and the river. They live in cramped unhealthy cottages with tiny windows, pretty and romantic only to the casual visitor's eye. The young sons can find no work at home, so are obliged to go into the towns. The percentage of those suffering from tuberculosis is among the highest in Germany.

All this I saw and felt during that summer. I spoke to any and everyone. The people lost their shyness as they came to realize how I had passed over to their side. If only I had the courage to do what I ought to do, I thought — but that is the hardest of all. I was no Red, but everyone would take me to be one. How was I to find my way out of the tangle? Good will and popular gestures are not sufficient. Without *deeds* everything remains empty and false and worthless.

I would seek further, I vowed; I must surely succeed where the goal was so plain. I swore a solemn oath; there must be no boundary stones in the Reich that was to come, with lions holding shields in their paws; there should be no more symbols of masters and slaves. There shall be only the one Imperial Eagle who divides and protects the Reich. Justice shall live under his wings, a free people in a free country.

I spent my nineteenth birthday at Freudenberg among the peasantry and tenantry, who drank my health in a glass of Loewenstein wine. My toast was to freedom in a new Germany.

Soon afterwards my mother and I adjusted our differences, and I went to Hamburg to continue my studies.

XII. *The Gate to the World*

*T*HE North German singer met me at the station and took me to some lodgings where the landlady spoke quite a different kind of German from any I had ever heard before. She did not seem to understand a single word of what I said in reply.

That was surprising enough, but I was to have plenty more strange and unusual experiences. Before describing them, however, I must make a few general remarks.

It has no doubt often been observed how much may hang on a single expression, a single characteristic. Sometimes it can make the history of whole generations, indeed of whole peoples. In 1914 we had acquired the habit of talking about 'when we still had peace,' and that split the world into two epochs so totally unconnected with one another that nobody expected them ever to become connected again. The year 1918 brought no change, and even in 1925 we were still using the same mode of expression. One talked of 'peace-time coffee,' 'peace-time quality,' 'peace-time materials'; in short, there was hardly anything over which one was not being continually reminded that we still had war. The prefix 'peace-time' had no reference at all to the years after the official conclusion of peace. Anyone who wished to obtain anything of good quality was obliged to express his desire in words that were almost a political confession.

I myself was no exception. I thought it very witty when people said, 'Peace broke out in 1918,' and 'Peace is a continuation of the war with different weapons.' That kind of thing was to be read in many newspapers, and it was freely

repeated by the Munich students. The worst imputation
that could be cast on anyone was to say that 'he may even be
a pacifist!' If anyone had said that of a member of my late
association, that would have been the sort of case in which
one would have been obliged to resign temporarily in order to
be able to fight a duel.

It was from such an atmosphere and such a manner of
thought that I came to Hamburg, to its hectic activity as
a great port, and its contact with all the countries of the
world.

Hamburg is the town about which every German boy
knows more than about all the rest put together. Only
Shanghai, Bombay, and San Francisco might possibly be
admitted as competitors, though I really don't know why
San Francisco. Probably it has something to do with the
Chinese quarter and the Golden Gate, which one imagines
as a portal leading to unbelievable treasures.

About Hamburg every boy has read all there is or ever
has been. The most important part, of course, is the harbour,
for here are to be found sailing ships on to which you may
smuggle yourself as a stowaway, and only appear a thousand
miles out to sea, covered with tar, very hungry, but with
'sparkling eyes.' While you are still stumbling over ropes and
barrels, the ship gets into a 'stiff breeze,' and in the east appears the 'dreaded bull's-eye' that can only develop into a
typhoon.

You are seized by hard sailor hands and dragged before the
captain, who is at first furious, threatening to have you keel-
hauled and wanting to know whether a damned land rat such
as you has ever heard of a cat with more than one tail.

Eventually, however, he calms down and growls: 'I
rather like the look of the boy. Give him a thorough wash
and feed him, and then we'll see what he's made of!' Saying
which, he points to the bull's-eye in the east, which has
meanwhile extended, halfway across the sky.

So then you are fed, and the mate gives you much good
advice; in the course of which he says that the *Santa Barbara*
is the finest ship in all the Seven Seas, and the 'old man' a

grand fellow, a real sea bear such as is seldom found in these days.

After food comes the storm. The topmast falls overboard first thing, and the men have to lash themselves to the steering wheel. A great many other things happen too. But in what is left of the ship there is every opportunity of becoming a great hero. And then it is not very long before you command a ship of your own, which is in every way much better than the old *Santa Barbara*.

On the other hand, you may have bad luck and get on to an English freighter in Hamburg, and be obliged to run between Cronstadt and Liverpool carrying rum and corn. Things do not improve until you are hired by a Yankee, get mixed up in the Boxer riots, and rescue a German regiment from a trap that has been set for it by the treacherous yellow-skins. You return covered with glory, and all the other boys who stayed at home are green with envy.

It is true that Hamburg also harbours many dangers and more temptation to go astray than other towns. But if you are wise, you do not fall for them. As a reward you get to know a patrician who is the head of an old shipping firm. 'Anyone who is sensible in youth will be a very wise man by the time he grows old,' he says, and from that day onward there are no heights to which you may not rise.

Hamburg men are never landlubbers. If one of them ever goes to live inland, he soon misses 'the salty taste on his tongue,' and in his dreams he sees the ships sailing down the Elbe to the mouth of the river where the seals are sunning themselves.

That is what Hamburg looks like to every boy, and even one who has no wish to go to sea, who would have no use for a patrician if he met one, and would find nothing to do either in Tierra de Fuego or at the Cape, longs to go there and expects to find it the open door to a thousand marvels.

With similar feelings I too arrived in Hamburg, with an indefinable expectation, and a thrilling pleasure at the great adventure.

But — and this while I was still in the train — it occurred

to me that I had heard much against this city at home.

Hamburg is a city of burghers, I had been told. It has no nobility, or at any rate no real nobility. The 'nobles' there are those who are the best chafferers and who have made the most money. And at the same time these people behave as if they belonged to Society! They are nothing but swollen money bags, republicans, tradesmen in a word, and opposed to all we stand for.

Not that this would have influenced me in any way now; but I must be quite honest; it did occur to me, and that always means something.

One's first impression of a new town is largely decided by the weather. Hamburg received me with a blue sky, and the trees did not look autumnal. I had hardly deposited my belongings in the house of the woman who spoke the curious German before I was out again to go and see the harbour.

I was not disappointed when I saw it, for it was full of ships of all sizes, and I even discovered several sailing ships.

All at once, amid all the confused bustle, I noticed one thing, the flags — the flags of the ships that were coming and going or lying peacefully together in docks or at anchor. Was this still a German seaport? It was a picture of the whole world. I had never before seen these flags in real life, and here they all were — the Union Jack, the Stars and Stripes, the French and Belgian tricolours. I even saw a Russian flag, red, with a hammer and sickle, and I should have liked to persuade myself that the men on deck looked quite different from all other men. The neutrals — one still called them so — were also represented. I saw Dutch, Danish, Norwegian, and Swedish boats. And amongst them all I saw many ships under the German flag, friendly and neighbourly, no matter whether the one beside her was English, French or Russian.

Theoretically one had known all this and been proud of the way we had regained our pre-war trade. But what it really meant one had not realized any more than that there had been a new peace since 1918, and that there was no sense in clamouring for the old one that had existed before 1914.

'Peace since 1918,' I said aloud, as if this was quite a new idea. What does it look like, peace?

That is what it looks like, like the Elbe over there! England and France and the rest over here with us, and we going over to them; there is one just setting off, her bow facing seawards, right into the midst of peace!

'That's just the kind of thing pacifists say,' a voice told me, and I hesitated; first they take away everything from us and then tell us to shut up, otherwise we are savages. Had we really lost all? Was not the esteem in which we were held greater than ever?

This had been predicted to me by the man in Weimar when I was only seventeen. Meanwhile the inflation was over, and my friend in Munich had said: 'We young ones must make an alliance with the young people in other countries. I'm sure they think as we do.'

Suddenly it all became perfectly clear to me. Where had we longed to go to in the days when we dreamt dreams? To India, China, and America, to all the countries that were distant, to all the peoples which are still alluring and mysterious. That is a dream which can only be fulfilled if there is peace on earth, so it is not true to say that every boy at heart longs for war. It is only other people who teach it to us by giving us swords and guns, soldiers and uniforms to play with.

There was so much about which I was still undecided, I felt at length, and I wanted to become strong and to have definite views. Above all I wanted to know what views I should like to have.

So this was the city of burghers that had always been a republic and had no decent traditions. How was it that there were Gothic churches here and many beautiful houses? Some of the streets were narrow and winding, but they were full of all that many people assert is only to be found in the royal cities of Vienna and Munich.

I stood before the portraits of old senators, reigning burgomasters, high dignitaries of this first German world-republic. They seemed no more distant, no more alien to me than the pictured men of past days whom I had seen in South Germany.

And then the new parts — a mixture of German and foreign, of near and far, modern buildings that were reminiscent of photographs of New York. It was easy to understand why these people were proud of their city and would not change it for any with crowns and coats of arms over its doorways.

The University of Hamburg was founded after the war, and seemed a little strange after Munich, because the building is new and much smaller.

I was pleasantly surprised to find that few students seemed to belong to associations, and that there were few whose faces were hacked about. On the other hand, there were numbers of young men like those who had been described to me as 'not fit to be members of a corps' in Munich; they belonged to the Youth Movement, Black-Red-Gold-Republicans, even Socialists.

Here too the students stood in groups round the notice boards in the entrance hall during the intervals, but the largest groups were to be seen by the boards which bore Republican or Labour symbols. Very few stood by the swastika board, nobody took much notice of them, and they looked rather sulky.

There was a freer spirit in the lecture-rooms than there had been in Munich. I saw students speaking to one another without introduction, and the same happened to me. One young man began to speak to me and asked me something, and when I replied he was obviously pleased at my Southern dialect. He wore a black-red-gold ribbon in his buttonhole. Later on it transpired that he was called Peter Vogt, a member of the Reichsbanner Black-Red-Gold, and one of its youth leaders. But by the time he had told me that, I already liked him, and so I replied, as if to excuse him, 'Oh, well, it doesn't matter.'

He looked at me in some surprise and said:

'Are you a legitimist by any chance? I ask because only those without any political ideas take up legitimism.'

No, no, I said, it was all quite different, and I really had nothing against the Reichsbanner.

At the moment I remembered the student who had been thrown out of our association in Munich because he joined the Reichsbanner. I had regarded it as perfectly proper and had said that this behaviour was abominable. But I would not mention that to Peter Vogt; I must wait and see what he had to say.

One way and another this Reichsbanner had been drawing a fair amount of attention to itself lately. There the Social Democrats, the Democrats, and the Centre had joined together to defend the Republic; and of course all those had joined it too who strictly speaking could not be called patriots. Ebert, the President of the Reich, had been connected with it during his lifetime, and now of course all the 'Republican' Ministers were, like Severing and Braun and Doctor Wirth.

'Republican' may be a very fine term, historically and so on. One may let it pass in the case of Venice and of course in the case of Rome and Athens — and how about Hamburg, I wondered? But as regards Germany it is just another term for 'Red'!

So I asked, though in the hope of being contradicted, 'Are you a Social Democrat?' And he replied, 'Of course. What did you think?'

So Peter Vogt was a member of the Reichsbanner and a Social Democrat. And I — what was I, when it came to that? Conservative, German National, Monarchist, Liberal? I was not sure, but at all events I was opposed to what he stood for! It would be interesting to find out more from him. So I said I wanted to see him again soon, and somehow felt disquieted as I said it.

From that time onward I was with him during every interval. It was not always very pleasant because his political remarks were made quite loudly at times. Once I felt obliged to say to him, 'If I'm not ashamed of being seen about with a Red you might at least have the tact not to compromise me in public!' There was a coolness between us

183

that lasted for three days, and in the end I apologized.

On the following evening he came to have supper with me, and found me in a bad mood. It had just been made known that the Left had suggested taking a plebiscite on the subject of dispossessing the former reigning princes of their properties. They had received millions from the German Republic, and that was to stop now, especially since there was some reason to suspect that they were supporting anti-republican activities with the money. This, at all events, was what the Left Press said, and of course Peter was of the same opinion. 'What do the princes matter to you?' he said. 'Have you yourself anything to lose?' That annoyed me very much, and I said it was a case of principle.

There we were again. The principle of unprincipledness, he called it, and thought it was abysmally funny that anyone should want to stand up for people of that kind.

'You know,' he said, 'I don't believe that you are really anything like as reactionary as you make out. You only think you've got to talk like that.'

'I'm not reactionary at all, but I don't want a State with no German traditions, with no real patriotism, like this Republic. I've often thought about it and sometimes I've even been near to becoming a republican myself — quite recently at Wertheim, for instance — and then somehow I felt that it wasn't right after all.'

'Simply because you've got no ideas of what the Republic is. You've sometimes come over all sentimental and felt that "after all the workman is a human being too," and then you imagine that that is sufficient.'

He said that he was sometimes anxious about the Republic himself, because it was much too lenient with its opponents. In a sense, even, he must agree with me that princely blood had its value. Cemented with the foundations of a republic, it gave it stability. That had been seen in France, where every restoration had eventually come to grief over the Jacobin traditions of the people.

I had bought a bottle of red wine for this evening, which we now opened. And I suggested that we should have no political — or at all events only semi-political — conversation for the rest of the evening.

So he began to tell me about his Youth League. It contained about a hundred and fifty boys, mostly the children of working-class parents, but also some from the secondary schools. Their position was very difficult, because the schools in Hamburg were very reactionary, and anyone who was pro black-red-gold had all his school-fellows and most of the masters against him.

Then he told me something that took my breath away, something that delighted me beyond measure, if only it was true — but it must be true! Peter Vogt knew Waldemar Claus, my fair-haired friend from Gmunden. He was living in Hamburg now, learning his job in a factory. He was going to be an engineer. This evening we could not get hold of him, but tomorrow morning for certain.

'What are his political views?' I asked Peter.

'Undecided at present. I hope he will join us one day. He's been out camping with us several times; the boys adore him. At all events, he certainly is not reactionary.'

'I suppose that's another one for me!' I said; and he replied, 'Well, why don't you come too sometime?'

'I should have to sleep on it,' I said; but the truth was I was terrified, simply terrified of meeting these boys. I suppose I was afraid of being laughed at if I did the wrong thing — as I certainly should among people who regarded the nobility as strange and rare zoological specimens.

Anyhow, tomorrow I was going to see Waldemar Claus, and on Sunday I might go out with them. Hang it all! Had I not seen and experienced enough to have plenty to talk about? And was I going to be shy of a crowd of boys just because they wore republican colours, and wouldn't admit that there had once been princes and counts of the Holy Roman Empire?

Peter Vogt grinned all over his face when I said so, and went home.

On the following day I really met Waldemar Claus again,

and for the first hour we were so happy to see each other that we couldn't think of anything to say. He had really changed very little in all these years. He was as cheerful and boyish as at Gmunden, and it was easy to believe that the boys liked him.

Now all we wanted was Dertlgruber and the rest; but Peter Vogt was a first-rate chap too, and one couldn't stay on at school for ever. 'Do you remember our prairie fires? We can't do that now when we go out on Sundays, otherwise the boys will do it too, and we shall be responsible. It's extraordinary how quickly time passes. It seems such a little while since we could have done with leaders ourselves!'

Then came Sunday. The boys were to rally at a point about an hour's walk outside the town, by the river. When I arrived Peter Vogt was there already, wearing the green shirt of the Youth organization of the Reichsbanner, and with a haversack over his shoulder. Round him were some fifty boys, all dressed as he was; only Waldemar Claus was wearing a Boy Scout uniform.

Once again I felt as I had done in 1923 in Munich. I was amazed at the spirit and the comradeship amongst these boys. Now they stood orderly in rank and file, looking very smart, though not as if they were simply a military formation. One of them was given the banner to carry, and when it was unfurled they all saluted it and began to sing a song the words of which I could not follow.

While they were singing I stood beside Peter Vogt, but all at once I felt absolutely alone. There were the boys and here was their leader. They belonged to a different world with which I had no connection. Nothing that I knew and nothing that they represented seemed to form a link between us. Yet it was a song that all the youth of Germany was singing. I found that out later.

It may be thought that it should not have been so very difficult. I was almost of an age with them, Peter Vogt liked me and Waldemar Claus was an old friend. I could still see him close beside me and thought of all that there had been between us. Now I felt as if I did not really know him at all.

186

He stared in front of him, looking straight at his little troop, and sang with them:

'With us marches the new time.'

But I belong to the old, I thought, and I felt as if they must all notice it. This grew so strong in me that I could not stay. I simply dared not, lest they should not accept me as one of themselves.

The song came to an end and they were ready to start; it was the last moment. I turned to Peter and Waldemar and said I couldn't come. 'All right,' they said, and none sought to detain me. I climbed up on to a slight hill and nobody took any notice of it. I looked back and not one of them had turned to look after me.

'You must see this clearly,' I said to myself. 'Today you have been beaten, with everything you come from. Those boys down there might have been your friends if you had been worth anything. But you failed; and you have probably lost someone who has been your friend for many years, for you have stood still while he has gone on.'

When I met Peter and Waldemar again in the course of the following week, they said nothing about the excursion, just as though they had agreed not to. So I had not the courage to say anything either; and for a long time neither of them entered into any serious conversation with me at all.

At about this time I did something rather incautious: I told a man who was an adherent of Ludendorff something of my Klagenfurt adventure. Meanwhile Ludendorff had become a kind of prophet, almost the herald of a new religion, a zealous and aggressive religion, that had set itself the task of converting the erring German nation.

The first result of my mention of the prophet's fight was an invitation to have coffee with them in the afternoon. The party took place at a house situated in a comparatively prosperous district. When I rang the bell, the door was opened to me by a maid with the severe air of a sergeant-major, who conducted me through a long passage to a room from which came the sound of several voices. I had just time to glance inside a half-open linen cupboard and to observe that each shelf had a white edging embroidered with proverbs in red. One of these proverbs ran:

> 'As yours was kept, dear mother mine,
> So shall my house be, clean and fine.'

My host was a well-known lawyer. He wore pince-nez, kept the back of his head shaven, and had a short, well-pomaded parting. His face was a whole crossword puzzle of sabre cuts, obviously from student's duels. His wife wore her hair in coils over her ears and had on a petticoat with a zigzag embroidered edge, as was easily ascertainable.

The visitors consisted of an officer's widow with hair piled high over a wire frame, an official from an insurance company, and a coal merchant who was presented to me as a captain of the Reserves. The room, in which the tea-party took place impressed itself so strongly on my memory that I can still describe it accurately.

On the coffee table lay a silk crocheted cloth; the coffee things were white with a gold border. In the middle of the table stood a flower vase with a thick stem. The sofa behind the tea table was covered in red plush, and its back was divided into three parts, on each of which hung little crocheted antimacassars, to keep the grease stains from the plush, which might be caused by hair pomade. There were also two red plush arm-chairs, but the remaining chairs had slanting wooden backs covered with plush. The seats were similarly made and gave an air of upholstered softness. For the officer's widow a thronelike chair had been set which had red-covered arms to it.

A coloured shawl lay halfway across the grand piano which stood at the other end of the room. This shawl must have come from Naples originally; it had a design of solid scarlet half moons on it. On top of the piano stood a vase of trembling grasses and a dish of wax fruits.

Then there was a table supported on three interlaced legs that looked as if they were bamboo. The top of the table was made of stiffly plaited straw, and surrounded by a border of overlapping semicircular wickerwork. The whole thing was gilded and for the moment was not in use.

Each of the two doors was covered with mauve velvet curtains, held back by mauve and gold cords. Beside the door through which I had entered stood two book cupboards with glass doors and green curtains. They appeared to be locked. On top of one of the cupboards I noticed an owl made of brass, standing on one leg, as with the other one it held a mirror. On the base of this figure was engraved the word *Sapientia*.

I only saw two pictures. One represented our host in the uniform of a lieutenant; below it hung two crossed rapiers, a shrapnel helmet, and one riding glove. The other was an oleograph called 'Before the Battle'; in the foreground upon a rocky eminence stood a knight gazing into the dawn, while from behind the rock emerged a forest of spears.

A little later on I observed a polished shell on the second bookcase, a selection of starfish, and a metal Chinese junk about eight inches long.

Above the coffee table hung a lamp with a yellow silk shade. It was upheld by three cupids whose hinder portions appeared to act as supporting balloons. The ceiling was adorned with a rich pattern of stucco fruits, slightly obscene in effect.

The only thing that really got on my nerves was the wall paper. It was striped green and white, rather like a shirt which had once been sent home to me from the laundry in mistake for one of my own, and which I had worn for the best part of a day until the irritation at the neck and arms got to be more than I could bear.

While we had coffee the plaited golden table was adorned with a plant in a pot. The stern-looking maid brought it in and departed, walking as if in goose step. This plant had hairy leaves and a mauvish-blue head of flowers, each head consisting of numerous small blossoms. To this day I have never enquired the name of that particular form of vegetable life.

As I arrived I heard the lawyer say to the officer's widow:

' ... and nobody realizes how dangerous the Jesuits are,' and she replied:

'Yes, indeed, the Jews are rather overrated!'

In the summer of 1924 I had, it is true, left the Church, and not without considerable inner protest; but that was not directed against the Christian teaching of the Church but against certain particular episodes in the administration which I had taken to be general. A year and a half had passed since then, and I no longer felt altogether happy when I considered the matter. I never could bear hearing non-Catholics speak against the Church; in such cases I instantly forgot that externally I was no longer a member of it myself.

I did not at all like what they had said about the Jesuits. Many of my relations, my father among them, had been brought up by them, and when we were first at Gmunden I myself was to have been sent to one of their colleges. So the scarred lawyer and the stout lady seemed to me to have gone too far, and I said:

'I don't know exactly what you are talking about, but you don't seem to know much about the Jesuits.'

'A great many people know nothing at all,' the lawyer replied, 'but *we* know all. Ludendorff knows and he tells us. Their power will thus be destroyed.'

They were all looking at him, and seemed as if they were under the spell of some imminent revelation, which, however, was delayed by the lawyer's wife.

'Hubby,' she said, 'don't let yourself get too excited. Aren't you thirsty for your coffee?'

'Dearest Madam, do let him go on,' the officer's widow chimed in, raising both hands and moistening her lips. 'He is so marvellous when holy rage overcomes him, and we do want to know everything!'

And so then we really did get to know everything. Doctor Schott, the Munich man, with his fairy tales was an ignoramus in comparison. How indeed should he be anything but ignorant when the Hitler party as Ludendorff asserted, was so permeated with Jews and was directed by so many secret Jewish forces that even good men were immediately perverted when they joined it?

Now, one has to imagine the world in the following way. It is divided into two camps, one good and one evil. The good one consists of Germany, in so far as it believes in Ludendorff or may still be brought to do so. Other things being equal, other Teutonic peoples are also included in it, although this is very doubtful in the case of England, which has been too far permeated by the venom of evil.

As regards the forces of evil, these have on tactical grounds been formed into three parts or 'columns.' First the Pope, together with the General of the Jesuit Order, the Jesuit Order itself, and the remaining Christian organizations; second, the Bolsheviks; and third the Jews and Freemasons, who were found everywhere. These were in fact no more than tactical subdivisions; in essence they were the same throughout. 'I dare say you've never heard anything about all this? Extraordinary! A young man like you goes to a university and crams Roman law and perhaps even Canonic law, that they took straight out of the Talmud, and of course never realizes that the hand of the enemy is at our very throats. And no wonder, with all the Jew professors, Mendelssohn-Bartholdy and all the rest of them.'

On that same afternoon I discovered in addition that Moscow, the Vatican, and Paris (where the secret 'Pope' of Freemasonry is established) were all connected by private telephone lines, thus enabling the Pope, the head of the Freemasons, and the chief of the Communists to discuss how best to destroy Germany.

'You have no conception of the danger that surrounds Ludendorff. Only the other day a man stood outside his house looking up at the window. And what do you suppose he did next? He stretched out his hand like the Rabbis when they're giving the Jewish blessing, the "broche" — you know; now you can imagine what that meant! Luther, Schiller, Richard Wagner, none of whom are alive any more, could tell something about that!'

To conclude we had a fairy tale. It was most significant

that Doctor Schott should have omitted this particular one!

'I was saying so to you just now; so attend carefully. It is the story of Snow-White who lived beyond the seven mountains with the seven dwarfs, and her stepmother hated her. What are these "mountains"? *Montes* in Latin. "Beyond the mountains"? *"Ultra montes,"* therefore. That's where the stepmother is — Rome. That is obvious, isn't it? The stepmother hates the German Snow-White, who must die in order that Rome and Judah may live. The seven dwarfs are the German people, small as yet because they are held down by conspiracy. Only Snow-White could make them into giants, and then that would mean the end of Rome.

'The tale goes on to say that the stepmother brought a poisoned golden comb which she pressed into Snow-White's hair. Snow-White sank down as though dead.'

'As though dead,' they all repeated, the coal merchant, captain of Reserves, the insurance agent, the officer's widow, and even our hostess with the embroidered petticoat. 'Yes, as though dead,' the lawyer proceeded, raising his voice; 'and now you know the whole secret of the Aryan race. Now you see whither it has been enticed. For the poisoned comb which the stepmother pressed into Snow-White's hair is, of course, the Roman imperial crown, only described more cautiously.'

At this moment I behaved as no one should behave whom a story-teller has invited for coffee. I burst into a fit of laughter before I had had time to swallow my last mouthful. It hit the lawyer, the coal merchant, captain of Reserves, the insurance agent, and even the officer's widow right in the face. And the more I tried to regain possession of my faculties and to stop choking by drinking more coffee the worse it got, until finally the whole company broke up in the most embarrassing confusion.

When I got home that evening and was thinking it all over, I looked at the scars on my left hand. I stared at them for a long time and reflected, 'They're with you for life, simply because you let yourself in for a fool's game once.'

This is about all that is worth saying about external events at Hamburg. Perhaps I should add that my studies progressed much more satisfactorily than they had done in Munich, and that I made up in six months there what I had missed during the whole of the previous year. Moreover I made the personal acquaintance of my tutor, Professor Mendelssohn-Bartholdy, which was later to be of great importance in my life.

I attended Professor Moritz Liepmann's lectures on criminal law, which I shall also never forget. The first modern German criminal procedure was based upon his suggestions, which did not start with the idea of revenge and requital but with that of making the asocial elements into useful members of the community by precept and example.

For the first time since I had been at Bordighera I saw the sea again during my time in Hamburg. And in doing so I very narrowly escaped a serious accident.

I had gone one Saturday afternoon to the mouth of the Elbe with Peter Vogt and Waldemar Claus. There was a sailing boat there that the owner allowed us to borrow. Since it was already late and the weather did not look very promising, we had really decided to spend the night in the boathouse and not to go out until the following morning. Owing to the affair of the excursion in which I had not joined, I was still not on quite the same terms as before with the other two, although I was making every effort to erase the bad impression. I had told them all details of my latest Ludendorffiade — to show them that I had definitely seen through the petty bourgeoisie with its radicalized plush sofas, and was going to make a serious attempt to acquire sound political opinions.

The story had of course amused them both enormously, and they had become much more cordial again. But somehow I felt that they were still not altogether sure of me. Moreover, they had become even greater friends recently and used often to discuss ideas and events in which I had no part. As a result I was anxious to show them that I possessed courage and enterprise, and so I began to urge them to come out on the water that evening after all.

The wind was blowing off the sea and the tide was coming in. The light was growing dim and several ships had already lit their lamps. The only piece of clear sky lay beyond the wide mouth of the stream. At first they refused, and with good reason, but at last they gave way, and of course the inevitable happened. When we were in the middle of the stream the wind turned and the tide with it. We were driven out to sea, and should have been drowned but that Peter Vogt managed to keep the boat in the lee of a sand-bank, until after hours of effort we were able to cross over to the left bank.

We obtained shelter in a fisherman's hut lighted by flickering oil lamps, while rain and wind beat against the little smudged windows. Neither Peter nor Waldemar said anything about the adventure, but I felt quite clearly that this was not the brand of courage that they wished to see in me.

I suddenly realized too that I could not go on in the way in which I had been doing. I must make some radical change, otherwise I should be trailing the last of my Gmunden egg shells for years to come. Worse still, I should miss making contact with those of my own age who had spiritually overcome the war.

I discovered what to do when I returned to the university shortly after the sailing episode. Announcements were pinned to the notice boards about Geneva University. There were courses in German, which would allow me to count a term at Geneva towards my degree. Moreover there were pictures of Geneva and a map of the town, with a particularly blue lake, and Mont Blanc, which appeared to lie directly behind the town and to be entirely covered with snow.

My mother had just raised my allowance from fifteen pounds to eighteen pounds[1] a month; and that, turned into Swiss francs, made quite a respectable sum. Why, therefore,

[1] Eighty dollars.

should I not go to Geneva? We had spoken of it years ago in Munich, and I still remembered every single word of what had been said:

'First we must send over ambassadors and then make alliances with all the young people in England and France, and with American boys, with all who have suffered as we have suffered without being accounted heroes, with all whose world was destroyed by the war and who want to build up a new and better one.'

That was certainly the right thing to do. Hamburg was the first step. I had seen the flags of all nations there. Geneva should be the second. There I should meet the peoples of all nations — and I should find out whether it was really true about peace and whether it was really possible to break down the barrier between Germany and the rest.

I wished the other two could have come to Geneva with me. But Peter was obliged to stay in Hamburg and Waldemar wanted to go to the Technical College at Charlottenburg later on. One day, he said, I should certainly come to Berlin too, and then we should meet again. In any case, it was ridiculous that I should never yet have been to the capital of the Reich.

Before I left I once more visited all the places I had grown attached to, and on my last day as on my first I spent a long time down at the harbour. I thought to myself that there had never been a greater step in my life than when I came from inland in Bavaria to this city that was the gateway to the whole world.

Surely I should find out now whether I was strong enough to find my way in it.

XIII. *Human Beings and Foreigners*

ON APRIL 1, 1926, I arrived at Geneva and rented a room in the Rue d'Italie, only a few minutes away from the southern shore of the lake. So I was living in a truly 'foreign' country for the first time since my childhood; for I do not count later visits to the now Italian South Tyrol.

In fact I was almost, though on Swiss soil, in an 'enemy' country, for western Switzerland had during the World War 'behaved' scandalously towards Germany because it is very 'Francophil.' Many years had passed since we heard those words; nevertheless they stuck in one's memory.

I have often had the same experience. Political propaganda is evanescent; one sees through it and it is quickly forgotten. But what sticks in the memory is what one hears casually at home or at school; for example, during mathematics or athletics, where one is not on the look-out for political conversation and consequently picks up passing remarks without subjecting them to any test of accuracy. That's true, one thinks, otherwise it would have been said with greater emphasis.

Moreover, while it is easy to revise one's political opinions, it is very difficult to bring oneself to admit that *everything* that one has heard and believed is false, and that the picture one has made of the world is out of proportion simply because one does not realize that there are thousands of details that should also be revised and set in their proper place. Even when one's brain tells one that something is not right, there still remains a certain attitude of mind towards things — mistrust or liking, some prejudice for or against. I had experienced this in connection with the words 'war' and 'peace,' and I was to experience it again with everything foreign I met in Geneva.

What was it that had been instilled into us? Which of the non-Germans were 'decent'? Our former allies, naturally, and the Swedes, who took our side in the war and whose Queen was reported to have said on one occasion, 'I am still a German Princess.' The Norwegians, on the other hand, were less worthy of respect because they sympathized more strongly with England. As for the Danes, they stole part of Schleswig-Holstein from us.

All the others were still worse. In Holland during the war, when a young girl spoke German in the street a man spat into her blouse. In Spain, too, nobody knew how to behave with the exception of the King, for they were all opposed to our submarine depots. Moreover, the wife of Napoleon III was the Countess Montijo, a Spaniard, and hated us. In the United States, it is true, a few decent people remained German, but they also were too weak in time of war to remain loyal to us. As for England, France, Italy, Japan, and all the others, every child knows what to think of them.

The Irish must not be counted amongst the English in this respect. Sir Roger Casement was virtually a German patriot. And in Belgium the Flemings are practically German, though oppressed by the Walloons and the French General Staff. Switzerland is divided in two, a good and a bad part. Although the friendly part is the larger, the hostile is far stronger in its enmity than the friendly is in its sympathies.

Every foreigner who does not form one of the small groups of decent people hates and envies Germany and desires its downfall. He does this all the time and does not allow himself to be deflected, least of all by what the pacifists call 'peace.' Out of cleverness (every foreigner is exceedingly clever, and at the same time stupid, because he is a foreigner), and if he is a Frenchman out of superficial politeness, he does not always show this, perhaps he even says that he has a high regard for Germany. But one must not be deceived by this.

197

Let us take England as an example. Notwithstanding the fact that Queen Victoria was the grandmother, and King Edward VII the uncle, of our Emperor, England unceasingly intrigued against us. England incited Russia, Italy, and all the colonial peoples against us, brought forward proposals of peace designed to weaken us in foreign affairs, and supplied money to the German Social Democrats in order to promote internal discord.

France, above all, who was completely defeated in military respects, has through President Wilson set up the League of Nations to enslave us for ever; because she is terribly afraid that the day of reckoning will come. Besides, Paris is a sink of iniquity in which no German should know what his compatriot is doing.

In short, it can be said that all foreign nations are lacking in ability and intellect, and they could have an apparent rise to power and civilization only at Germany's expense. They regard us as 'cultural dung,' and despise us because Germans wanting in a sense of national honour are continually trying to make up to them.

We can only gain their respect if we 'show them what we are.' Whenever a German goes abroad, therefore, he must lay stress upon his national characteristics. At the same time he should try to learn all about the other peoples. Up to the present we have always been too honest and too stupid. Only when we are indistinguishable from our enemies shall we be their superiors.

A popular saying shows the attitude towards the French: 'What a pity that they have such a beautiful language!' At home we were told that if a nobleman spoke bad French it was the same thing as if he were to eat with his knife.

Subconsciously, these were still my views when I came to Geneva, and at the time, I felt that Mademoiselle Jex was still haunting my thoughts. It is true that there were certain quite positive things opposed to this. These were not, I hasten to add, of a philosophical nature. They were mere superficialities, perhaps, but they were none the less impressive.

In Geneva were to be found other kinds of cigarettes, foreign inscriptions, cheap chocolate — and the children did not speak German. I could see from the promenade a striped mountain, Mont Salève, that lay across the French frontier. One had to have a special permit to visit it. Whilst I was looking at it I heard English and Italian voices behind me, and then two Indians wearing green turbans passed me by, to add to the confusion.

As I entered the University I heard a German student asking the porter, 'Où est-ce que je peux apprendre le langue français?' The porter replied: 'Pour apprendre la langue française, monsieur...' What German porter could have spoken like that? In a French restaurant on my first day in Geneva I discovered an *hors d'œuvre* composed of ten dishes from all of which the guests helped themselves as a matter of course, and as if they were eating Tyrolese dumplings or sauerkraut.

Tobacconists and other shops were open on Sundays as well as week-days. In the tourist offices I saw advertisements of motor tours to Paris, Milan, and Madrid. One advertisement even read, 'Visitez l'Allemagne!'

Germany from the outside! Doesn't one always think in terms of maps? Up till now I had been sitting as it were in the middle of a great map bearing the word 'DEUTSCHLAND' across it. Hamburg lay somewhere above the S and Munich directly beneath it. Now I found myself far to the left, sloping from the initial D, and quite other countries had their inscriptions around me.

In those days I hardly spoke a word of English. 'How do you do?' and 'Good morning' were the most I could say beyond merely 'Yes' and 'No.' My French seemed to me to have grown very rusty, and I was afraid to speak it because I remembered the story about the nobleman and the knife. Before I uttered a sentence I used to say it over in my mind in every possible tone of voice and variety of accent. It was long time before I realized that I could still speak French quite well.

At the university I entered my name for a great many

lectures given in French, and especially those delivered by Professors Logoz and Rappart on international law and international criminal law. I also went to German lectures, and lectures on Swiss civil law. There was no time left over in the week for more.

The German student I had overheard talking to the porter was by no means the only fellow countryman I met. In those days there must have been at least fifty to sixty German students who were divided into two political groups, a Right and a Left Wing. It was not possible here as it was at home to distinguish them by the colours and bands they wore. Moreover, their financial circumstances afforded no clue to their political sympathies. On the very first day of my stay in Geneva I was astonished to meet the son of a well-to-do merchant somewhere in Central Germany who told me he was a Radical Socialist. He kept away from the Communists, he said, because they were too reactionary for him.

At the same time I got to know another student named Gerd ——, who was a small and lively youth with a whimsically clever face. His father was a mining engineer and he himself had grown up amongst coal miners. Nevertheless he was a moderate Conservative. There was also a group whose members were individually of little importance. Together they were opposed to the League of Nations and to a policy of understanding and reconciliation. Their leader was a rosy-cheeked, baby-faced ex-officer who wore a monocle. Another group were their deadly enemies, and were the passionate champions of everything that the first group detested. They were led by a youth from Berlin who wore sky-blue shirts and intended to go into Parliament later.

There were also two Nazis. One wore riding boots, and generally carried a hunting crop that was greatly envied by the Radical Socialist from Central Germany. The other evidently had had his clothes made to measure, and in the presence of foreigners used to say, 'Naturally I don't agree with everything that Hitler does. But...' He was preparing to enter the diplomatic service of the German Republic.

So far I had met only Germans, and my friend Gerd had

had the same experience. We came to the conclusion that this was not what we had come to Geneva for, and determined to join the *Union Internationale des Étudiants*, a club for students that admitted foreigners, where one could indulge in tea, talk, and bridge.

We were greeted by a young English girl who said, 'How do you do?' and we replied, 'Very well, thank you.' Then we were given cards to fill in and I said, 'Mais nous sommes des Allemands.' The English girl replied, 'Just sign your name here.' Therewith we became members of the Union, sat down in a corner, and talked to each other in German. At the same time we kept our eyes fixed upon a student wearing flannel trousers and a tweed coat. There could be no doubt that we had sighted our first Englishman. What would he be like?

The obvious things may be taken for granted. Naturally we knew what Englishmen looked like, what their language sounded like, and something about their literature. The important question was, what was our subconscious conception of the typical Englishman?

There is an amusing story by the humorist Wilhelm Busch told in verse that I had learnt as a child and often read again in later years. The story tells of an English traveller and begins:

> 'In der Hand das Perspektiv
> Naht ein Mister namens Pief.' [1]

Mr. Pief took a look at the countryside through his telescope and said:

> '"Schön ist es auch anderswo
> Und hier bin ich sowieso."' [2]

Unfortunately Mr. Pief held the telescope the wrong way, and therefore fell into a well that he thought was much farther away from him than it actually was.

[1] 'In his hand a telescope,
Comes a mister known as Pief.'

[2] 'There's many another pretty place,
And here I am in any case.'

I did not know the name of the English student. But for me he was Mr. Pief and nobody else. He must certainly have been born in Calcutta, have travelled in Canada, have spent two terms at Oxford, and gone fishing in New Zealand — of course, for 'there's many another pretty place.'

Another association of ideas dating back to my earliest childhood also came into my mind. Among the English children with whom we had played on the beach at Bordighera was a certain Tommy. When the Italian street urchins attempted to destroy his sand castle, Tommy shrieked aloud: 'Ne me touchez pas. Je suis une femme!' A remark that he repeated from that time onwards whenever there was a dispute of any kind, notwithstanding the fact that he was one of the oldest children on the beach.

I should not therefore have been surprised to hear these words come from the mouth of the student who was now approaching us. Instead he shook hands with a much firmer grip than we are accustomed to on the Continent, sat down beside us, and said, 'Have a cigarette?'

He was a nice, healthy-looking youth with brown hands and face. 'But one has to be careful with foreigners,' I thought to myself. 'One must not be taken in by a pleasant manner.'

I actually asked him if he had been born in Calcutta. Indeed I asked him so many personal questions that I might have been in Gmunden or Hamburg.

Of Calcutta there was no question at all. He had been born in London in 1906, and was therefore eight years old at the outbreak of the war and twelve at the time of the armistice. The events that he remembered best were the Zeppelin attacks and other air raids on London. His little brother had been killed during one of these raids. His father had fallen in Flanders in the autumn of 1914.

Here was my world, but from precisely the opposite side! My new friend — I will call him Herbert Lesley — was my age, and now my fellow student. Yet for him Germany had been the enemy. He could still recall it all in its horrifying reality — foggy streets filled with flying people seeking

202

safety in the Tube stations, burning roofs, the roar of burst-ing bombs, and the shrill wail of the sirens sounding the alarm.

'We are the only nation with a righteous cause. We are not fighting for ourselves but for the good of all,' we had thought as children. But we never stopped to think what those words meant and what was the nature of this 'good.' We thought only in terms of bombs and places to be attacked, of machines, and of enemies and foreigners, but never in terms of men and women and children.

'Do you hate us?' I asked him suddenly. A stupid ques-tion. For he was bound to hate us, not for his father's sake, for millions fell on both sides, but because of all the rest, because of his small brother who had been torn to pieces by a bomb on his way to school, because of the hell that we let loose in his native town, and because we had destroyed his childhood.

'Oh, no,' he replied. 'That's all over. And in any case you are no more to blame than I am for all that we did to you — even after the war by prolonging the blockade and when France seized your last milk-cow. At the time we said nothing. But nowadays when one thinks of it in England one is ashamed and says that nothing like it must ever happen again. Besides, you people in Germany have a new State that wants peace. We like this new Germany, your music, philosophers, and writers. I have read everything that Thomas Mann and Ricarda Huch and Friedrich Gundolf have written, and it was because I wanted to read Goethe, Rainer Maria Rilke, and Stefan George that I began to learn German.'

I not guilty? Yes! It was my fault, my greatest fault. What had I been thinking of for years past? At the end of the war I joined with Dertlgruber in stealing arms. True, I was only twelve. But since then nearly eight years had passed, and was I not still the same? The 'new State in Germany that wanted peace': I had done nothing to support it, I never wanted it. Hence I had helped to strengthen its internal foes and therefore I myself was in favour of war.

But war meant destruction; war meant weeping women, terrified people, sirens, burning roofs, dead children.

Herbert continued to speak. He did so in order to put an end to the awkward silence that had fallen between us. He told us an anecdote. He said:

'During an air-raid there was a terrific noise near our house, which is not far from Hyde Park. My small brother, who was asleep, woke up and asked, "Are those German guns?" "No, Albert," I replied. "Those are our guns." Thereupon he turned over in his bed, murmured, "How kind of them!" and went to sleep again.'

At this I made an absurd remark. I could not help myself. 'If we were to make a real peace here and now, Herbert, there would never again be war between England and Germany or indeed anybody else.'

'Certainly not,' he answered in serious tones. 'But you'd have to bring the French into it. Believe me, if we English people can get along with them, you should have been able to do so long ago. But probably you are always fighting because you are too like each other.'

Perhaps he was not altogether wrong. The Frenchmen that I met behaved quite differently from the English; they behaved very much as I did myself. They also seemed to have preconceived ideas, or to have had German governesses who forced them to lie on the ground, and whose nose one had to bite; or to have read books — there were some to be found even in the Bibliothèque Rose — in which German governesses beat children black and blue not merely as punishment but because they were animated by 'German national pride!' In any event it has always taken longer to win the friendship of my French friends than to gain that of Herbert Lesley and his countrymen.

Once gained, however, the friendship was lasting. How could it be otherwise? Take only these three lives, German, English, and French; fundamentally they had been the same.

Herbert, partly orphaned by the war, whose small brother was torn in pieces, and over whose birthplace enemy aircraft dropped their bombs.

Robert Leroy, a twenty-year-old boy from St. Mihiel, where not a house is left standing in the state in which he knew it as a child. He lived through the destruction and dissolution of everything that he had known in childhood. He had known the enemy troops and had been told that they had come in time of peace, animated solely by a love of destruction and a criminal lust for conquest. When he came home for holidays he only had to walk a few steps beyond the rebuilt town into the fields where he had played until he was eight in order to see old wire entanglements, uprooted fields, ruined orchards that bore no fruit, and withered bushes eaten away by the poison gas that is stronger than life itself.

And I myself? Once upon a time there had been a castle in Tyrol and a park that had been my world. The castle still stands, and the fountains in the park are still playing. But I had been driven away, and the war had taken away the ground from under my feet. There had been years of famine because the other blockaded us in order to bring us *their* 'good fortune' and *their* form of 'liberation' in 'the name of humanity' — us, the German and Austrian children who died of consumption, school-friends who never returned, my father who was wounded in France, the war cripples who still continue to throng our streets!

A mighty Germany was the land of my childhood. Now it is the weakest among the nations of Europe. Eight years have passed away since the war. Nevertheless, when our statesmen attend international conferences they still have to fight for the barest justice to be done to our country. 'We like the new Germany' is to be heard everywhere. But nobody does anything to render its continued existence possible.

We on the other side are filled with envy and the longing for new and worthless power. We might enjoy justice and freedom, a mightier weapon than all the armaments of war, and instead we have turned rebellion and murder into political weapons, a procedure even approved by myself at the time of the murders of Kurt Eisner, Karl Liebknecht,

and Rosa Luxemburg. Even Rathenau's murder in 1922 did
not call forth my condemnation.

Was this to continue? A hundred little countries, each of
which might be truly great if it would respect the territorial
integrity of the others?

Subsequently I met with the same idea again in Weimar,
clothed in other words: 'Germany, disarmed and vanquished, is today a greater moral and intellectual force than
ever before.'

Is it really so difficult to believe in this idea? More
difficult than to forget what happened in Munich, more
difficult than to be faithless to history and early experiences
at the peasants' grave, on the Kalvarienberg, and in Wertheim?

I talked over all this with Gerd very thoroughly without
either of us reaching any definite conclusions. Everywhere,
we discovered, there were the older people who had learnt
nothing and forgotten nothing, there was the spectre of
Versailles and of those who had called it into existence, and
in our country all those who regarded their yearning for
another war as patriotic self-sacrifice.

We ourselves stood between the generations. Our willingness, our faith, everything we had to give counted for
nothing. Everyone thought us too young and said that we
had had no experience of life; and we were too old to identify
ourselves with the Present as those would be able to do who
were born after us and only knew of the war from books. It
seemed to be the same in every country and with the youth
of every nation, no matter which side they fought on in the
World War.

During the weeks that we spent in thinking over these
things the most important event that happened to us was
our discovery of the League of Nations. In the early days
of our stay at Geneva, Gerd and I absolutely refused to have
anything to do with it; to us the League was an infernal
creation full of French guile.

Since we had made friends with some foreigners, however,

we determined to examine the institution for ourselves. The first result of our investigations was a little surprising. We discovered that the wise men of the nations who were gathered together in Geneva not only talked amongst themselves much as if they were at school again, but also that they were continually whispering to their secretaries. In as much as there were some extremely pretty girls among them, we asked ourselves if this did not mean too much distraction for the good government of the world.

These were the months that preceded the entry of Germany into the League, and von Hoesch and Doctor Gauss were present as observers. I also remember Lord Cecil, Sir Austen Chamberlain, and Aristide Briand very well. But it was the interpreter who made the greatest impression on us. A delegate had hardly finished his speech in English before the interpreter stood up and repeated it in French, or vice versa as the case might be, with hardly any notes. Today I am convinced that he must previously have been given a copy of the very long speeches. In those days, however, we looked upon him as the man with the finest memory in the world.

Gradually we, and others from the group led by the rosy-cheeked officer, gained the impression that the League was a thoroughly humane institution that might one day render good service. At the time when the Spanish delegate declared that Spain would leave Geneva, we had already advanced so far in our regard for the League as to be angry with him.

At about that time we invented a new game. It consisted in trying to smuggle oneself into the most secret meetings of the Council. This was exceedingly difficult to achieve and usually ended in one's being thrown out. If, however, one was successful in getting inside and staying there for even a few minutes, one gained great kudos.

Those days in Geneva were the happiest and most carefree of all my university career. It was springtide for all the nations of Europe, and for us also. We often spent half the night on the lake, and one night (Midsummer Eve) we never went to bed at all. The English and the French boy and we Germans sat together by the lighthouse at the end of the long jetty and talked over our plans for the future.

I can compare these hours with those spent in our 'camp' at Gmunden. Once more the world seemed open before us; we only had to seize it to make it ours. When we had all become foreign ministers, or heads of states, in our own countries, we would meet again — best of all here in Geneva — and order the world anew. That would surely not be more difficult than had been the achievement of our present understanding!

In the course of this shortest night of all the year, June 21, another easier and more personal decision was taken. In the coming autumn Gerd and I would go to Berlin in order to pursue our studies in the very centre of the German Republic. For we should be better able to discover there than in even the great provincial universities what we had to do in order to find a new path for all of us to follow.

Our stay in Geneva came to an end soon afterwards. We all separated and went our own ways — youth from countries near and far — and we have never met since. Nevertheless I often think that each must have carried away something with him that he will not forget for the rest of his days, as myself and some of the other Germans did.

In the summer of 1926 I made my first trip to Italy. I must admit that during my travels I was not greatly concerned with the problem of Fascism or no Fascism, and indeed was disposed to see many advantages in Fascism, such as a renewal of ancient Roman traditions and forms and, as the well-known song says, the fulfilment of a youthful and heroic spirit.

At the time of my arrival in Rome an attempt had just been made on Mussolini's life. I was among the crowd that heard him speak from the balcony of the Palazzo Chigi. Although my knowledge of Italian was slight, his speech made a great impression on me and I said to myself: 'That's a different type of man from Hitler! One has only got to look at them both in order to see the difference!'

As the crowd dissolved to the accompaniment of wild outbursts of cheering, and I had made up my mind that every Italian was a Fascist, I fell into conversation with a young Fascist *Avanguardista* whom I had just heard shouting 'Duce! Duce!' at the top of his voice.

'Isn't Mussolini the greatest man who ever lived?' he asked me.

'I am sure he is,' said I, mustering my sparse Italian to try and make the answer sound more cordial.

'Or at least one of the greatest,' he modified his statement, and I replied, 'Undoubtedly.'

It went on as follows:

'Greater than Caesar! Or at all events nearly as great!'

'As Napoleon! Let us say, very much like Napoleon!'

'A very great man! He is certainly a great man!'

And then a longish pause:

'Do you know what he really is? A wild beast and the murderer of Italian freedom.'

After this I did not know for some time what to think.

My first sight of the Vatican was from the Capitol, a faint hemisphere, hardly connected with the earth, far beyond the city. Not until the evening of the third day did I stand at the gates of St. Peter's, and then they were already closed. Leaning against them I looked out across the vast court. In the fountains the shimmering rhythm of the rising and falling waters turned to misty rainbow colours in the moonlight, with the crucifix on top of the obelisk gleaming over all.

'*Vicit Leo de Tribu Juda*' — I cannot remember whether I had seen the inscription as I passed or whether I saw it from my present position. But I can see it clearly before my eyes when even I think of that hour. Many pilgrimages followed this evening at the gates of St. Peter's; inside the church, to the side chapel of the Pièta, and to the eighty-nine eternal lamps in front of the Crypto at the High Altar.

There are certain things that one does not care to express

in words and experiences that belong to oneself alone. So
I will say no more about these. My spiritual return to the
Catholic Church was accomplished during my visit to Rome.
Nevertheless, I have never ceased to believe that all of us
who serve the One Master should be bound together in the
bonds of mutual help and brotherly love.

From St. Peter's I went down three times into the 'Old
Grottoes' that contain the tomb of the Emperor Otto II.
He is the only one of the Roman-German emperors who is
buried in Rome. On his sarcophagus I saw a wreath of
laurels that an old lady renews in Ghibelline loyalty on
December 7 every year, the day on which the Emperor
died in 983.

My journeys and wanderings had taken a long time, and
I was obliged to think of going back north. Only at the
age of twenty is one sufficiently unselfconscious to take a
farewell of the kind that I made. At school we had read the
poem that Ovid wrote on the last night before he left Rome.
Goethe adapted it in German; and now that the end of my
tour lay before me, I went up once more to the Capitol and
recited to myself what I remembered of it:

> 'Cum subit illius tristissimae noctis imago
> Qua mihi supremum tempus in urbe fuit
> Cum repeto noctem qua tot mi cara reliqui
> Labitur ex oculis nunc quoque gutta meis.' [1]

I broke my journey only at Florence and Venice, spending
two days in each. Then I went on to Klagenfurt, to my
last visit to Rudolf Koenig.

There was an air of excitement about the place, for a new
master had just been appointed who was unusual in various
ways. He came from Wickersdorf in Thuringia, the most
modern school in Germany and the one with the fewest
rules; he was a Spanish marquis, of the family of the Duke
of Alba, born in Austria, whom I will call Fernando de

[1] 'When I remember that same fatal night,
The last that I enjoyed the city's right
Wherein I left each thing to me most dear
Then from my eyes there slideth down a tear.'

Avila, and he spoke of himself as a radical socialist. I met this man, who was eleven years older than myself, on the first evening of my visit, and we were soon on very friendly terms.

If I were really to describe him properly and as he deserves, I should have to write a whole book about him. I can do no more than enumerate certain of his characteristics, and I cannot vouch for its being a complete list. He was a mathematician, a historian, a classical philologist, a theoretical physicist, a geographer, with a thorough knowledge of each subject. He had an intimate acquaintance with German, English, French, Spanish, Italian, and Russian literature. The same was true of social economy, international economics, and sociology. I soon discovered that he himself wrote the most wonderful German lyric verse. Most of his poetry he kept in his head without writing it down, but he never forgot a line of it. He had several times in his life been very rich and very poor. During one of the latter periods, which still persisted, he had become a teacher, and so for the present he remained.

As far as one could judge, his clothing consisted chiefly of a raincoat. He always wore it, even in the house and at meals. He only removed it on special occasions, and then one saw that he was attired in a suit of black velveteen. Later on I found out that his wardrobe was full of a large variety of normal garments, which he used to brush carefully every evening. These peculiarities must have been the result of a shock he had during the war, for I never found any other explanation.

He had come home from the front once to find that his mother had gone mad, and nobody had told him. A disgusting smell assailed his nostrils as soon as he opened the door, and when he got into the living room his mother was sitting comfortably and happily by the fireplace.

'It was dreadfully cold,' she said, 'so I made a nice fire. Look ...'

He looked, and saw all his civilian clothes gently carbonizing.

To celebrate my arrival, Rudolph Koenig gave a banquet for all the pupils, and invited the Spaniard and myself to join him at his table. It was a waste of hospitality, because the Spaniard ate nothing at all and said he had a severe internal disease. After dinner he asked me whether I would not like to come into his room for a little while. He took an enormous sausage, weighing at least a pound and a half, out of the drawer of the table, and began eating it. At the same time he turned over the pages of the Court *Gotha*, turned up 'Loewenstein,' looked at me severely, and said:

'How do you come to be only in the Counts' *Gotha* and not in this one?'

'For several reasons,' I said, and first of all told him my family history; secondly, I said that since the year 1919 the Court *Gotha* had been the private property of the 'Union of German mediatized princes,' of the board of which my uncle was chairman; thirdly, that the whole thing was a dirty business anyway, because the Loewenstein-Wertheim family had no laws about equality of birth; one of our cousins married a certain Katharine Schlundt, the daughter of a soap-boiler in Wertheim — my father always called her a 'girl from the lower commercial ranks' — and she and her daughter were listed as princesses in the Court *Gotha*.

Hence, I concluded, I would not permit myself to be worse treated by the *Gotha* than the daughter of the soap-boiler, and should carry on the fight for my right to be mentioned in it, even if it should last for ten years.

Avila had not stopped chewing throughout the recital and had continued to gaze at me severely. Now that he had almost finished the sausage, he returned the tail-end of it to the drawer with the Court *Gotha*, and said:

'My dear fellow, you are perfectly right. Such a fight is a worthy fight — against the Court *Almanach*. Continue the struggle unceasingly; do not allow yourself to be put off it. Gather your forces, but not paper ones! What use is your princely passport to you, your father's princely certificate of birth, the official acknowledgment of your rights? Throw

212

them away! The only things that count are *deeds!* Listen, and learn from a most instructive case:

'I know a young man, a member of a princely house, of whom his cousin said that his father's marriage had been with a woman of unequal birth. He might have his title, but the rights of the mediatized princes? Absurd! The young man listened to this for years, until at last he had had enough of it and got married. And whom did he marry? The illegitimate daughter of the family cook. You can imagine the uproar that followed! A scandal in the newspapers, social boycott, and finally a family council. "Well," said the eldest member of the House, when they were all assembled, "well, my dear cousin, I was young myself once, a cavalry officer and all that — you take my meaning! When one sees a pretty girl..." "What do you mean, pretty?" replied the young man, "and what girl?" "The girl," said his elder, "hm, whom you married, of course." "But she isn't pretty," said the young man. "She's got prominent teeth, a bad figure, running eyes..."

'The family council was speechless. At length the head of the family smiled and said quite mildly: "Well, my dear cousin, of course that doesn't matter. One may be in love with a girl who, hm, isn't exactly a Venus of Milo. I dare say we've all done it in our time, eh?" "What do you mean, love?" said the young man. "Who says I'm in love with her? Have I ever said so?"

'At this even the old gentleman lost patience and said, "If you're not even in love with her, if she's ugly, and the illegitimate child of your cook, what in Heaven's name did you marry her for?" "Because," said the young man, picking up his hat, "I wanted to show you that I had the *right* to make a morganatic marriage. Who are the people who can make morganatic marriages? Only mediatized princes! I've done it, so I'm one of 'em!"'

When I went to bed that evening I felt a trifle confused, and did not know quite what to make of Fernando.

The next evening I spent with him was quite different. He told stories of the war and afterwards, when he had lived for a long time in the working-class quarters of Berlin. He had starved and studied and worked, but it was already before that time he had severed himself from his class.

'People who insist upon their rights,' he said, 'and who have done nothing to justify them for centuries! Have you ever looked closely at the pictures of Velasquez? His infantes and infantas — the wonderful colours of red and gold and silver, the garments of which each detail signifies power, and inside them figures which have lost all semblance even of intelligence — eyes, mouth, forehead, a sounding void, full of decadence and dullness. I don't know whether there is any reason at all in aristocracy nowadays. If there is, it is only because from its midst must come those who will destroy it.'

My experiences during those weeks were varied and the time passed rapidly. My birthday came — a year since I had been at Freudenberg, almost a year since I had gone to Hamburg; the end of that year had been no less eventful than its beginning.

Before I left there were other nights when I came to know French and German lyrics that were new to me. Stefan George, the herald of a new Reich and a new spirit:

'Neuen adel den ihr suchet
Fuehrt nicht her von schild und krone'[1]

Rainer Maria Rilke, the godly singer of beautiful death, some of Goethe, much of Hölderlin — 'it was he who invented poetry,' a friend of Avila's at Wickersdorf had said — and Baudelaire, Verlaine, Rimbaud, Mallarmé —

There we sat in a half-lit room, I and he, a little man, with a splendid great head and the most expressive mouth I had ever seen, and read. Until then I had never known what 'reading' could be: creation, moulding, poetry, a whole world of love and harmony.

What must he have suffered who had all this at his command? I realized it from his own works, dedicated to

[1] 'New nobility which ye seek
Do not derive from crest nor crown...'

his friend who fell in the war, works full of demons and men, of spirits of light and darkness.

One of them I shall never forget, about the heroic time of the Middle Ages which they praise. How simple, how easy, if I were my ancestor, starting forth to war with his lady's colours and whom the building of a chapel would save from hell and damnation. Nowadays dragons and giants are in our own souls. The battle is inglorious and without glamour, 'with blunt axe and closed vizor...'

Thus Klagenfurt became a farewell, an end and a beginning, both equally fraught with pain.

I went down to the school and talked to my former masters. I had been looking forward to it, but we had nothing to say to one another now. For them the world had come to a stop. Knowing that I had been abroad, they only asked me when the other nations were going to begin again and whether I, as a German, had been badly treated. One of them even wondered how much money Stresemann was being paid by France every year.

It was much the same with the boys. Until then my standards had remained those of my schooldays. Now a new generation had come up that hardly remembered me. Not until I spoke to the boys as I had heard Peter Vogt talk to his did I manage to establish some kind of contact; but it was a different sort, no longer that of a boy with his school-fellows.

As I left the houses with the red and blue balconies I felt that I should never see them again in just the same way. My forebodings proved correct. A fortnight after my departure Rudolf Koenig died of a heart attack. I grieved for him as if he had been my real father, and as though I now had to follow the path of my life alone.

During all the years that I had known him I had never left his house without some enrichment — the last time more than ever before.

XIV. *At the Threshold of Life*

I ARRIVED in Berlin on November 3, 1926, the Feast of St. Hubert. It was a clear autumn morning, with a pale blue sky and hoar frost on the trees.

I knew no one, had all the prejudices of a South German, and was confused by the bustle of the great city. Hamburg had been no preparation for it; it has too decided a character of its own to be typically North German, and at the same time is on the whole too old-fashioned to be a real contrast to the provincialism of Munich.

Somebody had told me of a residential quarter near the 'Bayrischer Platz,' and as that was the only name I knew, I enquired my way there by many different transport routes; when I finally reached my destination, I rented a room.

At the university I met a number of my Geneva friends: Gerd, the League of Nations enthusiasts, the baby-faced officer, and the two National Socialists.

The law course was accounted very difficult at Berlin University, and it was necessary to work very seriously if one was not to fail at the end. Hence this was an epoch in my life of which there is nothing much to tell. In common with the rest, I went to lectures, wrote papers, joined in a few debates, read newspapers in the reading-room, and abused the food in the students' dining-room.

Many of us had, in addition, all manner of love troubles; one went to places of amusement, which were very thrilling to me at first; then one got tired of them, and stayed at home in the evenings until one had been introduced to a few people.

At about this time I first met Prussian Junkers in any number. They were, as I soon discovered, very different from people of my class in South Germany.

There were many external differences to begin with. Our speech is broader than that of our North German cousins, and our behaviour, even in cases where we still cling to mediaeval custom, is nearer to the common people.

The High Nobility in South Germany, as well as certain baronial families in South and West Germany, are mostly of sovereign origin and have never treated the present rulers of their states as other than equals. I remember being told at Bamberg of the answer given by a Franconian nobleman when it was suggested to him to become a chamberlain of the King of Bavaria, since he was not otherwise entitled to appear at Court.

'Chamberlain?' he said. 'If I had the money I'd keep that sort of fellow, but I'm certainly not going to be one!'

The same feeling exists in the Rhineland and in Westphalia. The greatest statesman that Prussia ever possessed was the Rhenish Baron of the Empire, vom Stein, of whom it was said that he always regarded his ministerial relationship with King Frederick William III as a kind of treaty between two sovereigns.

Stein was a Liberal. He liberated the peasantry and the middle classes and became the founder of the modern State. Ricarda Huch even calls him 'Germany's secret Emperor.'

His downfall was due not so much to Napoleon as to a clique of Prussian Junkers who appealed to the King to protect 'the most sacred rights of the nation.' Since the words 'Red' and 'Bolshevism' did not exist in those days, they called Stein 'an agitator, a generation of vipers, and a Jacobin.'

Until Stein's time the Prussian monarchy had developed no democratic traits. It had for centuries relied upon the support of the army and the Junkers, from whom were drawn the officers and the higher civil servants. The South German monarchies, on the other hand, had never been without certain democratic elements, and there have always been some among the South German nobility, both in ancient and modern times, who have fought for the rights of the people. One knows of the revolutionaries Franz von Sickingen and Ulrich von Hutten, and of the leaders of the peasantry, Goetz von Berlichingen and Florian Geyer.

In the nineteenth century Ludwig II of Bavaria, for all his eccentric faith in his divine right, was a people's prince, and so were the King of Wuerttemberg and the Grand Dukes of Baden and Hesse. And the only Liberal reich chancellor of Bismarckian Germany was a South German dynast, Prince Chlodwig von Hohenlohe.

The fact that there were Liberal exceptions among the Junkers does not affect the general rule. As a class they were always a stronghold of reaction, and have ever been a source of surprise to every South German who has come in contact with them. I, in my turn, found considerable entertainment in observing the life and doings of these circles of Society; there was much which struck me as curious.

In Napoleonic days, as is well known, there lived a really great poet of Junker origin from the Mark, named Heinrich von Kleist, and a special celebration was to be held in his honour by the Nobles' Club (*Adelsgenossenschaft*) in Berlin. To inaugurate the proceedings an individual, by no means elderly, good-looking, and wearing the cross of the Knights of St. John, mounted the platform.

'We are met today,' he said, 'to celebrate, er, the memory, er, of our fellow aristocrat, Herr von Kleist.' I paid no further attention to his speech, but felt that the Thuringian Civil Servants should be induced to hold a celebration in honour of their 'colleague, Privy Councillor von Goethe.'

In the anterooms of the Nobles' Club that evening I had heard mention of a young 'Count Bernard von ——,' a very well-known South German name. Soon afterwards I met him first in one house, then in another, and then everywhere.

Count Bernard was about seventeen; he had a pleasing manner, and was obviously in high favour with various elderly gentlemen. He was treated with particular courtesy: 'How nice of you to give us the honour, Herr Graf ——.' The young man smiled most winningly in response, but seemed somehow to find my presence irksome.

There was something not quite in order; so much was clear. To begin with he said, 'The stove smells unpleasantly,' as if he were a footman. (We should say, 'The stove stinks.') Secondly, he used words like 'refined' and 'aristocratic,' and thirdly he folded his napkin after dinner, though he was not in his own home. Worse still, he addressed a lady as '*Frau* Baronin' instead of 'Baronin.' No South German would ever do such a thing, and if he did, so my father always said, you couldn't have anything to do with him socially.

That was just it. Personally one might see whom one liked, but one had to know whom one could bring together socially. No one seemed to know that here, and no one seemed to notice anything. The affair bothered me, and it was not long before he told me the truth, under a vow of secrecy. 'Count Bernard' was the son of a cobbler in Munich. At the age of fourteen he had been a lift boy, at sixteen he was discovered by a philanthropic Prussian Junker and taken to Berlin.

As in the famous case of the alleged Hohenzollern, 'Prince' Harry Domela, the boy had at first made no sort of claim to be anything but what he was. It was the somewhat romantically minded man from Brandenburg who gradually persuaded himself as well as the boy that he must be 'something better,' whereupon the youth at last decided to make a 'confession.' Since his mother had once been in service with the family of a count he adopted their name, and eventually a whole story was invented for him — artistic leanings, misunderstood by his father, ran away from home, and so on. After a year he was accepted everywhere and had picked up the social tone of his surroundings wonderfully. He showed me excessively funny letters which proved over and over again the immense reverence of those with lesser titles for a count. In South Germany it is quite immaterial what a man's title is so long as he is in Society at all.

I do not know how the affair ended, but I hope he has proceeded gaily on his career as Count, and has made many a mere 'Herr von ——' happy with it. At all events, when I wrote a long article about it some time later in the Berlin monthly *Querschnitt*, I altered the names so completely that I am quite certain it can have done him no harm.

Most of the Junkers I met were German Nationals, but there were also a few Nazis among them. The few who were members of the Republican parties and were thus deserters from their caste, were regarded as suffering from some nervous complaint. They were always referred to as 'poor So-and-so.' Later I came to know one of them, a certain Baron von Reibnitz; but he was a Silesian, so that he was not really one of themselves, and therefore need not be judged by such high standards. He was a Socialist and was Prime Minister of Mecklenburg-Strelitz, where he did excellent political and social work.

So far as my own political feelings went at that time, I used to be irritated by hearing German National talk; and one day when a Foreign Office official said to me, 'What is your objection to the SA and the Stahlhelm? They are quite decent people and by no means against the State, only against the Constitution,' I was seriously annoyed.

But there was no more to it than that. It never occurred to me to take an active part in any political work.

So I am afraid I must own that vast Berlin, the real, new Berlin, the Berlin of the Republican workers and Democratic burghers, remained a closed book to me. It therefore seems to me that it will be best to pass quickly over this period. Who would be interested to hear details of my intercourse with people of yesterday, and of what I did while I was a student of Roman and German Law, which libraries I studied in, or which articles of civil procedure I debated with my fellows?

I will note only one day, September 11, 1927, because it was on this day that I first met my wife. I shall give a perfectly unsentimental account of it, nor do I intend here or elsewhere to recount my own or my wife's personal feelings.

MY WIFE, HELGA MARIA

Soon after I left Klagenfurt, Fernando de Avila also left and returned to Wickersdorf. From there he used often to come up to Berlin, and he and I kept up a fairly regular correspondence. When he invited me to come down and see him at Wickersdorf, I accepted with pleasure, for I had long felt an interest in this school. It was the first in Germany to introduce co-education and democratic administration by the pupils themselves.

On the afternoon of my arrival he took me in to tea with the pupils, among whom was my future wife Helga Schuylen-burg. Just as we got to the door he told me a silly but very amusing story, and I was for several minutes too overcome with laughter to be able to speak a word. So I cannot im-agine that the first impression she had of me can have been a very good one.

Helga was of Dutch and Norwegian extraction, but had been living in Germany for years, and her cultural and his-torical ties were with this country. When I first knew her she was seventeen years old, and one of Avila's pupils. She was related to him through the Duke of Alba.

I wonder what we talked about at this tea-party? I suppose the same kind of thing that one talks about at all tea-parties. But when I was alone again I said to myself, 'What a pity, my bachelor days will soon be over; because obviously I shall marry Helga Schuylenburg.'

And so I did. And when we had become engaged I told her what my thoughts had been on the first evening. She said that at the same time she, of course in a modified way, had thought the same.

In considering the political passivity of so many of my year, very curious facts come to light.

Our studies of course had something to do with it, but there was something more besides; it was in fact the very thing that I had feared ever since the end of my schooldays. We were squeezed in between the war generation and the post-war generation, too young for the one and too old for the other. Only those of us whose sympathies were with the labour movement had any freedom of action. But even in the labour movement it was necessary to go very far Left — perhaps even to the Communists — if one were to make any sort of mark at the age of twenty-one or two. It is true that young Communists told me they had the same trouble with men who had been to the front, who knew everything there was to know and did not like giving the new generation any say.

I think that this did a great deal of harm to us, and probably to our whole country as well. The years 1926–1929 were peak years in Europe, years of real reconciliation, when Germany enjoyed a position such as it had not had for centuries. A nation of workers, burghers, and peasants was growing up, and a youth which was shaking off the limitations of its social origins. In the playgrounds, in the modern schools, on the highroads, in the hills, and on the lakes, a new race was in process of development, human beings who vanquished war by learning to control, to transform, to beautify, their own bodies.

Yet when I think of it, this new spirit must have affected us too. Among the students of at least the great universities drinking and rowdyism went out of fashion, the false romanticism of pre-war student life disappeared. In the bright lecture-rooms of Berlin University there was no room for the stuffy fumes of beer or the reek of carbolic on duellists' faces.

We began to have new standards for what was 'heroic' and what was bad form. Even we who remained passive in the political battles of the day took an active interest in the lectures in which the legal foundations of the new State were discussed. We debated passionately the project for a new and more humane Criminal Code, which should be based not on guilt and revenge but on improvement and education. We rejoiced that many ideas which had descended to us from an age of disgusting hypocrisy and reactionary ignorance were to be abandoned, and that capital punishment was to be abolished.

Moreover we made ourselves acquainted with a new set of ideas: the labour and social legislation. The Constitution of the Reich had laid the foundations for it and it had been developed on a magnificent scale. The laws of collective bargaining, of social and old-age insurance, of government arbitration in labour disputes, now all this seemed proper to us, the kind of thing to which one ought to agree, something that was obviously right.

We accepted this new State which had fallen into our lap as if it were a scientific discovery or a modern invention which one would not like to be without. But we did not feel at home in it.

I do not believe that among my fellow students there were more than two or three who felt that they had a really personal interest in the Republic — and this at a time when our proletarian brothers of the same age had already grown completely into the new political order.

Hence, even if we had not been prevented from any active co-operation, we should have had no idea how to fit ourselves into the new scheme of things. It is for this reason that certain of the middle-class young people did not wish to join extreme Left parties but who nevertheless were anxious to overcome their political passivity went to the other extreme and joined the Right-Wing Radicals, where it was easier to avoid competition with Labour Youth.

In November, 1928, I passed the State examination at the *Kammergericht*[1] in Berlin. Everything went well at the beginning, and there was nothing to show the complications which were to set in on the last day of the written examination.

I can still see the whole thing clearly. Thirty or forty of us were shut up for four hours in one of the large rooms in the Law Courts, writing the answers to an examination paper. It concerned a most complicated legal case, so senseless that anyone would drop it at once if it occurred in real life. At last it was finished, and nothing remained but horrid fears of wrongly quoted paragraphs of the Civil Code. And after that one had even to fix all the pages together. A needle and thread were supplied for this purpose at one's desk, and I

[1] The Supreme Court of Prussia.

thought of all the times when I had torn my trousers as a youngster and tried to mend them without anyone's finding out. Even in those days it was hard to get the thread through the eye of the needle.

So I rose and carried my papers, the needle, and the thread up to the supervisor's desk. A man was sitting there whom I took to be a clerk and who would be certain to know how it was done.

'I simply can't do this on top of everything else,' I said, and handed the whole thing over to him. The students sat up in boundless astonishment. They all laid down their pens and waited to see what would happen.

The man at the desk also looked rather surprised; then he picked up the papers and began to sew busily. When it was finished he found it was all wrong and had to be done over again. Afterwards they told me that he was a Judge at the Kammergericht, and if I got him for my viva, things might be lively.

I did. But it went off all right, although in one case that I cited I completely mixed up A, B, and X, and he said to me:

'You have a perfect genius for confusing the persons!'

What the actual legal relations should have been I have never to this day found out. When the bell went we were still arguing about it, and before I knew where I was my university days were over, and there was one more school which I had outgrown.

A few days after the examination was over, I went to Meran, and there in my beloved South Tyrol, among the mountains of my childhood, I questioned my conscience:

What have you done so far? Have you done all the things which birth, experience, and circumstances should have induced you to do? You are now twenty-two years old, and have been to universities for which many another yearns in vain. You have been abroad and have had the opportunity of bursting through the ring that war had drawn round yourself and your friends . . . . You have lived and worked in Germany. But have you learnt to know your own people?

Those were the fundamental questions, and an honest answer to them filled me with shame and remorse at the amount of time I had wasted.

What was I to do next? What occupation should I follow, after all I had done to prepare myself? There were various possibilities — lawyer, career as judge, diplomatic service, government administration — or something mercantile. I did not know what the answer was yet, but I felt that I should soon find it out.

The weather was warm, despite the fact that it was evening and the first week in December. I went out, along the riverbank all along the promenade, where there were very few people.

I slowly climbed the winding path up the Tappeinersteg — everyone knows it who has ever been in the South Tyrol — until the town with all its lights lay below me. I saw the transparent whiteness of the peaks of a mountain and the pale shimmer of villages and castles on distant hills. Then it was that pictures came to me from the faint memories of past years, and with them everything which had been overlaid with other cares but never forgotten.

My answer stood before me as a giant, it stretched out impalpable hands towards my soul, and filled all my mind, everything that I desired and felt. I knew with a certainty surer than mere supposition, greater than simple recognition, that all I had been thinking of in the way of careers was nothing; it was flight, it was flinching from the path, it was the death of my truest self. I knew that I had not been born to interpret laws but to improve them.

Did I intend to be an official and to carry out mechanical duties? Or a diplomatist and maintain the country's relations, when what the country really needed was to be liberated — internally more than externally? Or a merchant, to earn money for the sake of money, simply as a gesture of defiance because I had been taught that noblemen should not go into trade?

No, that was not the way to conquer the past; not by denying history and my birth, not by casting off tradition, could I be free. It is that which you remould and revive which makes you free.

What shall I call it? In what words can I clothe this experience? I will call it the voice of the Law, the angel who guards our footsteps, the daemon whom none can escape; let him who meets him hold him fast and until he gives his blessing....

Peter Vogt wrote in a book that he gave me while I was in Hamburg: 'Philosophers have merely interpreted the world in different ways. The important thing is to change it.' It was a saying of Karl Marx. And so I had taken no notice of it at the time. Now I remembered it, this deepest, most Christian admonition to duty and service and responsibility.

'The important thing is to change it'; that implied deeds, and sacrifice, which knows no end. Should I succeed?

I did not return until late. But that very night, between December 6 and 7, I headed a sheet of paper with the words:

'The Constitution of the New Reich.'

And many thoughts followed the first this night.

I must give the salient points of this Constitution here, because from that time onward there was no thought, no decision, hardly even a journey or a holiday, that was not in some way connected with it. No external occurrence could make any change in that, either at that time or at any time in all the years that have passed since then.

In so far as this Constitution — which aims at a general European future, a Western Reich of free nations — has room for a German 'foreign policy,' it is based upon the following lines.

Germany, true to its historic mission as heir to the Holy Roman Empire of the German Nation, regards it as its duty to promote the peaceful union of all European peoples.

Germany, in the multitude of its races and civilizations, is in itself an image of the Occidental Oecumene. Germany's intellectual prominence in Europe is greater than any

226

military glory. In giving the example of disarmament and co-operation with all, upon the basis of international law and international arbitration, it will convince even the most stubborn chauvinists in the neighbouring countries, or at least will cause them to disarm by the pressure of public opinion.

Once this has been done, European nations will be sufficiently established to protect themselves against the temptation of Communism or the pressure of Fascism.

Two things are necessary for this: complete economic and political democracy with a strong democratic leadership, and a social justice that is greater than that of Communism.

The present parliamentary system alone is not sufficient for political democracy, because Parliament does not represent all the popular forces. Still less, of course, would these be represented in the reactionary mirage of the so-called Corporative State, which has recently been haunting the minds of hypocrites lusting after power and pretended Democrats, and which is vaunted by them as a 'Christian solution.'

In order that all popular trends may be represented in the life of the State, the people must be gathered into comprehensive and autonomous associations, similar in structure and organization to that of the Reich as a whole.

One such association should consist of workers, another of the young up to the age of twenty-four, and a third of those who are responsible for industries and enterprises of all descriptions. The free election of representatives and leaders will be guaranteed by the Constitution.

Among the workers, trade and professional unions have important functions to fulfil, as have leagues, schools, and universities among the young. A special and most carefully worked out system applicable to every walk of life among the people provides for a continual influx of new forces and the attraction of all particularly suitable and talented persons, wherever their homes may be.

That various associations should overlap is an advantage, and not a disadvantage, because a man's relations with the

State are different according to whether his status is that of a youth, a worker, or a young worker.

The representatives of the various associations will be united in a second Supreme Governmental Body, which shares the work of legislation with Parliament.

Private property is a loan by the community to the individual. If the individual administers it badly, he may be deprived of it by a strictly regulated legal procedure.

The land of the Reich is the common property of the people of the Reich. Peasant properties are to be increased, large estates to be broken up. Internal colonization, which would make room for millions of free people within Germany, must be carried out.

Collective organizations for the cultivation of small and medium-sized peasant farms, and for the sale of their products, will be brought into being by the Government.

There shall be legal maxima for property and income which may not be exceeded by anyone.

A Central Economic Council of the Reich, consisting of representatives of workers, burghers, and peasants, under the chairmanship of the Head of the Government, shall organize the systematic production and distribution of goods.

The Reich believes in free trade.

The cost of education shall be borne by the community. The schools — built as far as possible outside the towns — shall be based upon collaboration between teachers and democratically organized pupils.

The imperial idea in German history is welded into the structure of the political organization.

The highest office of the Reich shall be handed on by the adoption of a successor in co-operation with the whole nation.

It will be a Christian Reich, Christian in its every act, not merely boasting of its religion or degrading it to a formula. That is to say, it will respect the liberty, dignity, and life of the individual. Thus the Reich is in absolute contrast to Communism and Fascism.

When capital serves the community thus, and the 'capitalist' will of necessity be changed into a trustee, the proletariat will be deproletarianized and the social injustice of Democracy will disappear, which in its present form lead to the sham solution of either Fascism or Communism.

This act will mark the beginning of a new civilization, for where there is misery and oppression, hatred and barbarism will arise.

The first steps to be undertaken in foreign policy towards realizing an Occidental Community are fresh agreements with Germany's neighbouring States, especially with the Western Powers. Then a general office to deal with the economic and foreign affairs of all the democratic nations of Europe might be planned within the framework of the League of Nations.

Austria is a part of the Reich, in accordance with his history, and as was planned in the first drafts of the German and Austrian post-war constitutions, which were only altered under external pressure. This inclusion would strengthen the Catholic, Socialist, and Democratic forces, and make any attempt at a Fascist *Putsch* impossible.

Laws and constitutions always sound very dry, so I will not go into further details. Instead I will spend a moment over the fundamental ideas and the kind of spirit that I should like to see immanent in our nation and in all nations.

Under the influence of the materialistic view of history, the working class has been alienated from Germany's Christian tradition, and to a large extent believes that a State can be built up on a purely utilitarian basis. Faults, mistakes, and blindness on the part of the Christian churches have aggravated this condition.

A large section of the middle classes, again, has never got beyond a somewhat empty form of liberalism, or has succumbed to nationalistic reactionary tendencies.

Anyone who has ideals or believes himself to have them is driven into the arms of Right or Left Wing radicalism in Germany. The Right believe that it is possible to create a 'new spirit' by means of militarization and regimentation, by the dictatorship of a party and a megalomaniac nationalism. The young generation of the middle and upper classes finds this the more attractive system because their parents tell them of the good old days in Germany when there were black-white-red flags everywhere, and the people could take a pride in their 'shining armour.' That this helped to bring about war and collapse has long been forgotten or is intentionally suppressed.

The principles of government of the Left are no different. Communism too has its militarism, its regimentation, its dictatorship. But it is understandable that sections of the working classes and certain types of intellectuals are attracted to it.

The German Republic, which stands between the two extremes, does not yet appear to have found its own solution. It cannot be done by simply talking about democracy and making peace resolutions. The sacred fire of the love of freedom, of passionate enthusiasm for peace must be kindled in the nation.

Peace is more than merely not waging war. Peace means work, service to the community, religious experience, travel in foreign countries, and the abolition of social evils.

Today, in 1928, I said to myself, our direct military expenditure runs into six hundred million marks a year, and another two hundred million marks are being spent for indirect military purposes. Who shall protect us against the risk that some other government will spend ten times that amount on armaments?

This amount of money would enable us to rebuild our slums within a very few years. Garden cities might flourish where today there are narrow streets and dark tenement houses. There is no end to what could be done. And this is no Utopian ideal, no dream of the future. Nothing is needed save the spirit that in law and action will fundamentally transform what is static and traditional.

Before returning to my chronicle, I will, disregarding possible scoffers, say a few words to explain my new religious attitude, just as I have spoken above of the 'matter-of-course Catholicism' of my childhood, of the religious crises of later years, and of my experiences in Rome.

No one who regards Christianity as a thin aesthetic veneer, as a pretty philosophy, or as something concerned 'only' with religion, has any community of spirit with Christ. His life, death, and resurrection are only fulfilled by those who recognize Him in all human relationships, in politics, economics, education, in every drop of our blood, in every piece of food that we eat.

Therein lies the solution of the social problem. It is only necessary to accept literally and to understand the meaning of what He says: 'My flesh is meat indeed, and my blood is drink indeed.'

Social justice, international law, national requirements: for all this the right form is found, once the unity of all in the Mystic Body is recognized.

Anyone who does not admit it — and how few of our statesmen, sociologists, and philosophers do — may make laws, give constitutions, rearrange the balance of power in the State, and make international agreements. It will all be dust, mirage, and destruction.

'To the Jews a stumbling block, to the Greeks foolishness' is the beginning and the end of human and governmental wisdom. The deliverance of a spirit that has grown barren, of an intellect that can only destroy, that has grown too clever to be wise, that passes by simple things in order to stumble over what is complex, that is full of doubts because it is ashamed to believe, that continually seeks new systems only to throw them aside on the morrow; of an understanding grown rigid, netted in its own mistaken thoughts, without love or mercy: deliverance from all this, change and liberation, can only be effected by the power that is still hardest for men to understand, because there is no human image for it: by the Holy Spirit whom to send the Son was crucified, rose again, and ascended to Heaven.

During this time of insight, Advent had approached. Before it was fulfilled I wrote to Helga, whom I knew to be in

Paris, and suggested that we should go to Florence in order to spend Christmas there together.

I have known Christmas in many towns, but I think it is most beautiful in Florence. There is a festive spirit over the whole town, in the street markets, at the wax chandlers, in all the churches. Before the dim altars that are never without worshippers, innumerable lamps and candles are burning; while anyone looking across the landscape from the hills outside the town can already see a faint flush heralding the spring over the dark pines, cypresses, and vineyards.

At a silversmith's on the Ponte Vecchio I found a piece of jewellery as a Christmas present for Helga, a Saint George, the human prototype of the Archangel Michael, such as I had worn myself as a child. On December 27 we got engaged. Soon afterwards she went to Holland and I to Rome. From there I wrote and said that I should like to be married in Palermo, a town dear to us on account of its Hohenstauffen history.

Three weeks in Rome and one in Naples revived in me the feeling that is never altogether absent in Italy — of the unity of culture and the common history of the North and South throughout the centuries of Christendom.

We remained in Palermo almost two months, making numerous excursions round the island, to the cliff gardens of Taormina, the ruins of Segesta, and the temples of Agrigento.

Once too we went to Messina from Reggio de Calabria, across the narrow Straits in which there are more dolphins than waves. It was a gruesome feeling to go through this town, remembering the tidal wave that had reached me as a child at the other end of the same sea.

We also saw the mosaics in Cefalù, in the Capella Reale of the palace at Palermo, and in Monreale. It was there that I remembered my dream experience of Byzantium.

On all these visits we spoke of the spirits of Norman kings and German emperors as though this were still their realm and we in it as their guests. So much of the past became intermingled with our lives that it is almost impossible now to separate them. It seems to me now that it must have been much as it was in the days when I possessed all the kingdoms of the world in the park at Schoenwoerth and beyond, and again when I bestowed estates and provinces upon Waldemar Claus.

We were married on the morning of April 4, 1929. But we did not exchange rings until the evening of the same day at the tomb of the Emperor Frederick II in the cathedral at Palermo.

There was a stormy sea on the following day when we sailed for Naples. Then we proceeded to Rome and Florence. After a few weeks' glorious spring there, we returned to Berlin in May.

Soon afterwards I went to Hamburg and asked my former tutor, Professor Albrecht Mendelssohn-Bartholdy, to be allowed to write my doctor's thesis for him. I chose as subject a comparison between Italian Fascism and the Constitution of the German Republic.

I like to think back to this period, when I read about the German Constitution and the history of its birth in the Berlin libraries with real knowledge and understanding for the first time. I came to comprehend the nineteenth century's heritage of freedom, the constitutional struggles in France, Belgium, and England, and the history of our own revolution in 1848.

Did this not link up clearly with everything that I had felt as a child, of which I babbled before I could speak it? 'A Republic with an Emperor at its head,' with justice for the people, liberty and happiness for all. The best men had hoped for this, and yet it had collapsed. Reaction triumphed, absolutism, Prussian bayonets; thousands had to go into exile, to France, and to the United States.

At the same time I read Heinrich Heine — an exile of his own free will — in order to understand the spirit of those times, without which our own could not be imagined.

> 'Denk ich an Deutschland bei der Nacht
> Bin ich um den Schlaf gebracht,' [1]

---

[1] 'Think I of Germany at night
I lie awake till dawning light.'

233

he wrote, and spoke for many to whom their fatherland had been closed because they believed in liberty and equality.

Emigrants — exiles because of their love for their country, persecuted, oppressed, suffering, hoping, ever waiting. I was told that in the American regiments, whose entry into the war decided the issue against us, there were many sons and grandsons of the exiles of '48 — Germans, whom Germany had expelled.

I was seized with a kind of shudder, like a dark cloud over the brightness of the Berlin summer and over the black-red-gold flags of the Republic, which had flown back to the towers and masts of Germany in 1919 from misery and persecution. What should I do if I had to leave thee, my fatherland, not to return for long years, like those to whom we owed our present freedom?

But that would never happen. Freedom is firmly rooted in our soil now, it is the foundation for our future, the brazen tablet of our laws; it lies before me, in the book of which the first words are:

'The German nation, united in its peoples, and animated by the desire to renew its Reich in liberty and justice . . .'

It is headed 'The Constitution of the German Reich,' but the people call it 'The Constitution of Weimar,' after Goethe's town, where the National Assembly created the new State and out of the old hopes, longings, and struggles showed the way into the future.

I read of all this during the summer. It captured me like a dream come true, strong and intoxicating, like the experience of a great happiness.

This was when the first stones were already loosening in the edifice of this State beyond the confines of the library, in the country and in the seats of power. I noticed nothing. So much sacrifice had already been required, I may have thought, that everyone would rally to protect the German Republic if ever an enemy should come to wrest our freedom from us again.

XV. *Land of Promise*

*W*HEN I had finished the German part of my work we went back to Italy.

We rented a house above Florence, not far from the Piazzale Michelangelo, which had once been a monastery. The former refectory was our drawing-room. It was a glorious Gothic hall, and large enough for us to receive numerous guests. But it had its drawbacks.

Anyone who thinks Italy is warm in winter is not speaking from personal experience. One feels the cold worse there, than in northern countries because one is expecting to be warm. When we had people to see us, we had to arrange them in three concentric rings round the stove. Between the circles we put oil stoves, and even then it was as well for everyone to keep his coat on.

Our economic situation was not altogether easy at that time, because there had once again been all manner of family strife, and as a result financial losses. Hence we were only able to afford to keep a peculiar Italian maid called Claudia, who came to work or not as it suited.

Once we had invited a large party to tea, among them an old lady who was greatly feared by all Florence. If we offended her there was sure to be a great deal of unpleasant talk. So it was very important that Claudia should be present.

Of course she was nowhere to be found, not a sign of her either to wait at tea or even to open the door. The only thing we could do was to get a friend to station himself in the entrance hall and to wait until everyone had arrived.

When the bell rang, he opened the door and pretended that he had just arrived himself — he hung his coat over one shoulder to make it seem more likely.

Claudia did not reappear until the following morning, and her reasons were perfectly valid: 'We had a wedding at our place,' she said, 'and I got so drunk that I should only have been a scandal anyway.'

I continued my thesis in the National Library and at the University of Florence. I went to work quite objectively, and forced myself to study the Fascist system, not with any preconceived opinions but purely on the basis of its own ideas and from the effects it had had on the country. I believed myself able to say some things in its favour, but I felt forced to reject it unconditionally as a whole, both in idea and in effect. It gave me final proof that every dictatorship, even though it may achieve external success, is worse than the worst democracy, for there are always possibilities of evolution in the latter which are destroyed by dictatorship.

Above all, in the life of nations it seemed to me that only democracies could contribute towards the peace and well-being of the community, while every nation ruled by a dictator was obliged sooner or later to seek refuge in war.

In the course of my work, which took me the whole winter of 1929–1930, I thought over carefully what I was to do when I returned to Germany. I thought I would confine myself to theoretical work: first, finish off the draft of my Constitution, and then expand the ideas in my thesis into further writings. I purposed keeping altogether aloof from the political struggle of the day, in order to be perfectly free to work for the maintenance and perfecting of the Democracy.

With these plans we returned to Berlin, once again in the month of May, and took a flat in Südende, a pretty residential suburb. Our friends soon came to see us here. There was Fernando de Avila, who brought one of his pupils, called Volkmar, with him, various of the Geneva people, including a Communist whom I will call Heinz — he had been a school-fellow of Helga's — and suddenly one day Waldemar Claus, with whom I never had quite lost touch since we met again in Hamburg.

I had known him for many years now, but I had another surprise when I met him this time. His thin face, in which the eyes were the most telling feature — dark blue with black lashes — was still tanned by the sea wind of his years in Hamburg. He had a forcefulness of expression that was too exalted to be hard. I never seemed to have noticed his hands before. Now I observed that they were slender and strong, such as I had only seen once before on the statue of a Portuguese cardinal who had died young, in the Church of San Miniato near Florence.

Under the influence of Peter Vogt he had meanwhile become a member of the Reichsbanner. When he came to see us he very often wore the uniform of a Youth Leader, which looked on him like a suit of flexible armour, needing neither ornament nor addition.

From him I heard what was going on in Germany. Beneath an apparently calm surface, a continual guerilla warfare was in progress between the Radicals and Republicans, meetings were broken up, attacks made in the open streets or from ambushes. Very often National Socialists and Communists were united against the Reichsbanner and other constitutional associations.

So he had after all decided to descend into the political arena, I said.

He was very glad to have done so, he replied, because now he had found a form of fellowship that was above class and calling. In the Reichsbanner one very often did not know to what party the members belonged, and if all went well, it should be the germ of the democratic State community of the future.

'Of course we still have a few old stodgers among the leaders,' he said, 'who have never advanced at all, but we shall manage them all right.'

'Are you the only intellectual among them?' I enquired.

'Not the only one. We have a few men who have their

degrees, and quite a good group at the university in the Republican Students' Union (*Republikanischer Studenten-bund*). But still there are too few. It would be a good thing if some more intellectuals would join.'

'Aren't they looked on with suspicion?'

'Yes and no. It takes a little while for the workers' lads to get used to them, but then they make first-rate leaders.'

These were serious matters which must be carefully thought over. They were certainly not as simple as Walde-mar supposed. Firstly, I was still far from convinced that I should find the right way of treating them. Secondly, there would be a fearful hullabaloo — I could imagine the headlines in the newspapers. A prince in the Reichsbanner, allied with the Social Democrats . . . !

But somehow it must be done, none the less; theses alone would not be sufficient.

After I had pondered it all, I wrote an article entitled 'The Third Reich.' I said that the National Socialists had no real idea of what it meant to be German. The Reich whose history they wished to ape had been a Christian community of European nations. But if Hitler came to power, there would immediately be oppression and war.

I said nothing to anyone about this article, but left it lying on my desk, where a friend of mine who was one of the sub-editors of the *Vossische Zeitung* saw it. On the following day, July 12, it was published.

The effect was rapid. All the Right papers published furious replies — the National Socialist of course more violent than any. The *Völkische Beobachter*, for instance, said that the National Socialists were, it is true, peacefully inclined; but if Germany was only able to survive if all the other nations went to the devil, they would not care.

I also received many letters, signed and unsigned, friendly and otherwise; in short, it was another arrow in a hornet's nest, and Waldemar said that now I should have to go on fighting whether I liked it or not.

There might not have been quite so much excitement over it if my article had not happened to burst into the beginning of the election campaign. Brüning, the Reich Chancellor, dissolved Parliament on July 18, and then began a turbulent and exciting time.

Before long there was not an empty space left on walls or hoardings. Placards of all colours, containing all the promises in the world, with attacks, mockery, prophecies, and appeals, were everywhere, such as Germany had never seen before. It was as though the end of the world were at hand, and a thousand different religions were trying at the last moment to entice as many souls as possible into their respective paradises.

I hardly saw Waldemar Claus in these weeks. He seemed to be on duty day and night, guarding meetings, canvassing, making speeches. He was not even in Berlin for the great festival of the Weimar Constitution on August 11.

I shall never forget this August 11 in the middle of the election campaign. In company with the man who had published my first article I spent the whole day, starting in the early morning, watching all the Republicans gathering in every part of Berlin for the festivities.

At lunch time I saw President Hindenburg in company with Gröner, the Minister for Defence, leaving the Reichstag where the members had met for a special session.

As Hindenburg — this was the first time I had seen my childhood's idol quite near — passed down the guard of honour, hundreds of thousands of people broke into cheers that seemed never ending.

Still more impressive were the masses who demonstrated along Unter den Linden in the evening. Once again I stood on the steps of the Reichstag building and saw the endless train of workers and burghers, marching in procession, led by the Reichsbanner with flags and torches.

A few days later my second article appeared in the *Vossische Zeitung*. It was called 'Celebration of the Constitution during the Election Campaign,' and gave a description of my own experiences. 'Something has been built up in the hearts of the German people,' I said, 'which will be lasting. If the spirit of this August 11 is preserved, the Reichstag that has

239

just been dissolved may be the last to collapse on account of disunion among the Republicans.'

This article brought me a special visit from Waldemar Claus, which I shall always remember. I was very pleased to see him, for what could he do but praise my attitude? Instead he said abruptly:

'Your articles? Are you really satisfied to go on writing newspaper articles and theses while others are in the thick of the fight? I used to think that there was good stuff in you, but I see you are afraid of the opinion of your own class. Don't you see that they have been your enemies ever since you have been able to think for yourself? — reactionaries, great estate owners, men who have failed to move with the times — in politics they are no different from what they were in the old days at Gmunden.

'No? You're not afraid? Then you are still nothing but a dreamer and a visionary as you were ten years ago. I know exactly what you are going to say: that I joined in all your plans. So I did. We were in our 'camp' together; we lay on our backs and stared at the sky, and divided up the world. We were going to make everyone happy, and there should be no more misery, and nobody should be hungry any more.

'Wherever we went to see how our laws were being carried out, the people would cheer and shout "Long live Hubertus!"

'All Germany was to be ours and then all Europe. And when everything was fulfilled a new Golden Age had dawned, and all tears had been dried, then we should sail across the sea, and you would lay down the crown by the withered tree that would burst into bud and blossom.

'I remember all that exactly. I have not forgotten a word of our conversations. We had discovered a book then with an old saying in it which we read over and over again, after you had taken me to the Kalvarienberg. There you told me about your November evening, what you intended doing and how you came too late. Then you told us that the hour would still come for us — and the old verse would tell us when:

240

'Doch wird das Streiten einst so gross dass niemand es kann stillen,
Kommt Kaiser Friedrich hehr und Wild zu uns nach Gottes Willen.
An einem dürren Baume hängt auf er seinen Schild.'¹

'You see, I can even remember the verse, in High German
or Middle High German, just as you prefer.

'And now mark what I say! Even now none of that seems
ridiculous to me. I believe in a Coming Reich, with all the
glory and the purple and the gold, just as I did when I was
fourteen. It is only on account of what is to come that I am
capable of working in the country all day and every day and
very often at night as well; and because one would be worthless if one contented oneself with dreams while in real life
the people are perishing.'

'You are right,' I said. 'But give me a little more time.'

'How much more time do you want? You said that in
Hamburg, and from Italy you wrote the same. We are in
1930 now, can't you realize that? 1930!!! European history
is in the making.'

'I know, and you may rely on it, I shall be there too.
We can't do anything positive yet — not even you with all
the work you do, because at the bottom of their hearts they
still look on us as children. The other day a fellow in my year,
a brilliant law student, went and put himself at the disposal
of the Social Democratic Party. Do you know what they said
to him? "It's fine that you've come, comrade; you can
distribute election papers at once. In ten years' time perhaps
you may understand something about the Party!"'

'That's no argument. I know just as well as you that there
are plenty of old stick-in-the-muds at the top who try to keep
us out of everything. But if we play the injured innocent and
do nothing practical we shall never have any say. Moreover,
it is simply our duty to take our places in the front line and to
help just as much as any proletarian — whether they accept

¹ 'When fighting becomes so great,
    That none can ever still it,
    The Emperor Friedrich, wise and free,
    Shall come to us, for God doth will it.
    He hangs his shield on a withered tree.'

us or not. If you think you're too good for it, you ought to be ashamed to face the boys in the factories, and all the unemployed in the streets, who have never heard of the Holy Roman Empire of the German Nation, but who know what the country expects of them today.'

When he was about to leave, I held him back.

'Waldemar,' I said, 'we can't part like that. You know what I think, but you see it is very difficult ——'

'When you've made up your mind,' he answered, 'let me know.'

'And until then,' I asked, 'what terms are we on?'

He made no reply, and when I tried to say something more myself, I couldn't.

We stepped back into the room from the door which was already half open, and since neither of us wanted to end our farewell, it took longer than all that we had been talking about before. At last came the moment when we said goodbye, and we both knew that this day had closed something that had filled the whole of our youth.

All that happened afterwards can be told in a few words. On September 13, the evening before the elections, Waldemar Claus and his group were standing at the entrance to a Republican meeting. Everything had passed off quietly and they were saying that they would soon be able to go inside too.

But just as someone was asking him for a match, there was a burst of shooting, and when a few of the boys ran across the road towards the wall from whence the shots had been fired, they only saw two or three forms vanishing into the darkness.

No one was hurt except Waldemar. They lifted him up. He was unconscious and his green shirt was red with blood. They carried him carefully into the Trades Union building that was close by, laid him on a table, and stood round, not knowing what to do. There was no doctor there, only a Red Cross man, who tried clumsily to tie up the wound. One of those who were there told me afterwards that Waldemar sat up once and said:

'What are you thinking of? Go back to the meeting, there's no one there to look after it. I can be alone when ——'

242

That was Waldemar Claus, the fair-haired companion and friend of my boyhood. Now he is raised above all the wise and learned who yet live, who will never fathom the secret of what he has seen — Death.

It was twenty-four years since we had come from the Unknown into the midst of all-embracing life. But he has gone back again to where we were before our childhood — when everything still lay in the future for me, the first time I said 'I,' the World Ash, Schoenwoerth, the night of Messina, the war and all those who died in it . . .

Millions had died, friends and intimates around us; and still death remained something strange and incomprehensible. As when we first went to school and saw those who were going to enter for their final examinations and whom we looked upon as beings of a different order. Then it was our own turn, and for a moment we stopped and looked at ourselves as if from outside.

The same thing happened the first time one loved. Could it really be oneself? Was it no longer only other people who could do it?

And so we shall be very proud one day when we ourselves come to die, after having thought all through life that death did not concern us. One will be proud, and those who stay behind will somehow feel shamed.

That was what I was thinking as my tears poured unchecked from my eyes, over and over again, even after weeks had passed. And I still think it now that I have no more tears, although so many followed him, men of my own age, and younger ones whom I had taught and who could now teach me.

What are the standards? Who is great? My answer is: 'He whom his last hour does not find unprepared, because he has done all he could, and who still took on more in order to do that as well.'

You, Waldemar Claus lived so and so died. But I was left behind; and I wondered what I could do in order to have the right to call myself your comrade again.

This happened while the first foreboding of terrors to come shuddered through Germany. The new Parliament was to meet on October 13. I had received information that the National Socialists were planning riots for that day, possibly even a *Putsch*. Curiously enough, the police seemed to know nothing about it or not to take it seriously. What was to be done? If the enemies of the Republic were planning to overthrow it, the forces who had sworn to defend it must be called upon. That is to say, the Reichsbanner.

How was that to be done? One could not simply go up to them, could one, and say: 'Good day. I am Prince Loewenstein. Oughtn't you to be doing something about the Nazis?'

At the same time, something would have to be done, because more and more information was coming in. It was October 12, and tomorrow was to be the great day. Helga was also of the opinion that one could not just stand by and do nothing.

'I'll tell you what I'll do,' I said to her. 'I will simply take the car and run over to Magdeburg to see Otto Hörsing, the Chief of the Reichsbanner, and tell him what I know. At all events I shall have nothing on my conscience then.' Helga approved of the idea, so I got out the car and went off. I still remember what an uncomfortable drive it was; hundreds of cars were coming into Berlin and hardly any of them dipped their lights.

That same evening I saw the Police Chief at Magdeburg, who was a friend of Hörsing's, and on the following morning I saw Hörsing himself. A black-red-gold flag hung in his room, and a portrait of Ebert, the late President of the Reich. Hörsing was an elderly man, of working-class origin, who had become a leader of the Social Democrats, then *Oberpräsident* of the Province of Saxony for a number of years after the war, an office that he filled with justice and great circumspection. He received me with paternal kindliness.

When he saw me looking at the Republican symbols, he patted me on the shoulder and said:

'That eagle is surprised too. This is the first time he's ever seen a prince!'

I told him what I knew and was amazed to find that it was news to him. Not only that. He did not even take it seriously.

I own that in consequence I felt an almost childish pleasure when even on my way back to Berlin I heard what had happened there. There had been Nazi demonstrations on the largest possible scale, numbers of shops in the main streets had been wrecked, and there had been various other acts of terrorism, the worst that had been seen in Berlin for years.

On the following day I saw Hörsing again. He had come to Berlin for the opening of the Prussian Diet.

'What are your plans actually?' he asked me. 'Are you going to remain a political free-lance all your life, write an article occasionally, and come to Magdeburg, and then go back to idleness? I shall introduce you to the district leader of the Berlin Reichsbanner. He'll tell you what to do.'

Thus, two days afterwards, the most momentous hour of my life struck.

'You know what you have to do,' said Helga as I was leaving the house, 'but do you realize exactly what it is going to mean to you? A breach with everything that has ever been, for you at least — for me, Germany has always been a democracy.'

Yes, I realized what it meant. It meant permanent estrangement from the greater part of my family, and especially from my old uncle; he would certainly turn against me, and there would be no prospect whatever of a real reconciliation. It would also mean a permanent separation from my father. True, he took no interest in politics, but he still looked on the Republic as an abomination — a son who was a Republican would no longer be his son.

What my brother Leopold's attitude would be was not quite clear. I had just had a letter from him saying that he had — practically for certain — found a post for me in the German Press section of the League of Nations. The matter was to be decided in a week or two. He would not be pleased at my risking such a chance, for Geneva would also have been very useful from a monetary point of view.

I was still receiving a fixed allowance from my mother, and

I had just been given a fairly large sum in cash, which would be quite sufficient to settle us most comfortably in Geneva.

But that was not so terribly important — Geneva or not, a settled income or not. What was most important was that we had hitherto had friends, acquaintances, many personal connections; and all that would be lost, nobody would be left except the two of us — Helga and I. But instead we should have the comrades of the man who had died, a countless number, a whole people.

So I was not afraid, and I knew that Helga would help me. She was four years younger than I, the war had been less of a burden to her. Now I understood what she had meant as she said good-bye. Her childhood in Norway was so completely different from everything with which I had grown up. Her first experience of Germany was when she was ten years old and the Republic was the legal form of the State. All this gave her greater freedom, her actions were not determined by so many things which are hard to overcome.

Yes, she and I, we should be alone — with all the millions whom we had chosen. One is always alone if one lives for many and is bound to them all.

Did my decision imply more than that? Infinitely more. I should no longer be the end of a line, no longer the last link in an endless chain. I should be a beginning, a founder, a pioneer for many who would come after me.

So I drove through Berlin one morning in the early autumn on the second day of the twenty-fifth year of my life. Every tree in the Park and down the Linden, every patch of grass and every house filled me with joy. This was Berlin as it was soon to be mine — full of life and striving, without servility or concealment, straightforward and free. Even the sky looked different from what it usually does over a great city, and I liked it even better. It was light blue and polished, with a few little white clouds that had no business to be there, and knew it.

The office of the Berlin Reichsbanner lay some distance behind the *Schloss*, in a part which I had never before visited

246

Over the entrance I saw a board containing the words: 'Reichsbanner Black-Red-Gold. Association of Republican Ex-Service Men and German Republicans. Second Floor.' I went across a courtyard and then upstairs until I came to a second signboard.

I knocked and went in without waiting for an answer. I found myself in a room with a counter halfway across it. Behind it was a file for documents, a desk, and a copying machine at which two green-shirted young men were busy. I said as I had planned:

'Good morning. Can I see Herr Neidhardt?'

One of the young men did not look up at all. The other took a moment before answering:

'Comrade Neidhardt is engaged.'[1]

So I sat down and waited. On a table lay some newspapers with pictures from the community life of the Reichsbanner, scenes from the last elections, and a long article entitled 'The Princely Enemies of the People.' They were not altogether wrong about that, I thought, but once a prince did turn Democrat they did not seem to be particularly impressed, or at all events they did not show it. In any case, things seemed to be turning out quite differently from what I had been planning as I drove up.

While I was still considering the matter, one of the young men came over and said:

'Comrade Neidhardt is free now.'

I was taken along a narrow passage, and at last found myself in the room of Arthur Neidhardt, the district leader, once a naval stoker and sailor, who said to me:

'If you are willing to be a loyal Republican, you are welcome.'

I have forgotten what reply I made. I only remember that the room was slowly filled by numbers of men in grey uniforms and with the dark faces of workers.

They were in front of me and I faced them, quite alone. What I possessed and what had happened before I was born

[1] Comrade (Kamerad) in Germany is a general term. The Socialist form would be 'Genosse.'

did not count here. What I was to be I must acquire anew; I must burn much that I had once worshipped, and worship what I had once burnt.

All the men stepped back save one, who read something aloud to me, and another next to him who held a black-red-gold flag. I saw them as through a veil and yet quite near I heard the voice as though from far away, and yet within my own soul:

'... to serve the German Reich, the Republican form of State, the rights of the people; to defend liberty and equality; to be a good comrade both now and in the hour of danger.'

Now they were all round me again, as long ago, almost twelve years. They came with torches over the misty hills, on an evening in November. Their fathers and brothers had been killed, they were mouldering somewhere on the Isonzo, in the Volhynian swamps, in the ice of the Carpathians, in France and Flanders, on all the battlefields of Europe and beyond the seas.

These were the host of the future, champions of Right, the living, those of tomorrow, in a land that belonged to my brothers, weak and strong, young and old.

I shall be with you, I thought; I have chosen — you and the freedom for which we have all yearned. The millennium that lies behind me has weighed heavily upon me, but a new one has now begun, one fate for you and me, be it victory or death and exile.

'Do you swear to keep this faithfully?' I heard the voice say, and as the circle closed round me I raised one hand in an oath and with the other I grasped the flag, saying:

'Yes, I swear it. Faithful unto death to the German Republic and its colours black, red, and gold.'

These were the words with which a period in my life came to an end, that had lasted for twenty-four years, and a new one began.

Since then many people have asked me what it was like when I awoke from the first intoxication of republican enthusiasm into reality — an idealist and a dreamer in a State that was soon to face its final struggle.

It is indeed a curious tale. If I remember rightly, I hardly knew then what politics were. I went into this German Republic with a lightness of heart and a faith in which the gloomy forebodings of earlier months vanished completely.

My diary and newspaper articles of that time bear clear witness to this. It is for this reason that I have decided to publish certain extracts from them. Perhaps they may also give an idea of how the true picture gradually emerged and how, amid all the hopes and disappointments, manifold experiences, and an everchanging fate, one thing remained unchanged: my ardent love for the German Republic and the ideas of the Constitution of Weimar.

This I felt from the first to the last day of my struggle in Germany, and it will be so as long as there are men who believe in liberty, peace, and justice. Hence the moment when for the first time I professed my faith before the world really brings to an end the story I had to tell.

All that happened afterwards, and my fate today, was determined by the stars that stood over October 16, 1930, the day on which the past was conquered.

From the Diaries of the 'Red Prince'
1930

30 October, Berlin.

Now I have been in the Reichsbanner for a fortnight. My first task was to write a series of pamphlets addressed to youth and to the middle and working classes, which are being distributed by the hundred thousand in Berlin.

The Right newspapers are already filled with sarcastic remarks: 'The Show Aristocrat of the Republic,' and 'The latest Reichsbanner sensation — the Red Prince!' The word 'Red' has already been tacked on to my name on another occasion many years before. It was as little justified then as it is now. But I will accept it as a title of honour merely because *they* apply it to me!

On the day following my entry into the Reichsbanner I had a uniform made for me: a green shirt, grey coat, breeches, shoulder-straps, belt, and a cap with a black, red, and gold cockade. My father would say, 'A thing like that is not a uniform!' Nevertheless I shall not let this trouble me. I am not going to appear in any way different from my proletarian comrades.

Our maid Gertrude, who is altogether very 'refined,' watched with horror while I tried the uniform on. The following incident occurred the next day. At eleven in the morning some people came to look at the flat. As I had gone to bed very late the night before, I was still in my bath when I heard Gertrude's voice saying, 'And do you think that merely because His Highness has joined the Reichsbanner His Highness would get up as early as any vulgar person?'

Since members of the Reichsbanner ought to belong to one of the parties composing the Weimar Coalition, I have joined the Catholic Centre Party. The religious aspect is obvious. From a political standpoint Catholicism is one of the most powerful democratic and social forces.

On meeting Neidhardt again a day or two after my entry into the Reichsbanner I told him that I was writing a memorandum containing the suggestion that the Reichsbanner should organize a League of Youth to unite the young generation between ten and eighteen years of age in a non-party democratic organization in order to prevent their joining the Nazis and Communists. I proposed that the League should be called *Vortrupp Schwarz-Rot-Gold*.[1] Neidhardt agreed with my suggestion but said: 'It won't be done as quickly as all that. You don't know the way our organization works.'

4 November.

Yesterday was the festival of Saint Hubertus — my patron saint. Always an important day in my father's life because it marked the beginning of the autumn hunting season. It has also become an important day in my life — for quite another reason. For the first time I visited a meeting of members of the Reichsbanner. No one bothered much about me. I was introduced as 'Comrade Prince zu Loewenstein' and a few people addressed me with the familiar 'Du.' The meeting was followed by long political discussions. I was dreadfully afraid lest somebody should ask my opinion or that I should be called upon to make a speech.

5 November.

My memorandum on the *Vortrupp* is finished. Neidhardt thinks it is good. Acting on his advice I got in touch with the *Republikanische Studentenbund*.[2] All the members are in the Reichsbanner and the majority derive from the Youth Movement. Nowadays there are frequent clashes in the University between them and the Rightist students.

[1] Advance Guard Black-Red-and-Gold   [2] 'Republican Students' Union.'

26 November.

I have met my first American — Oswald Garrison Villard of the New York *Nation*. He had seen my name in the newspapers, and was very charming when I met him. I was wearing the uniform of the Reichsbanner and had not had time to change into civilian clothes. He said, 'That is the uniform that we love in America.' He is one of those Americans of German origin who are champions of German Democracy. It would indeed seem that post-war Germany is very popular in America.

2 December.

An eventful day. I called upon the Prussian Minister of the Interior and the Secretary of State for the Interior, Doctor Abegg.

I liked Severing very much. He has a magnificent head and is undoubtedly a sincere Republican and a clean fighter. I told him about my proposal to unite all young Republicans in an organization. He seemed to approve of it. I was very glad to hear that. State support enables things to be done more easily. Besides, the youth of Germany will realize that the Republic is taking an interest in them.

25 December.

Yesterday was the first Christmas Eve on which I had my own Christmas tree. So one is really grown-up at last!

31 December.

The last day of this eventful year. I enter the New Year confidently. Troubles and dangers will indeed be many and great. Nevertheless I believe in the ultimate victory of our cause, even though we are still looked upon as too young to achieve anything worth while. We shall soon be so powerful that we cannot be ignored.

1931

2 January, Hamburg.

Yesterday I motored to Hamburg in order to make the final preparations for my examination.

Today I saw Peter Vogt again. He already knew that I had become a republican. It was a happy meeting despite the fact that our joy was touched with pain in recalling the days when there were three of us. One is already old enough to have one's own dead...

8 January, Hamburg.

I bought the *Berliner Tageblatt* this afternoon and found that an article of mine 'Youth and National Socialism' had been published as a leader. Beside it on the same page was a long report of the funeral of a member of the Reichsbanner named Willi Schneider who had been murdered by the Nazis. Among other things the reporter said: 'The funeral was one of the most impressive demonstrations of sorrow that the capital has ever witnessed and at the same time an imposing republican protest against the Fascist terror.... A guard of honour from the Reichsbanner kept watch over the coffin, which was covered with a black, red, and gold flag.'

10 January, Berlin.

Doctor Joseph Goebbels has honoured me with a leader in the *Angriff* entitled 'His Serene Highness Talks to Youth.' The writer devotes two columns to proving what an ass I am because — his meaning is easy to read between the lines — I am a member of the wrong Front and not of the National Socialist Party!!

Volkmar, who was present as I read the article, said: 'National Socialism is a stage in development through which every post-war German boy must go if he is worth anything. Though he is *not* worth anything if he sticks to it, for then he has not learnt to think things out.'

11 January.

Volkmar's criticism of National Socialism is undeniably just. But it has to be formulated more precisely. Of course there are many good forces among the National Socialists. 'Not being worth anything' is more a general tragic guilt than a personal one. And what is worst is the way in which the Nazis cold-bloodedly make use of the idealism of their youthful followers for their own ends. There will be a terrible awakening one day.

28 January, Hamburg.

Yesterday evening I went into the country to attend a meeting of the Hamburg Reichsbanner. A Nazi meeting was being held in the same place, and some six hundred people had been concentrated there from the entire neighbourhood. At the close of our meeting somebody said, 'Let's go and break up the Nazi meeting.'

I must confess that I was afraid. It was the first time that I had taken part in any such affair — and in addition we only numbered fifty. On the way to the meeting, however, I was seized by another fear: the fear lest my comrades should notice that I was afraid. Hence I was the first to enter the Nazi meeting. But this had just come to an end, and there was nothing that we could do.

29 January.

I have been thinking about this matter and asking myself whether it was not more cowardly to be afraid that the others might notice that one is opposed to force? Also — is it permissible for a republican to take the law into his own hands? I think it is, in given circumstances, if the Government fails to act. The Constitution itself states, 'All power proceeds from the people.'

12 February.

I have passed the examination. It was silly, perhaps, but it did please me when I was addressed for the first time as 'Doctor.' This is a title which no one has had in our family before.

We have decided to go to Ascona for a fortnight. I had less than three weeks in which to revise all the law I had learnt at the University, and so I am now a little overworked.

17 February, Ascona.

A telegram has just arrived to say that I am to give a lecture at Würzburg — thank God with manuscript — on Italian Fascism. The meeting in Würzburg will be followed by a conference in Stuttgart of the *Republikanische Studentenbund*.

21 February, Stuttgart.

Everything went off all right in Würzburg. It gave me a curious feeling to wander through this city — 1916, 1925, and now 1931. It really would amuse me to hold a meeting of the Reichsbanner at Wertheim! Perhaps Uncle Ernst — he is said to be frightfully angry with me — would let himself be convinced that my present conduct is no more than the fulfilling of the obligations laid upon me by the historic past.

Students from all over Germany are gathered together in Stuttgart. They all report a great increase in the number of National Socialists among the students at the universities. At the same time Communism also seems to be making headway among them.

22 February, Stuttgart.

The conference closed yesterday evening with a great demonstration on the part of the *Republikanische Studentenbund* in which the Reichsbanner, the *Sozialistische Arbeiter-Jugend*,[1] and other republican organizations took part.

As I entered the hall the chairman handed me a tele-

[1] Socialist Young Workers' Association.

gram saying that I had been elected leader of the Republican Students in Berlin. 'Now of course you must speak,' he said. 'After all Berlin is our most important group.'

Speak! I have never done so — at least never without manuscript — and certainly never at an important meeting. Impossible.

But a voice beside me is saying: 'The next speaker is the newly elected leader of the *Republikanische Studentenbund* in Berlin, Comrade Hubertus, Prince zu Loewenstein. He belongs to a family that is known to everybody in South Germany. He is the only one of his name, and actually the only German prince, to join the ranks of the people.'

Now I am standing on the speaker's platform and looking down into the hall. I see no faces but only an enormous crowd of people clapping and cheering. Suddenly they arise as one man.

Over the railing of the platform, to which the enthusiasm of the people makes me cling, there hangs a flag bearing the German eagle. It is not the only flag in the hall. The walls are bright with the tricolour of black, red, and gold; and on the platform behind me, upheld by Reichsbanner men, young workers and students, the flags are towering like trees in a forest. Everything swims before my eyes, in a new ecstasy. I feel as if there were a vast wave before me that I must command if it is not to overwhelm me. Suddenly all fear leaves me and I begin to speak as if I had been accustomed to it for a long time.

'Comrades! The fate of Europe will be decided in these years. We whose childhood was broken by the war, we who have found our way to the German Republic, we have the duty of fighting with all our strength for peace and for the liberty of our people. We know that mighty forces are at work to destroy this State, that was born out of tears and blood, in order to make clear the path for a few men consumed by the lust for power, and also for the greatest of all crimes — War.

'This State, imperfect as it may be, is the sole hope of our people and the foundation stone of our future. It is the

257

task of youth to fill it with living democracy and true social justice — a youth which no longer knows any class distinction and which has learnt that privileged birth and higher education only create the obligation of greater self-sacrifice and better service.

'It is our task to defend Germany and all other nations against the horrors of another war. We demand therefore that the new criminal code shall contain the following paragraph: "Whoever incites to war, glorifies war, or characterizes war as a necessary instrument of policy is guilty of high treason against the Germany Reich."'

Minutes passed before I could bring my speech to an end. All had arisen once more. I felt the rustling of the flags as they dipped in greeting, passing over me like a storm.

23 February, Jena — on the way to Berlin.

My speech has given rise to a fierce controversy. It is reported in every detail by Right and Left newspapers alike. A Nazi newspaper contains the pleasant sentence, 'Why doesn't somebody make an end of this Red Prince?' Another newspaper writes: 'His condemnation of the fully justified desire for war that inspires our party comrades is itself high treason. He should be made the subject of a criminal prosecution.'

I only hope they do it! Then we shall see whether the Republic remains true to the Constitution, which in its preamble declares it a duty 'to serve peace at home and abroad.'

I am speaking in Berlin tomorrow evening. I think I have lost my fear of public speaking.

25 February, Berlin.

The meeting yesterday evening jointly organized by the Reichsbanner, the *Republikanische Studentenbund*, and the Republican Boy Scouts passed off very well. I repeated my Stuttgart demand, and said that the majority of those who hurled insults at democracy were just afraid lest they themselves should not be chosen in an election of leaders conducted on democratic lines. Hence they took refuge in an irresponsible dictatorship.

The President of the *Reichstag*, Paul Loebe, spoke after me, and was loudly applauded when he said: 'Unliberated youth, looking backwards, seeking the totalitarian State and a dictatorship, belongs to the other camp. A youth that looks to the future and goes forward fights for democracy and refuses to be servant or slave.'

28 February.

Suddenly things are moving quickly. The third meeting in one week! But the first with a purely proletarian audience in the *Reichsbanner Berlin-Ost*.

My subject was Italian Fascism. Naturally I was careful to point the moral for Germany. Once Fascism gains the upper hand it need not bother for years what the people think about it. Elections that can overthrow a government are only held in democratic countries. Under a dictatorship political espionage, revolvers, and terrorism rule.

1 March.

As a result of my having spoken in company with the President of the *Reichstag* my speech on February 25 attracted widespread attention in the Berlin Press from friends and foes alike.

The Nazis have seized this opportunity of attacking both myself and my republican ideals by means of a new and original argument.

'When the Third Reich is established,' their argument runs, 'the Prince will at once fall back to what he was in his infancy — a Count.' This article was signed 'Meyer'! It is really very funny because — though how should Herr Meyer know this? — it is as counts that we belong to the high nobility of the Holy Roman Empire! The title of *Fürst* and *Prince*, on the other hand, was only conferred in 1812 on my great-great-grandfather and his legitimate descendants by the King of Bavaria. It therefore descends legally to all members of the family, like a name. Besides, the Reich Constitution of 1919 made all predicates and titles of nobility a part of the family name and thereby placed them under the operation of the Civil Law. In consequence even the children of morganatic marriages have today a right to bear the full family name. How much more right must I therefore have to do so — as my father was born a prince out of a non-morganatic marriage?

This Nazi article is, however, interesting because it reveals the political connections of my Wertheim relatives. Uncle Ernst is old and will probably not live much longer. His nephew and heir seems to bear me a special hatred. He has already twice endeavoured to get my princely title changed to that of count. Each time his demand has been rejected by the Prussian *Regierungspräsident* in Potsdam.

Now he has appealed to the Prussian Ministry of the Interior. Hence the Nazi article is doubtless intended to employ political pressure.

The whole question is repugnant to me. It makes no difference to me whether I am entitled 'Prince' or 'Count.' But it has now become both a political issue and a question of prestige.

3 March.

This morning I got a letter from Helga from Ascona saying that she cannot return to Berlin at present, as her mother is ill. At the same time my mother wrote to me from Monte Carlo and invited me to be her guest for three weeks 'as a reward for taking my degree as a Doctor of Law.'

Thereupon I went to the *Gaubureau* and asked Neidhardt if it would be possible to start organizing the *Vortrupp* in the immediate future. 'It will be a long time before we get started on that,' was his reply. Hence I decided to accept my mother's invitation.

9 April, Erlangen.

I am very glad to have left the Riviera, and more especially because, even if it is unpleasant, one experiences things in Erlangen that nobody in Berlin even dreams of.

First of all it is impossible to talk with one's republican friends here without being spied on by a third party — for the town is controlled by the Right-Wing Radicals. There are eavesdroppers in all the streets and cafés. If eavesdropping does not suffice, one is made the subject of personal attacks. In the University, in the students' dining-hall, in the reading-rooms and classrooms, attacks are continually made on republican students while the professors look on passively.

I myself have had a small taste of the local 'good manners.' I went with a friend to one of the reading-rooms and began to read a Social Democratic newspaper. Suddenly a man with a hacked-about face and a swastika in his buttonhole entered the room, made a rude remark, and trod heavily on my foot.

I laid the newspaper aside in order to let him see my black, red, and gold ribbon, and said, 'They didn't teach you manners in your nursery, did they?'

At first he was speechless. Then he saw a couple of Nazis behind him, which gave him the courage to say: 'If you weren't a republican, I should demand your card. As it is, you are not worthy to give me satisfaction!'

'That is all that was wanting,' I replied; 'no manners, boorish, stupid, and then talk about "satisfaction!" We know the type!'

For a moment it looked like a fight. Then my friend said to me, 'It's too silly, Comrade Prince Loewenstein, let's go.' On hearing these words the man with the swastika and his friends stood and gaped. Then I heard murmurs of 'I beg your pardon, Your Highness' — and it seemed to me as if I were back again in Wertheim. I was afterwards told that it was merely by chance that a republican newspaper happened to be on the table. Usually they are torn to pieces on their arrival in the morning.

Anyone who wishes to understand the *real* mentality of many of the Right-Wing Radicals must study the political phrases and cartoons that decorate the walls of public conveniences. Here is material for a psychologist! Nevertheless, even if these 'porno-political demonstrations,' as I have styled them, are valuable material for the history of the age, I blush to think that foreigners might see them.

12 April, Marburg.

It's much the same here as in Erlangen. It makes one anxious to think what will happen to the Republic when these students become its rulers and administrators.

The Right-Wing Radicals are already taking pains to secure the younger generations for their views. In the evenings they mix with older schoolboys, 'teach' them, and are looked up to by them. No wonder that each term sees more and more Nazis among the students.

It seems to me an unwritten law among the middle-class students that it is not 'well-bred' to be a republican and that it is 'not the thing to do' to wear the black, red, and gold colours. And when I last visited my old school in Klagenfurt I thought that time had stood still there because it is a little provincial town. But here in one of the 'centres of German culture' things are far worse. Here the date is again 1923, and some people would like it to be 1914 soon.

I am going to collect further data on this subject and then publish it all in the *Berliner Tageblatt*.

30 April.

My article on 'Youth and Democracy' with the sub-title '*Reichsjugendbund*'[1] was published yesterday in the *Berliner Tageblatt* as a leader. It was prefaced by the following editorial comment: 'This League seeks to bring together all the various sections of democratic youth in a single organization ... and has for its object the overcoming of all differences of class and birth among the young. The only way in which the muddy waters of unclean propaganda can be made to dry up is by giving the youth of the country a proper political education and by filling them with a sense of responsibility towards the State, pride in the Republic, love of freedom and of self-government.'

[1] Reich League of Youth.

9 May.

My report on the abuses and problems in the German universities has been published by the *Berliner Tageblatt* as an editorial. There is only one solution: 'The republican students must become an *élite* through their intellectual and sporting achievements. They are to be the republicans of the future whose motto will be: Give to all and help all. Destroy all pride of birth and all empty vanity in social standing. Only the elect of the people can form the new nobility of which the Republic is in need.'

11 May.

A flood of anonymous letters bearing such signatures as 'An indignant Erlangen student,' 'A disgusted Marburg student,' etc. A few write: 'If ever you come to —— again, we'll make mincemeat of you, you princely Bolshevik.' Other correspondents are especially enraged by my remarks about the new nobility. 'If you like to call republicans and proletarians aristocrats — that's your affair! May your ancestors turn in their graves! But don't ask us to do it!'

14 May.

The Prussian Ministry of the Interior has rejected my cousin's application and declared that after careful examination of the legal and other factors no justification has been found for any alteration in my princely status. This brings a long struggle to a final and victorious end.

The *Republikanische Studentenbund* has entrusted me with the arrangements for its conference in Northern Germany on June 20 and 21, and I have chosen Neustrelitz in the Free State of Mecklenburg as the meeting place, because I am personally acquainted with the Prime Minister, Baron von Reibnitz.

6 June.

I now speak almost daily at meetings of the Reichsbanner in Berlin and Brandenburg. At first my membership of the Centre Party was something of a hindrance. It cannot be denied that the non-reactionaries among its leaders are regarded as the exceptions.

After meetings held in the country one hears all sorts of things. The political situation there is far gloomier than in Berlin, since agitators have more success with the peasantry than among the workers. I am at times afraid that here the Republic is permitting an enemy to gather strength who will become a real danger, either indirectly or because he seeks to mobilise thirteen million voters against the State itself. The Reich indeed spends vast sums in aid of agriculture. But these will only become useful if they are directed towards the promotion of systematic co-operative evolution. At present the absurd situation exists in which the great landowners, who are getting the lion's share of public assistance, are spending that governmental money in subsidizing National Socialist and German Nationalist agitators, who are stirring up the peasantry and small farmers against the Republican Government.

All the customary methods of propaganda are brought into play — bands, military marches, demonstrations. Meanwhile the Republic and the republicans modestly take a back seat.

A short time ago I was in the town of Neubrandenburg, where I learnt that the following demonstrations had been held in the last few months. First, a meeting of a thousand members of the *Stahlhelm*. (Simultaneously the Communists organised a demonstration in which six hundred men took part.) Next a meeting of one thousand six hundred Nazis from Berlin. Finally, one held by the Right-Wing Radical *Jungstürmer* [1] at which Field Marshal von Mackensen was present. Since 1926 no republican demonstration has taken place in the town.

Theodor Wolff and Rudolf Olden of the *Berliner Tageblatt* understand this problem very well. I told them that I should like to write an article on the subject, naturally with many more facts and details than I had told them now. I proposed to call it 'The Radicalized Village' and to tell the truth very plainly.

[1] Storm Youth.

20 June, Neustrelitz.

While the majority of my comrades are already asleep I am lying in the hay and writing these lines by the light of a pocket lamp. It has been a magnificent day. I shall never forget it as long as I live.

In the early afternoon we left for Neustrelitz in two lorries decorated with fir branches and the black, red, and gold colours. There were eighty of us. We stopped in most of the villages on the way. Some of us had brought lutes, and we sang to their accompaniment. Astonished faces greeted us in a few villages — I think it was long since they had seen the republican colours — but in the end they all joined in.

At the frontier between Prussia and Mecklenburg we were greeted by a detachment of Mecklenburg state police. The roads and villages leading to the capital were decorated and people stood at their doors shouting and cheering. We were obliged to travel at a snail's pace because we were continually being joined by detachments of the Reichsbanner, the *Arbeiterturner*,[1] and other associations. Many people also followed us who did not belong to any republican organization.

At the outskirts of the town we got off the lorries and marched to the former palace of the Grand Duke, where we were given an official reception by the Prime Minister von Reibnitz and the Mecklenburg Government. Afterwards we marched off to our quarters, where we found sixty representatives of the universities of Hamburg, Kiel, Greifswald, and Rostock.

I opened our conference in the former Throne Room of the palace. Beneath the light of many candelabra and surrounded by flags and banners, the meeting took on the solemn appearance of a parliament of the youth of Germany.

The principal speaker was a much respected Reichsbanner man and Youth Leader who is the chief of the press section of the Police President's office in Berlin. His subject was 'The Reconstruction of the German State.' A strong Republic, he said, is the fundamental condition for the realization of

[1] Workers' Sports Club.

democracy. He looked upon the powers given to the President of the Reich as a grave danger to the Constitution. If ever a *coup d'état* were to be attempted, it would come from that quarter — though certainly not as long as Hindenburg was alive.

After this speech we held a torchlight procession in which thousands of people joined. We marched out of the town to a meadow on which a huge bonfire had been built for the Midsummer Eve celebration. One of us threw his torch into it, and as the flames mounted higher and higher, the crowd began to sing

> 'Brüder zur Sonne, zur Freiheit,
> Brüder zum Licht empor!
> Hell aus dem dunklen Vergangenen
> Leuchtet die Zukunft hervor.' [1]

It was the same song that had aroused my emotions years ago in Munich when I first saw a procession of the Workers' Youth. Now I was singing it myself, I was one with the people, a part of a living whole.

At the close of the first verse I stepped over beside the bonfire and spoke some words, as it were consecrating the beginning of the summer of republican Germany — words in which I spoke of our love of freedom and of our irreconcilable and enduring hatred of every form of tyranny. Then I fell back into the crowd and we all began to sing the second verse:

> 'Brüder in eins nun die Hände, [2]
> Brüder das Sterben verlacht!
> Ewig der Sklav'rei ein Ende,
> Heilig die letzte Schlacht!'

We shall be together for another whole day — I had almost said 'only one more day.' But I feel that we shall all take new strength with us from here.

[1] Brothers rise to freedom,
Rise to the sun, to the light!
Out of the darkness of past
There shines our future bright.

[2] Brothers, with hands now together,
Brothers make laughter of death.
Holy this our last battle
That slaves may have freedom of breath.

22 June, Berlin.

Once more I am in Berlin. The second day at Neustrelitz was as beautiful as the first. The speeches were excellent and gave us much inspiration, for they covered all the more important political questions, and that of a new social order. At the final meeting in the former Throne Room I had the task of summing up the results of our deliberations. I said something as follows: Freedom and Democracy are empty words if there is no social equality. Christianity calls for the expulsion from the temple of the New Reich of the money-changers — the lords of capitalism. Only when class distinctions have disappeared from among the youth of the country will it at length be possible to create a free and happy Germany.

All the time I was thinking, 'If only Waldemar Claus could hear me . . .'

2 July.

My article on 'The Radicalized Village' has been published as a leader in the *Berliner Tageblatt*. The evening papers were already in a great state of excitement over it. One that represents Conservative landed interests even appealed to the President of the Reich to protect German agriculture from the 'attacks' of the Left.

6 July.

The Prussian Minister of Education, Doctor Grimme, has issued an anti-terrorist order to the Prussian universities and colleges. It seeks to check excesses and to protect the freedom of studies at the universities. He emphasizes in it that the high reputation of German intellectual life was at stake both at home and abroad.

The effect of the decree upon Right-Wing Radicals was astounding. They at once declared that the Minister had 'inflicted a blow upon academic freedom'!!

On the same day a meeting was held at the University of all the various political groups among the students, from the Communists to the Nazis.

A Nazi was the first speaker. To listen to him one would

have thought that nothing was dearer to him than democracy and freedom of speech. Phrases like 'suppression of national forces,' 'police batons used against free students,' etc. poured from his lips.

A Communist followed him. Lo and behold, he supported the first speaker! He too thought it disgusting that the Minister should ignore the fundamental principles of liberty. He too spoke of 'police batons' — though this time as used against the workers! Finally he demanded the immediate withdrawal of the decree, and was loudly applauded by all the Nazis and Communists present.

Then I spoke, in the fashion in which one must speak when exceptional measures are necessary for dealing with exceptional conditions. The harassing of students loyal to the State and the Constitution could hardly be called one of the 'constitutional rights' of 'free students.' What astonished me, I said, was that the Minister had not intervened much sooner, since the application of democratic rights for the purpose of destroying democracy was absurd. And as to the workers who had been mentioned here: it was precisely the workers who justifiably refused to understand the happenings in the universities ——

At this remark pandemonium broke loose. Shouts of 'Shut up!' 'Toady!' 'Reactionary!' etc., rang through the room. A few left their seats and made for the platform.

I went on: 'As long as every Nazi beating-up and every Communist brutality is celebrated in the *Völkische Beobachter* and the *Rote Fahne*[1] respectively as the preliminary to a revolutionary world salvation, the ambitious desires in our radical student friends will increase until there will be no freedom of thought left in Germany.'

I was unable to finish my speech. One part of the audience began to sing the 'Internationale,' while another sang the 'Horst Wessel' song. Those who could not sing put their fingers in their ears. Some, however, put them to their lips in order to be able to whistle more shrilly. The chairman closed the meeting.

[1] The official paper of the Communist Party.

3 August.

Rudolf Olden and I went to see the faith healer and preacher, Joseph Weissenberg, who cures his patients with cream cheese and whose 'altar' is draped with a black, white, and red flag. His congregation was composed of hundreds of men and women of all classes and professions who rolled on the ground foaming at the mouth. A truly extraordinary scene to witness in the heart of Germany in the twentieth century.

I spent a pleasanter afternoon sailing with an English friend who is the Berlin correspondent of a great liberal newspaper. He told me that he had talked with many leaders of the republican parties, who discussed among themselves which would be the best city to take refuge in if Hitler came to power — Prague or Paris. They could not reach a decision. Personally I regard it as disgraceful even to discuss such a matter. In the first place, Hitler will not come to power. In the second, one should not cry out before one is hurt.

So many provincial newspapers have published articles from my pen recently that I can hardly keep track of the number.

What I liked best, however, was that the *Berliner Tageblatt* published a leader written by me on the subject of the Reichsbanner. Its capacity for self-sacrifice and its devotion to its task baffle description. The more I know of the men the better I like them. What marvellous men they are! It must surely be possible to overcome the internal crisis with their help. Moreover, I am daily learning to appreciate more and more the immense educational work done by the Social Democratic Party and the German Trade Unions. If only the Liberal middle class would give the workers stronger support. After all, its own liberty stands and falls with that of the workers.

9 August.

Today the referendum demanded by the 'National Opposition' and the Communists against the Prussian

Government was held. It was a failure because the Communist workmen refused to give their assent to the insane proposition of their leaders, namely, that the Communist Revolution could only succeed after the Republic and Social Democracy were destroyed and Hitler had come to power.

I spent the whole day in the working-class districts of Berlin in company with my friends from the *Vossische Zeitung*, and found that people were thinking the same everywhere. During the evening, news came in that the Communists had shot two police officers on the Bülowplatz.[1] Within half an hour of the deed we were at the spot, only to experience an uncomfortable few minutes. The police cordon that closed the approaches took no notice of our Press permits, and when we started to drive on, rifles were suddenly levelled at us.

I do not remember what came into my head at this moment. But I fancy it was a simple prayer like one I used to learn in my childhood.

I heard the click of the safety catches being released, and then nothing mattered any more. Indeed I was almost astonished when the officer in charge thought better of it, looked at our permits, and said: 'Go ahead. But if the police in there shoot you you can't blame it on the State. And if the Communists shoot you, don't blame us either!'

All's well that ends well. But I shall not readily forget that half hour. At every street corner one saw uniforms, rifles, machine-guns. Every now and then we were called upon to halt, and each time there came the click of the safety catches.

25 October, at —— in the Province of Grenzmark, West Prussia.

A Jewish member of the Reichsbanner met me at the station. He is the owner of the only store in this town of nearly ten thousand inhabitants. His house is a very cultured one and shows him to possess a sense of beauty — a surprising thing to find in this ghastly place.

[1] A square in the most Communist quarter of Berlin.

Conditions are even worse here today than they were in Gmunden in November, 1918. One could think that the last ten years had never existed. 'Come with me,' my host said. 'See things for yourself.' I went to the village school, where the head master was obviously not pleased to see me. But in the end my name accomplished what could not otherwise have been achieved: permission to be present during the lessons. I could not believe my own ears. The things that are taught to these children between eight to fourteen years of age by teachers paid by the Republic amount to high treason — naked and unashamed!

'This State,' said a teacher, 'was born of national disgrace. Its sponsors were Jews and traitors who had been bought by enemy money.'

A little boy was reprimanded: 'Anyone can tell that your father is one of the Reds. That's why you behave like a pig.'

And for this we had suffered the misery of the war, the collapse, the death of millions.

This is too much, and I refuse to look on inactive. The moment I am back in Berlin I shall publish these facts. 'And what will be the use of that?' said my host. 'Once we had a teacher who was a Republican. In consequence he was so boycotted by "order" of the neighbouring Junkers that he could not even buy milk for his baby. The Ministry of Education transferred him to Berlin instead of protecting him.'

And then in the evening our meeting. I was escorted by four Reichsbanner men. One of them remarked, 'The Liberals here daren't go outside their own houses.' We walked for a long way, leaving the last houses of the village behind us, and a bitter wind blew across the fields. 'How much further?' I asked, but without getting any answer. At long last I saw lights ahead of me that came from an inn standing alone in the midst of the fields like one of those robber haunts described in children's stories. This was where the meeting was to be held.

The hall where I was to speak was badly lit and icy cold. When we arrived it was about one-third full. A hundred men wrapped up in heavy coats were sitting as though carved out of wood. They all stared in front of them like statues that have been boarded up for the winter. Meanwhile five more Reichsbanner men wearing a uniform like my own had appeared in front of the platform.

'Shall I begin?' I asked the chairman. 'Not yet,' he replied.

We waited. A man came in and lit a fire in an iron stove. It smoked but would not burn. Men in groups of two and three stalked into the hall. They all looked as though boarded up with wood.

In the end there were about three hundred people in the room. I noticed that the chairman and the vice-chairman were exchanging anxious looks. I began to speak. Never before or since have I spoken for so long — and never to such an unresponsive audience. I tried everything — humour, pathos, military commands, exhortation — without success. The men facing me remained motionless, frozen, lifeless.

Two hours passed before their faces showed some slight signs of life. Some cleared their throats, others coughed — in approval or disapproval? Finally I could speak no more. I came forward to the very edge of the platform and called on the audience to stand up. They rose, their joints creaking like machines. I called for cheers for the Republic. One and all cheered with me, turned, and trudged out of the room.

'Now at last I can tell you,' said the chairman. 'With the exception of the few men in the Reichsbanner uniform, everyone present was a Nazi, or what passes here for a Nazi — poor agricultural labourers and farm servants who depend for their living in winter on the charity of their employers.'

10 November, at —— in Grenzmark, West Prussia.

A second journey in the eastern provinces after a brief stay in Berlin. Once again I am speaking night after night in country towns and villages and seeing things for myself.

Corruption must exist here on an unimaginable scale. Everybody resignedly tells stories of the enormous sums given by the Reich for the *Osthilfe* [1] — sums that find their

[1] Relief in eastern districts.

way into Junker pockets only. These sums are said to run into hundreds of millions of marks. Yet neither the Reich nor the Prussian Governments appear to know anything about it! I suppose that the local administration is also corrupt, and that that is the reason why the public hears nothing. The administration of justice and the police certainly appear to be already completely in the hands of the enemies of the State.

On their way home from one of my meetings two Reichsbanner men were attacked by Nazis and members of the *Stahlhelm*. One was dangerously wounded, the over severely. When the police arrived on the scene, they arrested the two Reichsbanner men and let their assailants go scot free.

If something is not done here swiftly and with determination the authority of the Republican Government will cease to exist. I shall see to it that something *is* done.

22 November, Berlin.

The *Berliner Volkszeitung*, which is a more popular replica of the *Berliner Tageblatt*, has published my report on conditions in the eastern provinces, under the title 'Chaos in the East' in large type. In the article I have published the names of all officials whom I know to be guilty of treason or dereliction of duty. I hope they will bring actions against me.

24 November, Berlin.

A meeting of the Republican Youth was held yesterday evening in the hall of the former Herrenhaus [1] as a demonstration in support of 'a strong Republic.' The seats beside the speaker's platform were occupied by the Prussian Ministers Severing and Grimme, who had to listen when I said:

> '"Nichtswürdig ist die Nation,
> Die nicht ihr alles freudig setzt an ihre Ehre!"' [2]

---

[1] The former Prussian 'House of Lords.'

[2] 'Contempt upon a nation
Which does not gladly sacrifice all for its honour!'

This is specially true of interior politics. A State is contemptible which allows its laws to be disregarded, which pushes impartiality *ad absurdum*, furnishing the enemies of the people with patents to commit crime and indulge in terrorism. If unwelcome consequences should come it will be the fault of the men who have let power slip through their fingers instead of making proper use of it at the right time.'

What could the two Ministers do except join in the applause? They could not behave as if it were all aimed at them.

25 November.

The Eastern Department of the Prussian Ministry of the Interior telephoned to me today and said: 'Your article has caused us much trouble. Why did you not tell us about it first?'

'Because in that case nothing at all would have happened,' was my answer.

But I also have some good news to report. The first local group of the *Vortrupp Schwarz-Rot-Gold* has been formed in Berlin with a membership of thirty boys. After a whole year — but let us hope things will move more rapidly now. I presented them with their colours and told them that within a year we must have at least one thousand boys in Berlin alone.

28 November.

There was another meeting yesterday in the chamber of the former Herrenhaus at which I took the chair. Severing was the chief speaker. He defended himself against my recent criticisms. Among other things he said:

'Anyone who is afraid of the possibility — the remote possibility — that Fascism should attain to power is a miserable cur. Everything must be done to prevent the rise of Fascism. But if it should triumph, we will go on fighting because we know that it is only a bad dream, a confusion of thought. Here we stand, coldly resolute. We know that the Fascist storm will hurl itself in vain against the cliff that is formed by ourselves.' Then, raising his voice, he added: 'The future is ours. Ours the victory over the dark forces of mediaevalism ——'

'Comrade Severing,' I said in closing the meeting, 'that is the spirit that the youth of the country looks for in its leaders. In my own name and in the name of all my friends — the millions of young people throughout Germany — I swear to you: We are ready whenever you call us!'

The meeting ended with the singing of the third verse of *Deutschland, Deutschland über alles* that begins with the words *Einigkeit und Recht und Freiheit.*[1]

19 December.

I have just heard that the headquarters of the Reichsbanner are going to send me out at the beginning of January for several weeks to speak at meetings in the industrial districts of Western Germany.

It is therefore all to the good that the greatest democratic newspaper in that part of the country, the *Dortmunder Generalanzeiger*, which is read by hundreds of thousands of workers, regularly publishes my articles. One appeared again today under the title of 'The Republican Offensive.' It contained stern warnings, a renewed appeal to the leaders of the Republic, and a rebuke to those who are anxious to let Hitler come to power in order that he may run himself out.

31 December.

The last day of my second year as a Republican. It has not been easy for me. Far more difficult indeed than it would appear from the entries in the diary, which I have just been re-reading. Above all I have had to learn to stand up to insults and defamations. At first it used to hurt me whenever I read the lies and reproaches — and I used to be ashamed of those who wrote them.

Subsequently I simply became disgusted and thought to myself, 'How dare they!'

[1] Unity and Justice and Freedom.

But now I have learnt that this is all nonsense. Since I have entered upon a fight and know what our opponents are like, I must not complain.

Whether what I have been able to do was worth anything, I really do not know — but I am glad of it, all the same! My article on 'Chaos in the East' has been published by fifty papers throughout the country, and I am told that things are a little better in the eastern districts. Not a single one of those whom I mentioned by name dared to bring an action for libel against me.

In addition I have organized many local groups of the *Vortrupp*, and in the first week in January I am to be officially appointed Leader of the *Vortrupp* for Berlin-Brandenburg.

It is certainly also important that I have learnt to speak in public. And that reminds me that years ago I decided that one must be a speaker if one wished to move the masses.

What I now need is time — perhaps two or three years — and then my work will be more firmly established and Germany will have become a stronger and more truly social democracy.

1932

14 January, Dortmund.

The first day off this week. On the ninth I left Berlin, and the same evening I spoke at Duisburg. Sollmann, the former Reich Minister of the Interior, spoke before me to the accompaniment of much uproar. In the interval between our speeches he said to me, 'Because you are a prince, the Nazis and Communists will keep quiet.' And he was right — despite the fact that I spoke much more sharply.

But already the next day, at a great meeting in the Wuppertal, a battle started during my speech. Since then no meeting has passed off without fighting.

The procedure is always the same. Several groups of terrorists take up their stations in the hall. At a given signal they attack the other members of the audience with rubber batons, lead piping, and knuckle-dusters, which they have smuggled in with them concealed beneath their clothes.

Sometimes comic situations arise such as the following. On their way home the other day some of our followers were attacked by Nazis and *Stahlhelm* men. As we came to their assistance, the wife of one of the Reichsbanner men was starting to beat a Nazi with her umbrella in order to liberate her husband, who was struggling in his grasp. The moment her husband saw what she was doing he forgot all about the Nazis, he suddenly became possessed of the strength of a bear, shook himself free, and grasped his wife, all the time shrieking desperately, 'Our umbrella, our umbrella, the only one we've got!' Thereupon his wife turned on him, hit him on the back with the umbrella, and shrieked in her turn, 'You idiot, do you think I'll let you order me not to defend you?' At that Nazis, *Stahlhelm*, and Reichsbanner men all began to laugh, and so went their several ways in peace.

15 January, Werl in Westphalia.

I enjoyed an unusual kind of success today. The meeting — proletarian like all the others — had gone quite well when a member of the *Stahlhelm* rose to speak, a certain Baron ——. He spoke less upon the matter in hand than about me personally. Among other things he asked if it was not a scandal that a Prince Loewenstein should fill the rôle of a champion of the proletariat. Probably, he went on, the cause itself was a matter of indifference to me, and I was merely lusting after power and desirous of imitating Caesar.

I answered him thus: 'You are making a great mistake. I am neither avid of power nor will I imitate anybody. But when you say it is a scandal for a prince to take up the people's cause, I can only say to you that it is a scandal for a nobleman to be an enemy of the people — a scandal that for my part I intend to avoid.'

Thereupon the workmen surrounded the platform and wanted to carry me shoulder-high through the streets. But this was impossible since I had to protect my unhappy opponent.

We had quite a good time, too, at Soest in Westphalia. On the same day the Nazis were holding a meeting that was advertised as follows: 'We are breaking open the doors to freedom. Speaker: The *Fehm* murderer Heines.' Are the doors to freedom, I asked my audience, to be opened by means of *Fehm* murders? At this remark a Nazi got up, seized a beer mug, and brought it down on the head of an old Jew, who dropped under the table like a stone. A second later the hall was filled with flying beer mugs, chairs, plates, and— men. One does not usually realize how light men are.

Finally the Nazis were driven out of the room. But the fight was continued in the street.

25 January, Dortmund.

Only another four meetings before I return to Berlin. I am tired but happy, for the results have been good. I think I have gained the confidence of the workers — that's why our opponents have organized so many disturbances, but they never once succeeded in breaking up a meeting. And that of itself says much: for throughout the Industrial District my posters were covered with swastikas and death's heads, accompanied by such remarks as 'Kill the brute!' 'Down with the Red Prince,' etc.

At a meeting in Gelsenkirchen on a Sunday morning things were very unpleasant. My opening words were the signal for the row to start. I heard the crack of revolver shots, shrieks, the crashing of chairs and of metal. Since, however, the sun was shining in my eyes, I was unable to tell who was victor and who was vanquished. I was therefore forced to stand on the platform waiting to see whether I was knocked down or could continue my speech.

After about twenty minutes the battle was decided. The terrorists were driven out and I was able to finish my speech.

I spoke again the same afternoon and evening. On every occasion the police intervened too late. It is quite obvious that if we do not defend ourselves nobody will defend us.

3 February, Berlin.

When I got home I found Helga ill — apparently a sort of nervous collapse. In the course of the previous night, first at two o'clock, then at three, and again at four, she had been rung up on the telephone and a voice said: 'You are expecting your husband, aren't you? Don't wait any longer. We smashed in his head for him today.' She had no means of testing the accuracy of this 'piece of news.'

21 February, Brunswick.

There is a Nazi Government in the Free State of Brunswick, and my lecture tour was held up through all kinds of chicanery on the part of the police. Nevertheless this evening was a great success. I have to hold nine meetings in five days!

I made use of the fortnight I spent in Berlin to organize the *Vortrupp* still further. There are already two hundred boys. I have appointed Volkmar as my deputy.

March 13 will be election day. Will it be Hindenburg or Hitler? Our motto is, 'Defeat Fascism by electing Hindenburg.' It is very fortunate that we have a man like him. His name has been accompanying me since I was eight years old.

28 February, Mannheim.

As a result of overexertion I returned to Berlin with a high temperature. The moment I went to bed the *Republikanische Studentenbund* rang up to say I was to go at once to Mannheim to attend a monster demonstration, at which Breitscheidt and I were to be the chief speakers.

I tried to say 'Impossible!' but it was no use — I simply had to go. During the entire journey I lay asleep in my compartment, and on my arrival I was almost too weak to shake hands with my comrades.

As the procession of a thousand men of the Reichsbanner entered the hall — the largest in South Germany — that was already packed to overflowing that evening, I was terribly afraid lest I should faint. And so I did in fact, but only on the platform, when I was speaking, and just after a sentence that was loudly applauded. The same thing happened to me three or four more times. I have no idea what I said.

But this morning the newspapers declare that my speech was the 'liveliest.' And I am quite well again.

10 March, Berlin.

Election speeches in Berlin, in Schneidemühl, in the province of Brandenburg, in Hanover and in Bremen — over and over again: 'Defeat Hitler and Fascism by electing Hindenburg; the election of Hindenburg means the salvation of Germany.'

Between speeches further organization of the *Vortrupp*. We are planning to have our first general outing at Easter. There are now local groups in nearly all the districts of Berlin, as well as a few in the provinces. I have drawn up a constitution for the *Vortrupp*, which I intend to develop along democratic lines but with rigid discipline. The ideal set before the boys is: 'You are the Advance Guard of the new youth of Germany!'

Easter Sunday, 27 March, Neuruppin.

The *Vortrupp* began its Easter excursion the day before yesterday. Sixty-three boys all in all — we had no money to take more. The most important thing, however, is that there are representatives of practically all quarters of the city, and also a few from the farthest confines of my district. The majority have already got uniforms — green shirts, black neckties with red edges, Scotch caps ornamented with a golden eagle, grey coats.

We have secured comfortable quarters, there is plenty of straw, and we do our own cooking. A mast has been fixed in the ground in front of our camp. Every morning the black, red, and gold flag is hoisted solemnly; every evening it is solemnly hauled down.

I have thought out a whole series of games which the boys like. They are not quite unmilitary, but I tell the boys: 'We no longer need this against the English and the French. But perhaps one day it may come in useful against the Nazis and the Communists.' I am also using the opportunity afforded me by the excursion of giving easy lessons on the subject of the State and the Constitution to the older boys. I am very happy because the boys like me and I like them. I believe that something can be made out of them — perhaps the future rulers of the Republic.

Easter Monday, 28 March.

Our sleep was much disturbed. We played at manoeuvres in the evening, and during the game noticed several suspicious-looking men lurking among the trees. At bedtime

I therefore posted sentries and gave orders that I was to be awakened in two hours in order to take the next turn in sentry-go.

Barely an hour had elapsed before I was awakened. A semicircle of men armed with darkened pocket lanterns was closing in on the house, which occupied a somewhat isolated position. Suddenly a stone crashed through the window, then another. Thereupon I went out of the house accompanied by Volkmar and three of the biggest boys, and called out, 'One step nearer and we fire!' The men stood still, and as the light came they disappeared.

Easter Tuesday, 29 March, noon.

The last day of the outing. It has passed off splendidly. I have now got sixty-three boys who for the sake of the cause will go through fire. We are going on another and longer trip at Whitsuntide. Meanwhile the various groups are to carry on their work and seek recruits.

10 April, Berlin.

This morning I returned to Berlin from another lecture tour in Brunswick, Hanover, and the Harz, just in time to vote for Hindenburg in the second poll of the presidential election.

The abuse that the Nazis have heaped upon Hindenburg is quite beyond description. Phrases like 'the candidate of the traitors; the candidate of the men who refused to serve in the war; the candidate of the criminals of November' were common.

There have also been some amusing episodes. A series of articles, for example, by Joseph Goebbels, in which he seeks to prove that Hitler is head and shoulders above Hindenburg, even as a man. In these articles there is to be found the following touching little story:

'When Adolf Hitler motors from Munich to address meetings in the country districts, his pockets are stuffed full with packets of cigarettes; and each packet contains a two or three mark piece. Every time he passes a group of hikers he stops his car. There follows a short conversation about their travels, and about where they have come from and whither they are going. Each youth is then given a packet of cigarettes, to his great astonishment, and sometimes he does not until the last moment realize with an access of joy that he has been speaking to his Leader.'

Hitler is thus contrasted with Hindenburg: 'It is true that he [Hitler] does not possess many another man's gift of being able to make a sentimental public exhibition of how much he loves children and delights to feed birds. To the depth of his soul, he hates publicity!'

Only one thing is wanting: that Goebbels should declare that Hitler has taken a vow of silence!

It appears to me to have been a fateful coincidence that on the very eve of this election I had to speak at Quedlinburg in the Harz. For that is the town in which my ancestor, the Emperor Otto the Great, the founder of the Reich, often lived.

A few hours before the meeting I went alone to the Schlossberg and saw in the crypt of the church the grave of the father of the Emperor Otto, Henry I — Henry the Fowler. He had to wage many wars against the barbarians who threatened German soil and Christian culture. And on this very day nine hundred and ninety-nine years ago he defeated his foes. The Nazis sarcastically pointed out this historical connection, and remarked especially on his war against the barbarians, 'who in those days behaved in Germany (so wrote the local Nazi newspaper) just as Hubertus declares the Nazis would like to behave in Germany today.' They mock at themselves and know not how.

12 April.

I have drawn up an exact programme of work for the *Vortrupp* and started instructional classes in the evenings for the leaders. At the outset many of the boys and subleaders were opposed to stricter discipline and any kind of authoritarian leadership. But it has been possible to establish both — indeed it is imperatively necessary if we are to hold our own against the Nazis.

22 April.

Wild rumours are in circulation: Hindenburg is going to dissolve the Reichsbanner! Some Nazis have denounced us to him and accused us of planning high treason! How can we commit high treason against a State that has the very Constitution for which one is fighting? Has Hindenburg forgotten that he owes his election to the votes of the Reichsbanner and the Social Democratic and Catholic workers? Seven men of the Reichsbanner were killed fighting on his behalf.

I have done something that will certainly be quite useless. But I simply had to do it. I have wrritten a letter to Hindenburg saying that the very men whose association he wished to suppress were his comrades in the war, and, like himself, placed themselves at the disposal of the Republic at the time when all the others who are now so 'nationalist' ran away.

27 April.

There is no more talk of dissolving the Reichsbanner. But that is not enough of itself: it must be made capable of action, and for that money is necessary. And money is exactly what we have not got. All we get are polite phrases and a friendly pat on the back. But we cannot equip our people with words alone against the *Stahlhelm* and the Nazis, who are liberally financed by the great industrialists and the great landowners.

I have talked this over with a friend who studied with me in Geneva. He has rich relatives whom he hopes to induce to do something.

30 April.

An important meeting took place this afternoon in the Democratic Club. My friend kept his word and induced his uncle to summon a meeting of a small number of very wealthy people. I calculated that those present — Jewish and non-Jewish — were worth three hundred million marks. They were all people who could not risk the advent to power of a National Socialist Government.

284

I explained the situation briefly. My frequent journeys throughout the country had led me to believe that confidence in the Republican Government was disappearing. Although this did not imply that the Nazis would obtain a majority by constitutional means, their strength was a temptation to the reactionary circles surrounding the President of the Reich to violate the Constitution.

Hence it was necessary to show the nation that the Republic had well-disciplined forces at its disposal that would not abandon the cause of Democracy without putting up a fight. For this purpose money was necessary.

'How much?'

'For the present, three hundred thousand marks and a little later another three hundred thousand.'

'And why should *we* provide this money? Such an enormous sum? First of all you are too pessimistic, secondly — well, and what if Hitler did come to power!!'

'Then you will probably lose everything — perhaps even your lives. I know Fascism and I know the situation in Germany. There will be murders, secret and public, political prisons, confiscation of property, and torture. No one will care a damn about the Courts of Justice because Special Courts will be established. The existing laws will be ignored because new ones will be made — and made with a fountain-pen and a block of scribbling paper — a fresh law to suit the need of every moment.'

The chairman then declared the meeting at an end. All those present said to me smiling, 'Thanks for this very interesting afternoon.'

Whitsunday, Guben in Niederlausitz.

The *Vortrupp* is on its Whitsuntide outing. This time we were able to take a hundred and thirty boys. Every penny for it had to be earned by the boys themselves. It is not like the Nazi boys, who get money from all quarters.

We have pitched our camp on a woodland meadow and are very comfortable and happy. A wonderful spirit of comradeship animates us all, because the boys have learnt to see something more than their 'leader' in me. They come to me with their private cares. I am gradually getting to know about all kinds of social conditions in all the groups — and there are already forty. The *Vortrupp* has achieved a membership of over a thousand — an aim that I had originally made for next November.

Many personal friendships have already sprung up between the boys. Some of them will last for a lifetime, like mine with Waldemar Claus.

Two fifteen-year-old boys, Norbert and Paul, are my most loyal followers. They are quite inseparable, and vie with each other as to who shall prove himself the best. That is the spirit of which Plato said that it would make an army invincible.

We are spending two more days together, and have decided to go into camp for a month in July on the shore of a lake near Berlin.

31 May.

Brüning, Hindenburg's paladin, dismissed by Hindenburg! Papen, the enemy of the Republic, appointed German Chancellor by the elected guardian of the German Republic. . . .

In power the 'Cabinet of the Barons,' supported not by the people but by the *Herrenklub*, among whose leaders are two cousins of my brother, Count Bodo and Werner von Alvensleben, and at least two or three Princes zu Loewenstein-Wertheim — my own cousins.

In the Gaubureau of the Reichsbanner this was noted and allusions made to it. I lost my temper, and told them that now I am devoted a thousand times more than before to the cause of the people and of liberty and of the Republic.

1 July, in the Camp of the Vortrupp, Erkner, near Berlin.

We went into camp today. The boys have been looking forward to it for weeks past, and I did not want to disappoint them.

Seventy boys are permanently in the camp, and at the

week-ends two or three hundred others will come out and join them. I have organized a system of communication with the nearest village in case of disturbance.

5 July, in Camp.

Since the last entry in my diary I have been in Berlin several times, and have drawn up a definite scheme of work for the Reichsbanner, for which there are prospects of financial support.

In the first place the Prussian Government must declare a state of martial law for the defence of the Republic in order to protect both itself and the nation against any attempts at a *Putsch* on the part of the Right — or of the Reich Government of Herr von Papen!

11 July.

We heard the news this morning of yesterday's Bloody Sunday — eighteen dead and two hundred severely wounded throughout Germany. Among them are the brother of one and the father of another of my boys — and I too have my own dead; Peter Vogt, who died like Waldemar Claus, and now I alone am left of the three of us.

In the evening we held a commemoration for the dead, with the flag flying at half-mast beneath a dark starless sky filled with heavy clouds. I addressed the boys — only a few words, for it is not seemly that a Leader should shed tears before his boys.

'Comrades: Whoever wears the black-and-red gold colours must now be prepared to sacrifice everything — even his life. I have written to your parents. Anyone of you who wants to go home may do so. It seems to me that another night is overshadowing Germany. An age of heroism awaits you such as has never before been known in history. But I believe and hope that the colours of Liberty and Equality will at last be victorious.'

Norbert and Paul, who were standing waiting for it, saw my signal. Once again the flag flew from the masthead, and there was not a single one who would have left us.

14 July, in Camp.

The last nights have been very disturbed. It began after Count Helldorf had addressed a Nazi meeting in Erkner and let fall certain remarks about our camp.

In great haste I caused trenches to be dug on the side of the camp nearest to the wood and demanded support from the local Reichsbanner in maintaining sentries round the camp. But I could not get in touch with any one. Hence I only had about five 'big' boys at my disposal, as well as my brother, Volkmar, and Hans Jürgen. Soon after the boys had gone to sleep we saw dozens of figures moving among the trees. They carried flash-lamps turned towards the ground, and came steadily nearer. In the last few days many boys' camps had been attacked by Nazis and the boys brutally beaten. So we knew what we had to expect.

Only bluff will be any good, I thought to myself, and gave the orders: 'Fifteen men here. Ten men take up position in the trench. Ten more in the square!' in tones so loud that they must be heard by those in the wood. As soon as I saw that they stopped their advance, I called out again: 'Put back the safety catch on your rifle! You must be mad!' That did the trick. As dawn broke at four o'clock the majority of our sentries could go to their tents.

16 July, in Camp.

I wish I could have a proper night's sleep. The constant necessity to be on guard by night is getting to be too much of a good thing. I have hardly gone to my tent to snatch half an hour's rest before somebody comes and says, 'Comrade Loewenstein, they're here!'

One hurriedly throws on one's clothes and dashes out. A faint glimmer of light shines over the square, all the tents are peaceful, and one might think 'What a marvellous night!' and 'How splendid for these city boys to be out here!' And then one catches sight of the menacing gleam of many pocket lanterns among the trees, and is reminded that it is war, ruthless and barbaric, here, only an hour's train journey from Berlin.

288

LONG LIVE THE REPUBLIC!

Meanwhile I have had barbed wire put up round the trenches and an old bicycle frame rigged up to look like a machine-gun. This has had a wonderful effect lately; especially when I called for 'water for cooling the gun' in a threatening voice. Naturally the boys soon began to talk among themselves about our nightly happenings. Now they all want to do sentry-go. They look upon the whole business as a frightful lark.

17 July, Berlin.

A friend came out to the camp this morning with the news that matters were coming to a crisis. Hence I went to Berlin and spoke with the Secretary of State for the Interior. In the course of the conversation I learnt that he had received some of the Communist leaders in order to impress upon them the necessity of changing their mad tactics against the Prussian Government if they did not want to pave the way for the Nazis.

I alluded to my scheme of work for the Reichsbanner and said that there was no more time to be lost. It was beyond question that Papen's Government was planning an anti-republican *coup d'état* against Prussia. The Secretary of State also seemed to take a serious view of the situation. At least he assured me that he did; but I do not feel as if anything will happen. I got the same impression at the headquarters of the Reichsbanner.

I should like to have a thousand armed Reichsbanner men — only a thousand — to arrest Papen and the members of his Cabinet, and Hindenburg as well if absolutely necessary; then the proclamation of martial law by the Prussian Government; then an appeal to the masses and the South German States; the distribution of arms to the people; and if absolutely necessary a summons to a general strike as at the time of the Kapp *Putsch* in 1920. In twenty-four hours there would be an end to all plans for a *coup d'état*, there would be no more traitors, and Germany would be a Republic in comparison with which Rome and Sparta were nunneries.

But we are powerless. We all — the 'wise men,' the

cautious men, the men with experience — are in control of all
the forces and means to power in the Republic. The curse of
millions will come upon them if they run away as did the
princes in 1918.

21 July, Munich, Hotel Baverischer Hof.

World history has been made between the present and the
last entry in this diary, to quote Herr Severing when he, the
elected representative of the people, capitulated before a
handful of traitors. What more can I say? Soon there will be
as many books about the July 20, 1932, as about all the other
events of recent days put together. But nobody will be able
to find anything more disgraceful.

I still have one hope: opposition on the part of the South
German governments. I flew to Munich with a document
stating that I was the representative of the Prussian Government — I only got it late at night — and was received by the
Bavarian Minister of the Interior. The negotiations are
going on well.

This afternoon conferences with the Trade Unions, the
Reichsbanner, Social Democrats — everywhere the same
indignation at the behaviour of Prussia.

My personal position here is very singular. I hold conversations by telephone with all manner of Republicans,
receive representatives of the democratic Centre and Left,
and at the same time the festivities for the marriage of my
brother Leopold are coming to an end in this very hotel!

His marriage to Countess Bianca Treuberg was a brilliant
affair, and quite in the old style. Long and friendly accounts
of it are to be found in all the newspapers, including even the
Völkische Beobachter, which had forgotten that Leopold was
my brother, and including the *Vorwärts*, which published it for
that very reason. In addition King Manoel of Portugal, who
was a cousin of my new sister-in-law, had just died; and the
relationship, as well as all other family connections, was carefully noted in many newspapers.

But what happens now? Since I have arrived the head
porter has become a pillar of ice, the waiters' greetings have

290

become less friendly, and if one of the managers happens to be standing beside me in front of the hotel when Reichsbanner men pass by and greet me with the salutation '*Freiheit!*'[1] he simply does not know what to do.

24 July, in Camp.

My journey has come to a successful end. Negotiations in Stuttgart and Darmstadt with the other South German governments have been completely successful. The Front is closed, and Papen can be overthrown *if* the Social Democratic leaders in Prussia only have the courage as defenders of the Constitution to make a public appeal to South Germany and the nation. We are all ready on that account to fight and, if necessary, to do more.

1 August, Berlin.

We struck camp yesterday. I went straight to Berlin to vote. That the Radicals would win with a Government of Reaction in power was beyond question. Only the Social Democratic leaders appear to have counted upon an electoral victory for the Republic!!!

The feeling among the Reichsbanner men and whomsoever else one talks with is desperate: for out of hopes of an electoral success Prussia let the time limit set by Bavaria, Baden, and Hessen elapse. Now Papen's high treason is 'legalized,' our action has been rendered valueless, and perjury and violation of the Constitution are become legal in Germany.

17 October, Vienna.

I spoke today at a mass meeting of Viennese workers, and brought them greetings from the Berlin Reichsbanner.

After the meeting I went with Doctor Julius Deutsch for a walk in the park at Schönbrunn. I remembered that as a child I used to play in the park with my brothers, and that the sentries presented arms to us because our footman's livery was virtually identical with that worn by the servants of the Bavarian Royal House.

[1] 'Freedom!'

In the course of conversation with Deutsch I learnt that it was he who had delivered the speech in Gmunden on that first of May when I had wanted to see our history teacher carrying a red flag.

After we had parted company and I was alone, I was arrested by a police official on a charge of 'speaking in such fashion as to endanger the safety of the State,' and taken to the Police Headquarters accompanied by an escort of forty policemen.

There I was told that I must leave Vienna within three days, and that they could not understand how a 'foreigner' could interfere in Austrian concerns. I replied that I did not feel myself a 'foreigner' in Austria.

By the time I was released the whole affair had already appeared in all the newpapers and there was great excitement. During the evening I learnt that all foreign newspapers had also reported the incident.

18 October, Vienna.

Today I visited the beautiful Vienna municipal buildings. The Vienna proletariat is probably on a higher level than any other in the world. The children here are not pale-faced and miserable as in other great cities. Nowhere else have I ever seen so many happy and good-looking people — people that come so near to the Greek ideal of a balanced mind in a sound body.

I who knew the grim Austria of the war and post-war years find all this doubly remarkable. I believe that we in Germany could learn much from it.

30 October, Münster in Westphalia.

My original intention had been to visit my once so conventual sister Sophie, who had meanwhile married a papal chamberlain named Count Arbeno Attems-Heiligenkreuz from Friauli, near Udine. But the Reichsbanner summoned me back to Germany.

I can no longer remember — everything has become so mixed up together — how many nights since then I have spent in a motor car or in the train, how many meetings I attended and in what towns. Berlin, Hamburg, Munich, Bremen, Berlin again, Schneidemühl, the Ruhr — the great final effort before the election on November 6.

If we win this time the Republic is saved: for a party like the National Socialist cannot survive defeat.

31 December, Berlin.

The most difficult and most dangerous year of my life is at an end. I end it with the knowledge that our efforts have not been in vain. On November 6 National Socialism received a stunning blow — two million less voters than in July. Its coffers are empty, Gregor Strasser has revolted against Hitler, and the Party is breaking up.

Then General von Schleicher became Chancellor and sought to render the Junkers powerless by revealing the Osthilfe scandals. Now we hope for a close collaboration between the Trade Unions and the Army — for a popular Front of the greatest dimensions. If it comes off, all danger of revolution is banished and we can start afresh.

The day before yesterday we held the Christmas and New Year celebrations of the *Vortrupp*, in which many Reichsbanner units took part. I spoke to my comrades, and my first words were commemorative of our dead. They died that we and those who come might be free. I then went on to speak about what it was necessary to do now that the most dangerous attack had been broken. Germany must not be a Republic merely in name. Our purpose was to make it within and without into a true People's State.

In common with its older comrades the *Vortrupp* was entering upon a year of Hope and Work. For — and in saying this I was telling the very latest piece of news — in the course of the ensuing months the post would be created for me of a Reich Youth Leader of the Reichsbanner, and the Berlin *Vortrupp* would serve as the model for the building up of a Republican Youth Movement throughout Germany. Within a year three hundred thousand boys would be marching beneath our banner.

In association with all who fought for freedom and justice this would be the force to lend weight to our words — the beginning of a New Reich that should possess true glory and live in peaceful rivalry with other nations.

Spring, 1933

30 January.

Today Hindenburg betrayed the German people and handed over the Republic to Hitler. What is coming cannot be foreseen: it may be blood and horror and slavery such as our people has never hitherto experienced. But whatever comes one thing is certain: I will never submit to tyranny which I hate from the bottom of my soul and with the whole inheritance and tradition of my name. Yes, that also plays its part; why should I seek to deny it?

To call that man 'Leader' and to shout 'Heil Hitler' would be as great a betrayal of history with its responsibilities and duties as it would be disloyalty to my oath to the Republic. It would be a disgrace to the honour, dignity, and pride of all the emperors and kings whose blood flows in my veins, and an insult to my comrades both dead and living.

I am of the opinion that one must answer Hindenburg's breach of trust with force. I said as much in my thesis for my doctorate, and I said it again this evening before a thousand members of the Reichsbanner: 'The President of the Reich is called upon to be the supreme guardian of the Constitution. If he fails in his duty, then it is the right of each individual to revolt — and there is not only the right but the duty to revolution!'

But I know already what will be said: 'One must avoid civil war at all costs.' Therefore they will prefer to be slaughtered without showing any fight. Oh! Germany — my fatherland!

14 February.

To all outward appearances little has changed during the last fortnight. A faint shade of meaning in the intonation of our house porter's 'Good morning,' after he had just addressed another tenant with a hearty 'Heil Hitler,' a clicking sound in the telephone (there can be no doubt that our conversations are being overheard), and the fact that the maid in the flat above ours — a flat belonging to a Nazi family — has orders not to talk to our maid; that is all. Otherwise everything goes on as before.

The *Vortrupp* holds its meetings regularly. On the twelfth we actually carried out an 'alarm manoeuvre' in Berlin and the Province.

I continue to receive leaders and political friends as usual, and to speak regularly at election meetings just as if the election on March 5 were an ordinary one. It is true that police and secret police are present at these meetings, and that whenever I begin to attack the Government I am interrupted; and also when people come to visit me the porter is standing by the door and notes the number of callers and how long they stay.

Fewer and fewer Reichsbanner and Socialist emblems are to be seen in the streets. On the other hand, there are more black, white, and red ribbons worn by those who for the time being are still ashamed to display the swastika.

It creeps upon us like an octopus, slowly and slimily, putting out its tentacles, irresistible...

19 February.

At the close of a political meeting today there was a mass demonstration of the Reichsbanner in the Lustgarten. Hours before it was due to begin the square was packed tight, while endless processions filled all the side streets. It was as if a dark cloud hung over those waiting. Not a loud word was spoken, only whispers, signs. Hundreds of thousands crouching to spring or to be crushed. I had stationed a thousand boys of the *Vortrupp* in front of the speaker's platform before the palace. So great was the crowd that the boys had to form a cordon in order to keep the platform clear.

There was nothing new in the speeches. But what was 'old,' the simplest concepts of civil and human rights, suddenly carried a new pathos. Whenever the word 'Freedom' was pronounced the crowds, starting from their stupor, broke into cheering that lasted for minutes at a time. It seemed to me all the time that they were expecting something more — a signal, the order to advance. After it was all over, the square still remained filled with people who could only be induced with difficulty to disperse.

As the Reichsbanner marched off in detachments, and I was about to dismiss the *Vortrupp,* I saw that half an hour still remained of the time allotted to us by Police Headquarters. Hence I mustered them again and gave order to march over the Palace Bridge and down Unter den Linden. A song suddenly started. First it came from the group in which the fair-haired Norbert and the more delicate Paul were marching. Then Volkmar's and Hans Jürgen's boys took it up. Finally, they were all singing:

> 'Voran der Trommelbube,
> Er schlägt die Trommel gut.
> Der Knab weiss nichts von Liebe,
> Weiss nicht wie Scheiden tut.
> Er trommelte schon manchen
> Zum Tod und in sein Grab,
> Und dennoch liebt ein jeder
> Den schönen Trommelknab.' [1]

It is an old song that has been sung by everyone in Germany who has been among boys, just as youth sings of Love and Death — the Unknown and the Mysterious. But now it took on another tone. Not that of boys who may sing of these things because they are far from them, but of boys taking destiny on them with every step, first-borns early grown

---

[1] The drummer boy leads on,
Loudly he sounds his drum.
The boy knows nought of love,
And nought of parting's pain.
Full many has he drummed
To Death and to their graves,
And yet there's none but loves
The gentle drummer boy.

mature, standing alone on a field of battle where none but they remain to hold the flag aloft.

I marched the thousand boys from Unter den Linden to the Gendarmenmarkt, and ordered those carrying the flags and banners to take up their position on the steps of the State Theatre. I ascended the steps and spoke:

'Comrades! Which of you who swore loyalty to this flag thought at the time that the day would come when the flag and the Republic which it symbolizes would be seriously threatened? Governmental crises and changes of government we have experienced often enough. But the foundation on which our State rests, the one certainty: 'The German Reich is a Republic. All authority derives from the people,' *that* is shaken for the first time. And what had hitherto been looked upon as dead and gone has become imminent again:

> 'Wer die Wahrheit bekennet und saget sie frei,
> Der kommt bestimmt auf die Hausvogtei.' [1]

That verse from the worst days of persecution before 1848 was taught to you in school so that you might learn how happy we are in comparison with those days. For who could be arrested until today, who could be made a political prisoner, merely for speaking the truth? But now the spectres of slavery have arisen from their graves, and there is nothing that they may not bring: military service, years of your life spent on barrack squares, assassination and imprisonment for all who remain true to their ideals.

'Another certainty was yours: no more war! The last lay far back in the past like a cloud that is slowly disappearing. Now it has returned. And if it comes you will be the first to go! Yes! This time it will be you!

'Within a month the history and the experience of the World War and of the fourteen years of German freedom will be swept away; in the twinkling of an eyelid it will be swept away, the new generation and all it had hoped of life.

'Therefore keep alive in your hearts the desire for freedom

---

[1] Who speaks the truth and makes it known
Straight in prison shall be thrown.

— the sacred flame — however much they may seek to destroy every memory of it in you who knew freedom as boys; to compel you; to corrupt you; to persuade you; to deceive you — so that no bridge may be left between the Democratic State of Weimar and those who will soon only know of it from the abuses of its enemies.

'You must never let the memory of the German Republic die. Not even if some day all that we have lived through appears to you as a dream. Then longing will be so great and the land of your youth will call so strongly that all barriers will be broken as by a mighty stream and you will regain your name: Advance Guard of the New Reich.'

This was Kalvarienberg. Now we all knew it. And as then, long ago, in the mist of a November evening at Gmunden the call came, anticipated and yet timely, so now it came again, still valid and yet no longer so, and valid again for the future:

'Long live the German Republic!'

The cheers came echoing back not only from the thousands in uniform but also from others who had filled the square. The echo resounded and grew and came back from the houses, and the churches, and all the stones of Berlin. Before it died away the flags declined around me, so low they sank that the golden eagle almost vanished in black and red.

Then I did something which one can only do without premeditation. When I wanted to embrace them all, the tricolour flag suddenly lay in my arms like a child and a rich treasure. I clasped it to me and could not let it go. And now it is the others, who raised the cry that I must answer as though it were meant for me alone.

'Long live the German Republic!'

20 February.

On the way to my election meeting this evening we learned that Göring had ordered the police ruthlessly to make use of their firearms against 'enemies of the State' — he said that not to shoot was worse than too much shooting. Thus

299

murder has been made a governmental principle, and Germany has ceased to be a State of law and justice.

24 February.

This morning in the *Gaubureau* we learnt of an attack on a member of the Reichsbanner and his wife in ——, near Berlin. We also caught some words about incendiarism before the telephone connection was suddenly cut off. I was asked to find out the facts of the case, and I took Werner with me.

When we arrived on the scene we found all the inhabitants out in the street. They were standing about in groups of two or more, speaking in undertones, whispering, their faces filled with terror and fury. I went into an inn and asked the local leader of the Reichsbanner to come and give me his report.

On the previous evening an SA meeting had been held in the neighbourhood. When it was over and everybody in the village had gone to bed, a detachment went to the house No. —— in which six families, including the Reichsbanner man R—— and his wife, were living. 'That's the house there!' said the local leader, and pointed across the street to where wet smoke was rising up from a collapsed house.

As he was about to continue a sudden noise arose and a woman forced her way through the people standing at the entrance to the inn. Before I could stop her she fell upon her knees, clasped me round the legs, and burst into uncontrollable sobbing only broken by confused cries: 'Help! They're murdering him! Can't you see that they are murdering him?'

She was an elderly woman, her hair was grey and thin and her face worn and lined. I stroked her head gently like a son his mother's. Everyone around us had fallen silent. Gradually she became quieter, or had no more tears left to shed, and then she told me the following story:

'Last night I woke up because there was a noise outside. At first I did not want to wake my husband, but the noise got louder, and when I stood up I saw framed in the window ——' She stopped in the middle of a word. Her eyes

became vacant, and held only the picture of the burnt
house outside, clouded by smoke. Her mouth — there were
flecks of froth at the corners — moved two or three times
before she suddenly screamed aloud, in a voice as if her
tongue had become a wooden clapper:

'A brown devil was standing there on a ladder, shooting —
shooting — shooting ——'

Somebody drew the curtains and the sight of the smoking
ruins was cut off from her vision. But something else was
in her eyes that came from within. I think it is like —
but no! I do not think it, there is no comparison, and I
only know that one must not look into such eyes.

And so it continued. Man and wife fled into the kitchen
and bolted the door. The Nazis burst it with a hand-
grenade. And when the man and woman jumped out of the
window to the ground two stories below they shot after
them. The man, who had broken his ankle, was twice
wounded. His wife managed to escape. Meanwhile other
Nazis brought up petrol, and soon the flames were shooting
up. Out of the other flats children, women, and men ran
screaming into the open.

I took down an exact statement of what happened and
heard the accounts of many witnesses. I also made enquiries
of the police. The woman's story was true in every detail.

Late that evening we had a discussion in the *Gaubureau*
at which Neidhardt, two other leaders, the lawyer of the
Reichsbanner, Doctor Guenther Joachim, and I myself
were present. The lawyer is going to have the wounded
man moved from the hospital in which he is now lying into
a private nursing home.

28 February.

The Reichstag building was burnt yesterday. And today
it is said that the Communists set it on fire. It is too silly
for words — as if the Reichstag building had been situated
on the top of a mountain and was to be seen by the entire
nation as a 'beacon'!

I was able to see what really happened because I had

arranged to call on Werner in his flat. At the moment I arrived he and Hans Jürgen were standing in the street very excited: 'The wireless has just announced that the Reichstag building is on fire.' 'Clever of the Nazis,' I remarked before we went by the underground to the Potsdam Square, where we took a taxi as far as the Brandenburger Tor. When we arrived there it was about 9.50 P.M.

The square in front of the Reichstag was filled to overflowing with SA men. For the first time they were acting as auxiliary police, and they were awkward and overbearing. So far as was possible we went around the building, and everywhere we saw the same thing: crowds of insolent and conceited SA men standing about all over the place and far down into the Tiergarten.

We heard one Berliner say: 'Look at that little brown monkey over there! He must have had to run hard with his short little legs to arrive in time for the opening of the fire!'

When we got back to the Brandenburger Tor we met an innocent young Bavarian Reichswehr soldier who did not know Berlin and wanted to know what was up. 'The Reichstag, my boy,' I said. 'That's where laws were made, and over it stood the words "To the German Nation." Now the Nazis have set fire to it so that they can make laws by saying "Heil Hitler," and tomorrow you'll read in your paper that the Communists did it.'

'But that's very wicked,' said he, and a sorrowful look came into his eyes.

I told this story to everyone who would listen, personally or on the telephone. But there was no reply from two numbers. 'Away from home,' was the operator's reply.

2 March.

Frau R—— and her husband, who is still in hospital, were arrested yesterday. The State Prosecutor has started proceedings against them for — arson! And because one has so far been accustomed in Germany to turn to 'legal remedies' we have got Doctor Joachim to lodge a complaint.

Terrorism has greatly increased since the burning of the Reichstag building. Not only is the propagandist activity of the Communists and Social Democrats subjected to pressure, also our Centre Party meetings suffer more and more from hindrances and interruptions.

For some days nothing has been heard of a number of friends. Paris? Prague? Or — somewhere in Germany?

3 March.

Brüning's enormous meeting in the overcrowded *Sport-palast* in Berlin was the last assembly of free citizens, the last appeal to reason, justice, and humanity. It was not he himself that spoke: it was the conscience of the world that spoke through his mouth.

His appeal to Hindenburg 'to protect the oppressed against their oppressors' was useless, at a moment when the blackest treachery in history had already been committed. But it is of importance for the records of the future.

His accusation against the oppressors themselves: 'Your greatest crime is that you have destroyed the feeling for what is right and what is wrong.' It is good that this should have been said once more before the curtain falls! I sat so near to him that I could see every quiver of his ascetic face — a defeated man, defeated by his own fault, but honourably and with a tragic greatness, as all those in Germany who believed in the incorruptibility of a patriarch and of the inviolability of an oath to the Constitution.

After the meeting I joined in the greatest spontaneous procession that the streets of Berlin have ever seen. Tens of thousands moved along as if pursued by dreadful sights, and with a mad note of fear — a last senseless longing — in their cry of 'Freedom!' Alas! only when one loses it does one know what it means!

Suddenly we heard whistles and brutal orders. Before one realized what was happening a hundred policemen were among us and striking down anyone they could reach with their rubber truncheons and the butts of their rifles. Nobody defended himself. But the crowds behind kept pushing

303

forward, and more and more people were caught in the affray. The police, led by a lieutenant with an eyeglass, were by now no longer standing on the pavement, but on human beings that turned and twisted, on women, old men, little children whose mothers could not leave them at home alone.

The cry of 'Freedom!' died away. Its place was taken by inarticulate and hardly human sounds that came also from the other side of the street, where the same things were happening, until everything became a confused, bloody mess — voiceless.

5 March.

Towards half-past six in the evening they made a last — and abortive — attempt to get our black, red, and gold eagle flag of the Republic, the only one that flew in Germany during this 'election.' Now we are as exhausted — Helga, Volkmar, and myself — as after a long siege. There was a scene yesterday afternoon like those I can recall from the stories of revolutions I heard as a child.

We were sitting and playing cards when a curious humming noise began outside that soon grew louder and louder. We went out on to the veranda and saw the street brown with people, who pointed threateningly towards the flag. We bowed slightly and smiled, whereupon they roared still louder, until first one and then another group went away shamefacedly. After a few minutes the street was empty. When the SA subsequently made other attempts, the police, who are still behaving splendidly in our part of the town, drove them away on each occasion. Until the last time, barely an hour ago, when they came almost too late.

Probably the whole thing was madness. But there are things that one must do if one is to retain one's self-respect.

14 March.

At about four-thirty this morning our bell was rung several times. I went to the door and asked what was the matter. The answer came: 'Open the door! SA and the police!' And at that time they hammered on it with the

304

butts of their rifles. I went to the telephone and asked for the Flying Squad. But it was a long time since March 5. 'Yes, yes,' was the reply. 'We'll come all right ——' The knocking became louder and we heard some mention of hand-grenades. Nevertheless we did not open. Instead we went to the window and looked down; a lorry filled with SA men stood in the street.

Several minutes passed before a police car arrived. We saw it rush up and the SA men making way in confusion. A short conversation followed between the police officer and an SA leader. Then the police re-entered their car and drove away.

Next the telephone rang. It was the local police station speaking: 'You must open the door. But wait a moment, and I will send a policeman.' A decent voice filled with shame and confusion. Once more endless minutes passed, again the knocking on the door, then the telephone rang. 'Now.'

I went to the door and opened it. A brown stream burst into the hall. 'You are early,' I said. 'Mind the china.'

Two candles that had been lighted the previous evening were still burning before a statue of the Virgin Mary. The Nazis recoiled slightly. Then they started to 'search.'

Bits of conversation. 'The boy just now — a proper Communist — well, he's —— ! The father said he knew nothing ——' The house-searching lasted for two hours. When it was over nothing much was left of Helga's or my clothes. They calmly helped themselves to all the loose cash in the flat and 'took into safe custody' whatever papers and letters they happened to find.

My arrest was postponed 'for the present.'

18 March.

The *Vossische Zeitung* reports that Doctor Guenther Joachim has disappeared from his home.

Norbert came this afternoon and told the following story: When he was coming out of school with Paul, a motor car with the Prussian official flag was standing before the entrance. An SA leader of high rank was leaning against the car watching the boys, and either nodding his head as if in approval or making a gesture of refusal. The moment he saw Paul he went up to him, grinned, and said, 'Come along!'

'You should have heard Paul,' said Norbert. '"Here! What's bitten you?" he said, and was just going on home when another SA man caught him and hit him. He hit me too because I kicked him, and he demanded our addresses. We didn't want to give them at first. Then we had to because they had police authorizations ...'

I asked Norbert whether he and Paul wouldn't rather sleep in our flat for the next few nights. Many people sleep in a different place each night. But he said that he must stay with his mother — and Paul too.

In the evening I got a telephone call from the Head Office of the Centre Party. I am to speak the day after tomorrow in Berlin-Neukölln, but only on the subject of 'culture.'

20 March.

This afternoon at three o'clock Norbert's mother rang me up and said I was to come to her immediately. I was about to ask what was the matter, but she had already hung up the receiver.

When I rang the bell, she opened the door without saying a word and looked at me. Her look was not that of a human being, because human beings are alive and have in their faces some kind of expression, at least sorrow, pain, or something. This woman had no expression. She was completely benumbed, like a mask; she did not move herself but was moved.

Her boy lay in a room with the blind drawn. His head was bound up.

'Norbert!' I exclaimed. 'Norbert!' I could not tell if he recognized me. His mouth moved, awry, with the corners torn and bleeding.

Suddenly he shook himself, stretched out his arms, and cried, 'Paul — Paul,' and nothing except this name. Then

306

his face became very solemn and he began to whisper as if he was an old, wise man who had to hand on a secret: 'There were many there, but one can't walk — you know — one always slips on the floor ——'

'Norbert,' I said, 'take hold of yourself. I must know what has happened.'

Then he looked at me and spoke in a sing-song voice. When he left anything unsaid, it was said by the face of the woman that stood behind me — the mother. I will try to set it down in a connected fashion.

At three o'clock in the morning shots were fired in the street, and then in the house itself. There was a noise in the neighbouring flat — a gurgling as if someone were drowning, and then silence. Suddenly there came a knock on their door, and immediately afterwards a shot was fired through the door. 'We'll open,' his mother called out, and opened the door. A man seized her by the arm and asked, 'Is that your son?' 'Yes,' she replied, 'but he is only just sixteen.' 'Keep your trap shut! So much the better...' Then Norbert was dragged over the floor, down the stairs, and thrown into a lorry.

His mother ran to the nearest telephone kiosk and rang up the police. 'Yes, yes, that's all right,' came the reply. 'We can't do anything about it...'

There were many others in the lorry. Norbert heard the command: 'To the Ulap' — The Nazi barracks.

There is a cellar at the Ulap entered by a ladder. Already at the top there could be heard a sound like the whimpering of children, and sometimes a shriek. It grew louder down below, and the atmosphere grew thicker. The cellar was lit up with shadeless lamps that hung on loose wires, and now Norbert saw many faces, SA men, brown-red, their caps on the sides of their heads, their sleeves rolled up to their elbows. Other figures were there too — naked, half-naked, lying, sitting, standing, with dripping or encrusted bodies.

He was pushed on, until he stopped abruptly. So did the others with him. Before them a man sat riding on a wooden stool, his hands tied behind his back, and his jaw bound down so that he could not move it. He was staring at two SA men, who were lighting cigars. 'There, you swine of a Jew! Now you won't stare after German girls any more,' said one of the men, as he put the burning cigars first into the one, then into the other, of the man's eyes.

The man could not cry out. But he groaned aloud, deep down in his throat, so that Norbert tore himself free and fell down. Somebody kicked him, he slid forward on the ground, and felt a sticky wetness on his hands and face. As he got up, he saw the other SA man at work with two bricks, and heard him say in a matter-of-fact way, as if he merely wished to make a statement, 'He is still a man, this Joachim.' And then it happened——

At that moment the tie slid off his jaws and the tortured man screamed, so much beyond anything ever heard that all else was silenced.

But then the scream was lost amid the cool deliberate movements of the SA wherever they were at work. One hit Norbert on the head, another on the breast and shoulders, his clothes were torn off him, and he lost consciousness.

On coming to himself he saw Paul in front of him. He was lying on his back, his arms were stretched out on each side of his head as if he were swimming, and indescribable things had been done to him.

'Paul!' said Norbert (he cried out the name as he told it all to us). Somebody laid hold of him — he thought it was the man who had struck him in front of the school — and then Norbert heard the words: 'Ah! there is the other!' Then everything vanished in a sea of blood and pain and shame.

His mother told me that they brought the boy home in the afternoon, and said: 'If you say a word about it ——'

When this had all been told, she made a sudden movement, the mask that was her face broke, she stretched out her hands with bent fingers and, laying emphasis on every word, she said: 'The day — Lord God — the day — with my own hands ——'

Then I went away and brought a doctor. Norbert will live, he thinks, but as a cripple...

I visited Paul's mother before going to my meeting. She already knew everything, because they had told her that she must not open the coffin.

When it was my turn to speak, all the restraint which I had been able to keep up through the day collapsed and the power of thinking returned too.

What I had intended to say about 'culture' I had long since forgotten — what is culture here? I shouted, wept, cried out what had happened, until my throat was dry and the glass in my hand broke 'like Germany's honour if we permit this shame' — those were my last words.

Secret police and SA men were stationed both inside and outside the hall. But nobody dared lay hands on me.

I have just telephoned to Bishop Schreiber of Berlin. He will try to do something for the prisoners in the Ulap, and above all for Joachim, because he is a Jew and our duty towards him is therefore all the greater.

22 March.

We buried Paul today secretly, and as if we were committing a crime. His mother, Norbert's mother, Helga, Volkmar, Hans Jürgen, and I were the only persons present. I laid a little golden eagle in his grave and a black, red, and gold pennant — the boy who together with Norbert upheld the banner of German youth.

Across the cemetery a loud speaker from somewhere near shouted out the news of the 'State ceremony' at Potsdam, of the alliance between the 'glorious Field Marshal' and the 'Leader,' and much about the awakening of the German people.

Awaken it will — of that we are all certain . . .

25 March.

The people in Berlin walk in a strange way as if they no longer had control of their limbs, or like the inhabitants of a captured city. Yet it is spring: the first blossoms are appearing in the Tiergarten; and the grass is growing green. It is the Festival of the Annunciation, and exactly a year since the *Vortrupp* left for its Easter camp.

Helga told me today that our child would be born in October — the child that we have longed for, hoped for, during nearly four years.

'My child' — how unreal it sounds. Nevertheless it is certain. She has known it for weeks past.

As a result we came to an important decision. Until the child is born we are going to leave Berlin and live in Schoenwoerth — where else in the wide world? A few weeks ago we were told that it might be to let. I wouldn't hear of it at that time.

But now I think it might be permissible — indeed we must go there, in order that just as it was my origin, so the new life may also begin there...

27 March, Gasthaus zum Dampfl, near Schoenwoerth.

Like a stormy sea beyond harbour walls, Germany was left behind after I had crossed the frontier yesterday.

A clear, sharp air filled the valley of the Inn. I drank it in like a new-born child drawing its first breath. The river was swollen with grey-green waves, which one seemed to be pushing back as one drove along the road, and the valley was like a great bed out of which Winter was coming forth. From Kufstein I looked across again and again, and now I am still nearer to the Wilde Kaiser on my left. He is heavily covered with snow, and his topmost peak that resembles the crown of the Holy Roman Empire is gleaming. For nearly nineteen years I have not thought about him. Then on the other side of the valley appears a soft ridge, brown with spots and wrinkles — the Great Cow. And now, quite clearly to be seen, at its feet — Schoenwoerth, with its broad central tower, Wotan's ash, the pointed, round tower that serves as a fire escape, the face turned northwards with the round, kindly eyes and the great wide mouth.

The road descends sharply and turns to the right to the bridge, against the wooden pillars of which the water is rising, and then passes by houses at the sight of which I found that Memory corresponds with Reality like two exposures made on the same piece of film. Now I am standing before the gate between the stables where the stork used to hang, and the castle. The stone armorial bearings are still there; the fusils of my family and my mother's coat of arms — a mailed hand holding three arrows — that cracked on the day she left.

The castle is uninhabited, and the red-and-white shutters are closed. The wild vine on the walls has grown thicker. I leave the carriage and walk along beside the wall of the drive — it is so easy to look over it! On that tree there my swing was hanging when we heard the news of Sarajevo. Below it on one side there appears the roof of the super-intendent's house which George and the others have left long ago. A powdering of snow is still to be seen at the edges of the paths, around the trees, and on the withered leaves lying in the middle of the grass.

It is a remarkable fact, and one of common experience, that if one has a great longing for something that has vanished, the next time desire meets with fulfilment it seems to join on as if without any interval to the last experience, even if decades have intervened between the two occasions.

I returned in 1914 when I was grown up to the land of my childhood, and now that seems like yesterday, or as if only a winter lay between.

When I came to the village inn kept by Dampfl, they all recognized me immediately — the mother, the son, the serving man. I saw photographs of my parents, my brothers and sisters, and myself, and even the old gramophone was still there, into which one had to put two pennies in order to make it play 'The Battle of Sedan.' I sat down and we began to talk, as if from the point where we had left off nineteen years before.

'Do all the children hereabouts look as if they were our brothers or nephews?' I asked Dampfl, after we had talked ourselves out, as a couple of fair-haired boys came running in, who could hardly be distinguished from the photographs of ourselves as children.

He grinned knowingly and said: 'That must be the air or the weather! What else could it be?'

An old peasant — I had thought him very old years ago — had the keys to Schoenwoerth. He was sitting on the seat beside the stove, completely enveloped in a blanket and a white beard, addressed me by the familiar 'Du,' and asked how were the boys and girls at home. He meant my brothers and sisters.

'Very well,' I answered. 'And now I am coming back again.'

'About time, too,' he said as we got up to go to Schoenwoerth.

Except that electric light had been installed, I found it unaltered, though it was filled with strange furniture and different pictures hung on the walls. Our coat of arms was still to be seen everywhere — on the 'Office,' over the doors and on the windows of the Great Hall.

I went over the whole place and into my most secret kingdom — the panelled room with the small leaded windows, the former armoury where the skeletons stood, and into my elder brothers' rooms in the new wing. But when I entered my father's room it seemed strange to be allowed to do so.

Then Dampfl said to me that it was lunch time, and that one could come back again in the afternoon. So I went out into the park and along the stream to the mill, where the weir still filled me with awe.

Hidden flowers bloomed in the wood and beside the little bridge by the tennis court beneath roots and dried leaves: snow roses and anemones. The scent of the earth was so strong that I felt strangely moved. Here and there beside the spring were a few crocuses, still a little pale, and as I sought among clumps of wild mint and dead nettles, I found yellow buttercups, and a very light cowslip. Then I looked up at the castle and at the middle of its face. I wanted to see the blue and white fusilly flag flying high above it where it belonged; and I knew what I had to do that afternoon.

It was quite a proper meal that Dampfl gave me: meat soup with balls of liver, 'Gselchtes'[1] with red cabbage and

[1] Smoked meat.

potato cakes, a glass of beer, and then dumplings filled with plum jam.

'What are things like here?' I asked Dampfl. 'How many servants will one need?'

'Only a few,' he said. 'I know just the right ones: the Hossacher Moidl as cook; Hansl from Brandstaetter down below there as manservant; Mariedl and Gretl could work as chambermaids; Franzl knows something about cars; Josef, Anton, and the Schorschl can work in the garden; the Hollas Anna ——'

'Stop!' I said. 'Who on earth else shall I take?'

'Your Herr Papa,' he replied, 'had sixteen in the good years — and very proper, too, for a castle. Besides, it doesn't cost much here. In Berlin you'd pay as much for two.'

Not dear, I thought; good! But still — sixteen servants? Or perhaps only ten. In any case I should have to devote my life to it.

As I said nothing more, Dampfl thought the matter was settled and suggested that we should return to the castle. This time we went up the stairs until we were at the top landing where the green and red guest rooms are. That was as far as I had ever been in my life.

'We can go this way,' said Dampfl. I followed him, a little hesitantly and undecidedly. The stairs that I was now ascending led to the balcony that looked like a mouth from below and to which I had never been allowed to go. Two creaking, rusty iron doors opened before me. I put my hand before my dazzled eyes. A single step more — and I was standing on it.

It is giddily high, so high that at first I did not look around, but then the picture cleared — the river winding into the far distance, the meadows, Dampfl's house, and the park all together in a space the size of a man's hand. My whole empire and all the kingdoms subject to it...

Sic transit Huberte — that was the throne of the world where you are now standing, symbol of supreme power and of the beginning of real, independent life. Far into the mountains everything now lies before you! And behind the mountains? There lies Germany — and your comrades lie bleeding, while you are becoming the lord of a castle. It was a bright kingdom — this park. But now you have seen the boundaries and it has become as small as a prison cell.

When you looked aloft a little time ago, you wanted to see the fusilly flag flying — a flag that you have inherited. Is that the only result of all these years? No! it is not. I will not be faithless to the black, red, and gold banner whose follower I have become, which I have gained for myself, and for which many of my friends have died. Therewith I knew what it was that held me bound with bonds stronger than the call of the past. I stepped back and closed the door myself. I walked out of Schoenwoerth without taking a backward glance, and thought to myself that it should lie undisturbed until even this present hour had become a dream again.

Meanwhile night had fallen and it was very still in the whole valley. I arranged my papers, diaries, and the drafts of the Constitution, in order to send them to Leopold in England before I returned to Berlin tomorrow.

I will collect together those friends of mine who have been scattered by the first blows of terror and summon them to join in the fight of freedom. The Weimar Constitution has been taken from us; what remains to us, then, except to fight for our rights underground? The better we do it, the more quickly it will be over, and whoever can still manage to come to Germany must try to remain there for as long as possible.

29 March, Berlin.
While I was away the following incident occurred. Early in the morning there came a knocking on the door. Helga opened it and was pushed aside by a crowd of SA men. 'Where is your husband?' one of them shouted. 'In Austria.' 'That's a lie.' 'I'll telephone to the police.' 'You won't!'

They dragged her away from the telephone. Two SA

men held her; the others searched the flat for two hours. As they were leaving Werner arrived. He fetched a doctor, but it was too late.

Our child will not be born in October.

4 April.[1]

I have been at the police station several times and assured them that I no longer take any part in politics. In any case I have had hardly any private life during the last few years.

Supplement.

Today we held the inaugural meeting of the new League. Its cipher is DL. Some of the local groups will be registered as football clubs. All the members are adult Reichsbanner men, with the exception of two groups composed of former *Vortrupp* boys. I have told them to join the Hitler Youth — no matter how unpleasant that may be.

8 April. Supplement.

At first we thought it was purely by chance that the bell was rung continually during the night. Now we know better. Each SA man who passes the house rings the bell of our flat. Sometimes this happens as often as fifteen times in a single night. Each time of course one gets up and has a look; one never knows ...

I met an acquaintance today on the Kurfürstendamm, who used to be a Democrat and has now gone over to the Black-White-and-Reds.

'What are you doing in Berlin?' he asked. 'You should have been in Paris long ago!'

One sees new faces in the restaurants and theatres, and the streets are full of newly rich owners of motorcars. Every lout of an SA man will soon have his own car. And it is easy to see how stuck up they are.

DL now has sixteen groups in Berlin and three in the provinces. We use cellars and back rooms as meeting-places

[1] The careful styling of this entry and similar ones is due to the constant fear of further raids by SA men. The 'Supplements' were written in the autumn of 1933.

— quite comfortable they are too — and also for hand print-ing presses and copying machines.

I went yesterday to visit Norbert and found the flat empty. The neighbours said that they had left Berlin and that nobody knew where they had gone.

10 April.

I met a police officer in the street whom I knew from earlier days. A nice, decent fellow. We started to talk and he asked me if I did not think that a little holiday in the South would do me good.

Supplement.

Helga went out today for the first time, only across the street. She wore Werner's old trench coat that he had left with us months ago.

She had hardly left the door before she saw an SA man. He stood still in astonishment, for on her coat were the three arrows that were the badge of the strictly forbidden 'Iron Front.' The man walked up to her, trod on her foot, and made a rude remark to her. Without hesitation she soundly slapped his face. The SA man was completely taken aback, stuttered, asked her pardon, and disappeared.

11 April. Supplement.

There is unrest in the SA, among both the rabble and the decent men. The rabble would have liked still more plunder-ing, while the decent men begin to understand that something is wrong with the Socialism of the Third Reich. They have already begun to push the proletarian elements into the background and to promote the 'genteel' ones.

We have therefore resolved that every member of DL who can do so will enter the SA.

12 April. Supplement.

Three of us were caught today, and I nearly fell into the trap too, but on the way to Tempelhof somebody warned me that the police had discovered our room there and were

lying in wait. This evening there was an important conference in K'House. I shall have to leave Germany. One
loses one's sense of proportion and any connection with the
world whilst one is there. Besides, people are needed in the
Saar Territory in order to work against the Nazis at the
coming plebiscite.

13 April.

Helga's mother has gone to the Tyrol, and writes to say
that she would like to see us both, or at least one of us,
because she wants to rent a small property in the Inn
Valley. At first Helga did not want to go, but I persuaded
her, because it is impossible for me to leave.

17 April.

Helga writes that she has found a pretty, modernized little
castle near Brixlegg in the Tyrol that is to let. It has a
large park with two small lakes full of fish, a vegetable
garden, and some forest. The rent is low, and we could
put up several of our friends comfortably. As I have not
been feeling well and have been suffering from insomnia for
some time past, I am suddenly greatly attracted by the
notion of a country life.

20 April. Supplement.

A friend of mine had a Chrysler to sell — the very car
I was looking for. I have just made a tour of the provinces
in it and visited nearly all the towns where I spoke formerly
and in which I have acquaintances. An understanding with
the opposition in the SA and with the *Stahlhelm* is in process
of development. We have also got one or two representatives
in the leadership of the Hitler Youth.

23 April.

Helga came back today. The lease is signed. As I shall
probably return in six weeks, I have rented two rooms in a
friend's house and intimated the fact to the police in due
form. We are very sorry to leave our pretty flat in which

317

so much has happened. But we really are in need of a change, especially Helga, and the flat would have been too large for me alone.

26 April. Supplement.

The flat is empty — and the parting is at hand. It is a frightful thought. Up to the last moment I hesitated, and would gladly have sent somebody else abroad and into the Saar Territory in order not to have to leave Germany. But it cannot be helped, and therefore I said good-bye today to my leaders.

28 April.

The last evening in Berlin. We drove through the town once more and said good-bye to the people, the streets, and the squares — the Brandenburger Tor, the University, the Lustgarten, and all the houses round about the *Schloss*. We also visited the theatre on the Gendarmenmarkt.

Everywhere swastika flags were flying, because the day after tomorrow will see the National Government's celebration of May 1. My life in Berlin has lasted for almost seven years. It is impossible to forecast what is now beginning from what has previously happened.

30 April, in the car before the frontier guard-house at four o'clock in the afternoon.

Helga is with Volkmar and Hans Jürgen in the German Customs, in order to have our hand luggage examined and complete the last frontier formalities.

Early yesterday morning we left Berlin and had a very easy journey as far as Bamberg. I had not been there since 1917, and this return was also a parting. Everywhere that I had been as a child we stopped: before my old school, where boys were playing in the schoolyard just as we had done; at the cathedral; and by the church built by the Emperor Heinrich the Saint and the Empress Kunigunde. And there it seems to me that today it is doubly sacred through the name it wears: St. Michael — 'Who is like unto God' — when men seek to make gods of themselves or of races and nations.

In all the villages through which we passed the people had been compelled to display the swastika flag. On a market-place in a village not far from Munich a black, red, and gold and a white and blue Bavarian flag were being burnt.

Munich itself — the city of the serene arts, the Athens of the Isar, the gay, beautiful town — was now covered with the ugly emblems of dictatorship, and crowds of heavily armed guards in uniform passed along the streets. For Munich was the last to be robbed of its legal constitution and subjected to the brown tyranny by a fresh breach of loyalty and the Constitution on the part of Hindenburg. So disgusting was the sight that we did not delay there any longer than was necessary.

Was that really our parting and the last memory of Germany that we should take with us? Thank God! Another awaited us shortly afterwards in a bright and cheerful village. It was the annual fair there. From a long way off we heard the strains of the village band, to the accompaniment of which young and old alike were dancing on wooden planks laid upon the ground. The houses were decorated with gay flags, white and blue, black and red, green and white, and over the streets hung paper garlands and fir twigs. At night the village was to be illuminated — we could see the boys busily engaged in hanging up Chinese lanterns.

These boys are having a splendid time altogether today. They can fire off their little cannons and crackers as often as they like. If they get dirty all over and black-nosed, no one can say anything today. The little girls — and the bigger girls too — look on enviously. *They* have to behave properly. The mistresses of the Guild of Mary and of the Guild of the Virgins keep a stern eye upon them.

The peasants are wearing specially fine green hats today with soft grey chamois brushes that are silvery towards the tips. They wear heavy watch chains ornamented with old silver coins and their widest green and brown braces. On these, and coming over the middle of their chests, hangs a portrait of King Ludwig II, the Fairy Tale King, who is believed by the peasants to be still living.

In front of a stall on the market there stood a singer surrounded by a crowd. He danced a *Schuhplattler* and sang a new song as an accompaniment that earned much applause. The crowd grew larger and larger, and the laughter was so loud that I had to push myself forward as near as possible to him in order to hear the words of the chorus:

> 'Und weht das Hakenkreuz im ganzen Gau,
> Bleibt unser Fähnelein doch weiss und blau!'[1]

Each time that the singer uttered the word 'swastika' he slapped his hands on his buttocks and turned them towards his audience. They soon learned how to do it, and there was no doubt that they all meant the same.

After this had gone on for some time, we walked round the stalls in the market; it was marvellous how many things one could buy there: linen woven by the peasants for shirts and jackets, silver buttons ornamented with the Bavarian fusils for wearing on Sunday waistcoats, cloaks made of felt with buttons of stag's horn, glass balls and beads, sugar candy, black and grey chamois *Lederhosen* with green embroidery (these were for tourists: a proper pair of *Lederhosen* must be old and well worn), blue suits for boys and white dresses for girls to be worn at their First Communion, shoes with great nails, alpine sticks — and many more things than can possibly be enumerated.

Next the village priest came up to us and engaged us in a friendly conversation. He would have nothing to do with politics, he said, because it had become a godless affair, and in his village such things would never have a chance. He then invited us to drink a mug of beer with him. If I had not had to drive the car, it could easily have become three or four.

As we drove away from the village, we could still hear the band playing for a long time. Everyone we met upon the road greeted us with a friendly smile and called out 'Grüss

---

[1] And may the swastika fly all the country through,
 Yet our flag remains forever white and blue!

Gott.' And then it was not long before the mountains grew high and we knew that the frontier was near.

I am about to cross it for the second time within a month. But this time will be different from the last and from any previous time. Where the Wilde Kaiser and his paladins stand is now exile. Whatever I formerly possessed will remain behind — the breath of seasons over the towns of my country and over its broad furrows, its men, boys, and women, the mothers of my people, at their daily toil, in struggle and need and misery — my whole country and all my youth.

All that I take with me is the flag to which I have sworn fealty and a dream of German freedom that longs to come true.

Now Germany will soon lie behind me, and I know that I shall never see it again — unless as a victor and greater than before.

FINIS

Index

323